LEAN ACCOUNTING

LEAN ACCOUNTING

BEST PRACTICES FOR SUSTAINABLE INTEGRATION

Edited by

Joe Stenzel

WILEY
John Wiley & Sons, Inc.

Library of Congress Cataloging-in-Publication Data:

Lean accounting : best practices for sustainable integration / edited by Joe Stenzel.
  p. cm.
  Includes index.
  ISBN: 978-0-470-08728-2 (cloth)
  1. Managerial accounting. 2. Organizational effectiveness. 3. Industrial efficiency.
I. Stenzel, Joseph, 1957–
HF5657.4.L42 2007
658.15′11—dc22

2006033471

Printed in the United States of America

10   9   8   7   6   5   4   3   2   1

CONTENTS

Part III   Lean Accountancy

6 ON TARGET: CUSTOMER-DRIVEN LEAN MANAGEMENT   121

Dr. C. J. McNair, CMA

7 VALUE STREAM COSTING: THE LEAN SOLUTION TO STANDARD COSTING COMPLEXITY AND WASTE   155

Brian Maskell and Nicholas Katko

FOREWORD

ENACTING, NOT IMPLEMENTING, LEAN MANAGEMENT

Managers always want to do something to improve how their organizations function. The combined effects of global competition, the growth in business books and magazines, and business consultancy has led to a never-ending series of fads to fix organizations. It often seems that these do more to confuse than inform people, leading to one change program after another, what the people at Harley-Davidson dubbed many years ago, "AFP," Another Fine Program (often translated differently internally).

"Lean" is the fad of the day. For a top team to not have its version of a lean management program is tantamount to managerial negligence. Yet, few of these succeed in achieving their intended outcomes, just as few process redesign programs succeeded, and, before that, few TQM programs. In fact, Dr. W. Edwards Deming, one of the pioneers of total quality, became so disgusted with the fad fetishes of contemporary managers that he refused to use terms like TQ, TQM, or Total Quality in the latter years of his life. For him they had lost all meaning: "They mean whatever people want them to mean."

The essays in this book represent the struggles of thoughtful and experienced people to get their arms around why otherwise useful ideas and tools can contribute to ongoing improvement in a few organizations and become mindless pabulum in so many others. Some of these contributors are good friends and long-time colleagues. While in no way summarizing their insights, the following three *core premises* capture a bit of where they are coming from, I think.

Genuine Reflection Will Always Trump Simplistic Solutions

Dr. David Cochran talks about the failure to establish agreement on important functional requirements. Why would this occur? It should be evident to everyone that such agreement is important, that forcing people to strive for goals they care little about is not likely to compel commitment or success. Yet, the agreement behind most lean initiatives is often token at best. It is not that people do not see the need for improvement. It is more the case that they usually doubt that this latest "AFP" is likely to address the deeper issues that frustrate them.

Deming used to say, "No reflection, no learning." But, what he meant by this is lost on most managers trained in the instrumental problem solving popular in modern management education. By these approaches, we first "externalize" problems to a set of symptoms, usually measurable symptoms. We then figure out clever ways to address those symptoms and then "implement" the respective solutions. But throughout, the process is limited by unquestioned assumptions, like, "We really do not need to understand how the problem has arisen," or "I am (or we are) separate from the problem."

When pressed as to why they do not reflect more on how the problem has arisen, the standard response is, "We just don't have the time to do this." But the resulting superficial solutions rarely ever achieve lasting change—something that people often readily acknowledge. So, they may not have the time to do it, but they have plenty of time to "redo it," often many times over.

Our experience has always been that there are deeper reasons than not enough time for why we shy away from reflection. Paramount among these is that people either feel unable or unwilling to confront the quality of conversation that is required. A conversation based on reflection on what exists that we "do not see," as Cochran says, may lead to seeing ways that we are part of creating the problems, or that management systems in place focus people in ways that reinforce the status quo, or that there are underlying issues of power and personality about which people, in effect, have "taken an oath of secrecy."

But failing to commit to more reflective conversation also masks our deepest aspirations and longings. It keeps people not only from talking about what is, but what they truly desire. Such conversations are difficult. They do take time. But they can end up saving much more time.

Systems Intelligence Will Always Trump Reductionistic Analysis

I am of the opinion that we are at the very beginnings of starting to wrestle with the profound implications of a systems worldview, and that this awakening, which started in physics, biology, and other basic sciences but which really has its roots in timeless ways of understanding common to native people the world over, will continue to unfold throughout this century.

That said, the time to start is now, and the benefits can be immediate as well as for coming generations. Tom Johnson points out that Toyota, the most studied company in the world, still outperforms virtually all of its competitors, many by a very long ways. How could this be? What are people missing?

I recall a story Professor Johnson used to tell about a colleague at Toyota's Georgetown manufacturing facility. He had hosted literally hundreds of groups of visitors who had come to study the famous "Toyota production system." According to him, the visitors would often say, "Oh, you have a Kan-Ban system, so do we." Or, "You have quality circles, so do we." Or, "You have process and value stream maps, so do we." Professor Johnson added, "They all see the pieces. What they do not see is the way they all go together."

There is an old saying in the systems field, "If you divide a cow in two, you do not get two small cows." Systems have integrity. While they are composed of elements, they are not defined by their elements but by how all these elements function as a whole. The easiest way to perceive a system is to look at its functioning and then begin to imagine how the different elements must interact in order to produce this functioning. As one systems biology teacher put it, "There is a world of difference between memorizing all the parts of a cell and learning how the cell *functions*, how it processes nutrients, how it sheds waste products, and how it maintains the integrity of the cell wall in the face of continual onslaughts."

These are the rudiments of systems inquiry but they are not as simple as they appear—in part because of complexity and in part because we ourselves—our mental models and our relationships with one another—are all among the elements of the system. So, systems inquiry is, by its nature, reflective.

Moreover, in a living system, these elements are continually being recreated, unlike in machine systems where the elements are fixed and simply decay over time. So, how we continually recreate our relationships with one another, form our interpretations of our work and reality, or shape our sense of shared purpose and specific goals—these ongoing activities are all part of the organization as a living system.

As soon as people start to contemplate this, their eyes cross and they can easily see the task as impossibly daunting. But look around. We see countless examples of very complex living human systems that function effectively. Sporting teams, symphony orchestras, jazz bands, dance troupes, and even many families and working teams. It is not that creating healthy living systems is impossibly complicated; it is the *way we usually think* about them that is impossibly complicated. Human beings have immense innate capacity for systems intelligence.[1] Our task is to understand this intelligence and how it either develops or stagnates. While rational and conceptual capacities are part of it, it is also an active intelligence that is evoked by *doing* things that matter together. In short, we build systems intelligence by continually and reflectively attempting to enact better ways of doing things. Systems intelligence cannot be broken down into simple rules or tools. It can only be learned, or as the Chinese would say, "cultivated."

Closely related to the folly of rules of systems intelligence is the naïve belief that the right measures will save the day. Measurement by its nature fragments. To measure someone's temperature is to capture one tiny facet of how one's particular mind-body-heart system is functioning at that instant. This is the difference between the physician as mechanic who looks at all the fragmented indicators and the gifted medical practitioners who also looks at the person as a whole. Managers need measures. All learners need ways to assess how they are doing relative to their aims. Very often measures can contribute to this assessment. But it is foolish to confuse the metric with the assessment—like confusing your temperature with your health.

Humility, openness and asking for help, from everyone, will always trump arrogance and the naïve belief in the next greatest tools or leaders

"There are no answers—and even if there are, we do not have them." This could serve as a regular mantra for all those serious about the journey. At one level, that we have not figured it all out is probably obvious to everyone. But we do not act as if this is so. Leaders regularly communicate that the new strategy is the right strategy—that the new change program or this new set of tools will solve our most intractable organizational issues—that the new boss will transform a mistrusting, non-reflective, under-performing culture. We bow to

---

[1] I am indebt to Esa Saarinen and Raimo Hämäläinen for the concept of systems intelligence: Systems Intelligence Research Group at the Helsinki Technological University, www.systemsintelligence.hut.fi. See, "Systems Intelligence: Connecting Engineering Thinking and Human Sensitivity," 2005, Hämäläinen and Saarinen (eds.). "Systems Intelligence—Discovering a Hidden Competence in Human Action and Organizational Life," Helsinki University of Technology, *Systems Analysis Laboratory Research Reports,* A88, October 2004.

humility and then act as if we have all the answers. Perhaps, it is because we do not know how to act otherwise.

Surely, regularly confessing ignorance and incompetence to your direct reports does not constitute a compelling management style. But confusing insight with "the answer," or compelling vision with "the plan" undermines an organization's genuine learning spirit.

One of the corollaries of adopting a systems perspective is that there is no complete answer, no definitive analysis. We have only working hypotheses, and we are inevitably guided by vision and intuition. People in leadership positions grounded in these simple truths can build an enormous sense of common undertaking and shared responsibility. As one CEO once put it, upon his retirement after a remarkable time of turnaround in a Fortune 50 business, "My greatest learning was the power of my vulnerability. When I could, at certain times, simply say, 'I do not have a complete plan and there are things about our business setting that I don't fully understand, it turned out to be a tremendously effective invitation to others. People started to realize that, "Phil does not have all the answers, and we all have to be part of figuring out what is needed."

****

The simplest way I know to summarize these three premises is that *We* are the organization as it operates today—what is visible, what is invisible, what is working, and what is not working. The structures and systems that dominate, both formal and informal structures, do so because we create them, day-by-day, hour-by-hour, by the way we think and act. No one is holding a gun to our heads. The rules we follow mostly take the form of habits we have acquired, habits of thought and action. And, most of these habits, especially the deep ones, are beyond our daily awareness. If the organization is stuck in counterproductive ways of doing things, it is because we are stuck, both individually and collectively.

This is the theory of "enacted systems"—that the systems that govern how families, organizations, industries, and societies work are created by their members. It is always tempting to find someone else to blame. Yes, there are external forces. Yes, there is history. These must be understood. But at some level it is pointless to attribute our fate to these. Comforting perhaps. But pointless.

Enacting alternative systems is not easy. It requires tools, methods, and guiding ideas —like those you will find in the following pages. But, the right tools used with the wrong spirit will amount to little more than symptomatic fixes, short-term improvements but little longer-term change.

Hopefully, appreciating these three premises will contribute to a learning spirit that can make the insights and ideas that follow truly helpful in enacting lean management rather than getting others to implement it. As this begins to actually happen on a larger scale, "lean" can take its place, not as "the answer," but as one more step in the long journey toward truly healthy organizations—organizations that, by their nature, contribute to economic, social and biological health and well being, for all.

Peter M. Senge
December 30, 2006

INTRODUCTION

Why are established lean enterprises so durably successful while so many attempts to become lean fail? The answer lies in the Anna Karenina principle, an extension of Tolstoy's observation: "Happy families are all alike; every unhappy family is unhappy in its own way." In general, this means that a deficiency in any one of a number of factors critical to overall system function dooms the new relationship. Human interactions with nature are replete with examples of this principle. When an otherwise healthy species of plant or animal is introduced into a new ecosystem, the new species must harmonize with many critical subsystems—longitude and latitude, rainfall, terrain, predators, competitors, and sources of nutrition. More often than not, the introduction of a new species fails because the new ecosystem cannot support the alien life form, or the newly introduced species significantly disrupts the balanced subsystems of the finely tuned native ecosystem.

Unlike the balanced scorecard, activity-based costing and management, quality management, or many of the other fine tools that can be integrated into the overall enterprise ecosystem, lean is an ecosystem unto itself—an entirely integrated set of subsystems (like a good marriage) that cannot be adopted in a piecemeal fashion to manage a limited number of enterprise activities. An enterprise might choose to become more lean, but its managers should not expect to become lean by borrowing here and there from an integrated system where all practices are interdependent.

No single person can master the many details of the many interrelated lean subsystems, so this book maintains an appropriate focus: to provide perspectives on the ways that established lean enterprises treat accounting and performance measurement practices as subsystems that support an integrated approach to product and service delivery. Each chapter addresses important elements of these two practices. The best way to introduce this book is to characterize its authors and define the premises that guide their experience and writing, and the best way to introduce the authors and the core theme of this book is with its first premise.

If the business of business is business, the business of the lean enterprise is continuous, sustainable adaptation and well-being.

This first premise sounds like a strategy, and that is just the point. While strategy has become a universal paradigm for organizational management, lean is a universally sustainable strategy that leads all other evolving strategic choices. Lean enterprises universally seek to deliver value to the customer by designing and endlessly perfecting value streams to meet customer needs with continuous workflow processes from order to delivery that aggressively identify and eliminate any form of waste that impedes work flow. Clearly, the implementation of such a strategy does not fall within the purview of any single individual or functional discipline.

As learning leaders of the annual Lean Accounting Summit, this book's practitioner and academic authors have made a full-time commitment to lean and to each other from many different accounting and performance measurement perspectives. Just as lean is a comprehensive enterprise strategy that depends on all employees working as informed decision makers, any thorough treatment of lean management depends on a balanced team of informed experts who share a common understanding of how each person contributes only one or two perspectives to the whole picture.

This book presents the collected insights of some of the most experienced lean accounting and performance measurement practitioners in America, but a single question dominates the organization and presentation of their insights: Why does a comprehensive understanding of the formula of lean principles embedded in the Toyota Production System continue to elude and frustrate otherwise intelligent people trying to implement it in their own enterprises? The answer to this question comes in part from our second premise.

Learning lean is not a matter of personal initiative alone and cannot be acquired from textbooks, classrooms, conferences, or seminars; people learn lean by working together as they actively practice lean principles in an enterprise culture committed to lean from top to bottom, side to side.

In every chapter the authors emphasize the importance of building a culture that levels the conventional information and authority hierarchies so typical of traditional economy-of-scale organizations. Whether the topic is leadership, process design, quality, performance measurement, employee motivation, or accounting, people throughout enterprises choosing a transformation to lean learn how to implement lean principles and reconfigure the workplace side by side. Lean is a transformation of the enterprise, not a transition. Each chapter discusses concrete steps that employees at all levels can use to accomplish the lean transformation together *in the workplace.*

This means that lean transformations cannot be sustained without first establishing the appropriate enterprise-wide culture, and an important reason why Western enterprises so frequently fail at lean transformations lies in the unwillingness of leadership to redefine their roles from financially biased commanders-in-chief to operationally informed facilitators and resource providers. Lean transformations depend on cultural transformations, and culture can only evolve when executive leadership understands the principles of the new culture it wants to build. Once again, each chapter describes clear steps for executive leaders and managers to use as they work with fellow employees to lay down the cultural foundations necessary to support sustainable lean processes.

Why bother? The answer to this question comes from many sources, but the third premise answers the question by capturing the essence of each source.

When followed as a comprehensive system, lean is simply a more mature way for organizations to function in the current business environment.

Although it was conceived in the economic poverty of World War II Japan, lean seems to have anticipated the newfound power that the Internet has placed in the hands of the customer, and everyone is scrambling to capture customer information for strategic advantage. Anchored in order-to-delivery process structures where customer orders eliminate guesswork and waste by providing the enterprise with full customer preference information, lean practitioners continue to perfect cost-effective customer satisfaction with processes that actually learn—from the customers, suppliers, and the enterprise employees who seek to perfect the processes that serve the customer. Wall Street increasingly values intangibles, learning organizations, and human capital. Lean systems by their very nature seek to optimize these three areas and represent a more mature means of doing business than traditional economy-of-scale enterprises.

Consistent with this premise, new sciences like systems thinking, quantum mechanics, and field theory have become increasingly more influential in the management science literature over the last 20 years. Managers at all levels and from all disciplines recognize the parallels between living organisms and human organizations, and one of the most important parallels is the importance of information sharing, connectivity, and relationships—cells to cells, cells to organs, organs to organisms—and the natural ways that a decentralized relationship structure of these elements promotes maximum efficiency and survival advantages. This organic perspective on the lean enterprise is built into the language of lean cultures where many "work cells" contribute to a "value stream." Traditional enterprises seem mechanical and inflexibly brittle by comparison.

In *Profit Beyond Measure* (New York: Free Press, 2000), H. Thomas Johnson distinguishes between two enterprise cultures: the traditional, financially driven, hierarchically structured management by results (MBR) culture and the lean, operationally driven, distributive management by means (MBM) culture. In MBR cultures, leadership focuses on quantitative results to achieve unlimited growth through command and control relationships (a tribal stage of organizational development). MBM culture leadership focuses on sustainable growth by building current and future relationships with customers, with suppliers, with fellow employees throughout the enterprise in a system where all these participants contribute to the ongoing perfection of customer delivery processes (a democratic stage of organizational development). Lean is more mature, but cultural change is the bottom line challenge. Each chapter addresses the challenges of evolving rigid traditional cultures and their organizational structures into adaptive lean cultures from the shop floor to the executive suite.

Because lean is a transformation of enterprise maturity, and because so many enterprises fail to make the total commitment to the steps that lead to lean maturity, this book presents the steps from the starting point of the traditional enterprise—financial command and control systems designed to support economies of scale. The primary components of traditional systems are strategy, quality, cost, and performance management methodologies. The authors contrast traditional understandings of these methodologies in terms of lean principles so that managers can learn to create a more mature culture and guide the enterprise-in-transformation to sustainable, integrated, interdependent work processes that incorporate the customer, supply chain, and employee learning.

The book is organized in three parts that remain consistent with the sequence that people can best learn how lean principles support a radically new enterprise structure and culture. Rather than jumping straight into accounting, Part 1 addresses the lean principles, enterprise design, and leadership characteristics that form the foundation of a successful lean transformation. The order of Parts 2 and 3 tacitly suggests another important characteristic of lean. Despite the obsession Western enterprises have with cost, cost is simply another highly specialized form of performance management. Part 2 sets the stage for an examination of lean accounting by focusing on performance measures in lean systems and how those systems motivate employees beyond the measures and results incentives so characteristic of traditional reward and punishment methods. From this platform, Part 3 provides a detailed examination of accounting relevance in the lean enterprise with a focus on the information that managers in traditional enterprises need to facilitate the transformation.

A recurrent theme haunts Western enterprises in lean transformation and serves as our fourth premise.

The *comprehensive* application of the lean principles embodied by the Toyota Production System guides the cultural transformation necessary to support the continuous, sustainable adaptation and well-being of the lean enterprise.

To their detriment, financially driven Western managers have grown accustomed to displacing their focus on universal enterprise strategies for continuous, sustainable adaptation and well-being with the tactics and methodologies designed to support strategy, as H. Thomas Johnson and Robert S. Kaplan describe in *Relevance Lost* (Boston: Harvard Business School Press, 1991). The many individual tactics and methods for strategy development, quality, performance, and bookkeeping are bought and sold in piecemeal fashion like commodities. This form of enterprise management lacks cohesion, consistency, and sustainability, and lean implementations eventually languish along with other poorly integrated management solutions of the month.

After more than 60 years of unwavering practice in lean principles, the Toyota Production System is the unquestionable gold standard of lean practices marked by continuous, sustainable adaptation and well-being that place Toyota at the top of a highly competitive marketplace. The authors make no excuses for learning from and writing about the longest-lived, most evolved lean practitioner. While many other enterprises have learned to adopt the lean principles of the Toyota Production System, expect to hear an in-depth treatment of the many different ways that Toyota uses its integrated system to maintain its competitive advantage from chapter to chapter.

The final premise of this book is primarily editorial and serves as a challenge to the reader: Traditional levers of control have no place in the lean enterprise.

Lean systems replace the notion of traditional control with system regulation, but high-level managers have little or no incentive to relinquish the status they enjoy as controllers—especially management accountants. Strategies for profit and financial results breed mixed agendas for all managers. Conscientiously applied lean principles provide an enterprise with a truly fiduciary culture where the fiduciary relationships among all employees are highlighted by good faith, loyalty, and trust—not control.

CHAPTER 1 EXECUTIVE SUMMARY

"Lean Dilemma: Choose System Principles or Management Accounting Controls—Not Both," by H. Thomas Johnson

Written by one of the world's most influential management historians and committed lean researchers, Chapter 1 analyzes the current business climate and discusses why it leads to so many lean initiative failures. Remaining consistent with all the book's premises, this discussion looks at the root causes of lean initiative failures rather than just the symptoms. Historical perspectives help people see and understand legacy practices that do not work well in emerging, more mature systems. Lean is based on a long history of committed practice by an organization from the Orient, and this chapter characterizes and contrasts the evolutionary sequence of two evolving business philosophies: traditional, financially focused command and control structures and lean systems. The inability to recognize and understand these different philosophies is the prime obstacle to successful lean transformation.

CHAPTER 2 EXECUTIVE SUMMARY

"Limited Production Principles: Right-Sizing for Effective Lean Operations and Cost Management," by Jim Huntzinger

Chapter 2 begins by analyzing the profound differences between traditional economy-of-scale production methods and lean limited production methods and their work process designs in terms of efficiency, waste, and adaptability. This chapter then introduces core lean principles and terms that all employees in a lean transformation must understand before focusing on how lean organizations appropriately size each element of their work processes to eliminate waste, facilitate continuous improvement, and optimize enterprise adaptability to changing business environments and customer preferences. This chapter concludes with a discussion of the implications of lean principles for enterprise accounting systems.

CHAPTER 3 EXECUTIVE SUMMARY

"Lean Strategy and Accounting: The Roles of the CEO and CFO,"
by Orest Fiume

Chapter 3 examines lean from leadership and strategy perspectives. The chapter begins with an overview of the critical relationship of strategy to the cultural characteristics essential for transforming a traditional organization into a sustainable lean enterprise and names the two people who must know lean principles well enough to make this happen—the CEO and the CFO. The chapter then discusses 12 critical aspects of the transformation process that the CEO must lead if the company is to successfully implement a lean business strategy. Finally, the chapter discusses the difficult task of the CFO in implementing a lean strategy. The CFO must be concerned with the same focuses as the CEO but also address other lean strategy implementation obstacles embedded in traditional financial accounting practices that undermine lean cultures—perhaps the most common reason for the failure of sustainable lean transformations.

CHAPTER 4 EXECUTIVE SUMMARY

"Creating a New Framework for Performance Measurement of Lean
Systems," by Bruce Baggaley

Chapter 4 takes a critical look at the book's second major focus, lean performance measurement. Since lean strategies are universally based on continuous, sustainable adaptation and wellbeing, many lean performance metrics are uniform across similar classes of lean enterprises whether oriented to product or service delivery. This first performance measurement chapter focuses on process measures, the first of two essential measurement categories for lean enterprises. The chapter begins with an analysis of the ways that traditional measures undermine lean transformations because they focus more on the shareholder than the customer. The discussion then moves to the ways that managers must structure lean performance measurement systems to enhance employee involvement and ownership to facilitate continuous learning and creative solutions to problem solving rather than the color-within-the-line mandates of traditional command and control measurement structures. Then, after describing the essential characteristics of lean performance measures and the way appropriate measures reflect core lean principles, this chapter concludes with the presentation of a starter set of lean measures.

CHAPTER 5 EXECUTIVE SUMMARY

"Motivating Employee Performance in Lean Environments: Respect, Empower, Support," by Frances Kennedy and Peter Brewer

Chapter 5 focuses on the second and most important of the two essential measurement categories for lean enterprises—employee motivation. Measurements motivate human behavior, and lean measurement systems borrow from a growing body of traditional research suggesting that people simply perform better when intrinsically motivated by their work rather than when extrinsically motivated by money, job titles, and working hours alone. This chapter describes the way that lean systems encourage employees to own and take pride in their work—with an enterprise culture that proactively takes formal steps to respect, empower, and support employee ownership of their work processes. In three parts, this presentation details the ways that lean managers involve employees in the creation and ongoing stewardship of the measures that monitor the quality and efficiency of the work they perform and the enterprise's processes themselves. This chapter discusses concrete methods that lean enterprises use to capture the most from their human assets—the collection of talents and ingenuity employees possess and can apply to their work if given the opportunity. Enterprises lose these competence assets when employees are constrained by the extrinsic rewards of traditional performance management systems; this chapter gives managers an alternative that embodies the best of core lean principles.

CHAPTER 6 EXECUTIVE SUMMARY

"On Target: Customer-Driven Lean Management,"
by Dr. C. J. McNair, CMA

Chapter 6 launches the third and most extensive part of this book—lean accounting—by discussing how lean accounting is a specialized extension of performance management that addresses the driving force behind all lean enterprise management decisions: the customer. Maturing the financial accounting focus of the traditional Western enterprise is the make-or-break point for the lean transformation, and the growing emphasis Wall Street places on the customer just might be the easiest way for the traditional enterprise to justify a commitment to the lean journey. Chapter 6 examines lean accounting and performance measurement from a customer-driven perspective and gives equal treatment to considerations of service and manufacturing concerns. The chapter begins with an analysis of customer economics and the impact of customer perspectives on lean accounting and performance measurement system design with plenty of proven lean implementation examples from successfully transformed enterprises. The discussion then turns to customer segmentation strategies for the market by showing how lean enterprises analyze and group customers based on a common set of preferences for specific product value propositions, again with many examples from actual practice. The chapter concludes with ways that lean enterprises act on the customer perspective by building it into their accounting and performance measurement systems.

CHAPTER 7 EXECUTIVE SUMMARY

"Value Stream Costing: The Lean Solution to Standard Costing Complexity and Waste," by Brian Maskell and Nicholas Katko

Chapter 7 addresses the crippling impact of legacy standard costing methods for enterprises on the road to lean transformation. Traditional enterprises continue to use these outdated practices from the mid-twentieth century, and standard costing methods are significant obstacles to a lean transformation because they support the traditional financially driven cultural values so inconsistent with customer- and employee-focused lean cultural values. After an analysis of the ways that standard costing undermines the lean transformation, this chapter presents the lean solution: value stream costing. A value stream is all the activities required to design, order, and manufacture a product or service from raw material to the customer and along with the work cell embodies the most important element of lean process and work flow design. Chapter 7 details how lean managers use the value stream as the focal point of all their cost management practices in terms of using cost information to manage the value stream, product costing, and implementing a value stream costing system.

CHAPTER 8 EXECUTIVE SUMMARY

"Obstacles to Lean Accountancy," by Lawrence Grasso

Before moving to Chapters 10, 11, and 12, which give practical steps that managers can take to transform their accounting practices, Chapter 8 presents a thorough analysis of the obstacles traditional enterprises face at the start of the lean journey from the standpoint of accounting system relevance. The discussion emphasizes how strategic, measurement, and accounting practices influence each other, creating a self-reinforcing cycle. Appropriate accounting practices inform and lead to successful lean decisions, and successful decisions lead to favorable results measures that reinforce an evolving strategy based on lean management. As a management accounting domain, cost and performance measurement is a positive force enabling lean. Since this self-reinforcing cycle works both positively and negatively, inappropriate information inhibits continuous improvement, and inappropriate measurement focuses encourage behaviors that subvert lean management. This chapter identifies the five primary obstacles to lean transformation with an emphasis on the strengths and shortcomings of some of the most recent accounting and performance measurement system innovations like activity-based costing (ABC), *grenzplankostenrechnung* (GPK), resource consumption accounting (RCA), and the balanced scorecard for the lean enterprise. Chapter 8 concludes with some practical steps managers can take to overcome the barriers to lean transformation.

CHAPTER 9 EXECUTIVE SUMMARY

"Lean Application in Accounting Environments," by Jean Cunningham

Chapter 9 pulls together virtually all themes from previous chapters discussing how to apply lean principles in the accounting environment seasoned by examples of practical, personal experiences. The central tenet of this chapter is that "effectively adopt lean" means first and foremost that the accounting function must adopt a new primary goal: *add value to the company bottom line for all activities*. To accomplish this goal, the lean accounting function must focus on three broad, overarching areas: (1) follow change and adapt accounting processes and deliverables; (2) establish how people use accounting information and supplement, modify, or eliminate reports to support the primary goal; and (3) seek out and eliminate waste in the accounting processes that do not add value to decision makers. After a discussion of the ways that accounting participates in Kaizen events, Chapter 9 presents a ten-step process that guides the accounting function through the early stages of the lean transformation.

CHAPTER 10 EXECUTIVE SUMMARY

"Sarbanes and Lean—Odd Companions," by Fred Garbinski

Chapter 10 addresses the lean perspective on a subject near the top of any manager's list in the American business environment: Sarbanes-Oxley compliance. It begins by describing how and why the auditors were handed the role they now enjoy in a post-Sarbanes world because it is management's responsibility, not the auditor's, to design and implement effective control processes. The discussion then addresses how a management-led process, such as a lean initiative with its standard work, continuous improvement, and team-based organizational tools, can and does meet the Sarbanes requirements, thereby appropriately realigning responsibilities for the integrity of financial reporting and compliance requirements. Lean enterprises repeatedly demonstrate how lean processes are more effective and efficient than processes used by traditional, transaction-based mass producers. With the underlying purposes of simplicity, availability, understandability, and capability, lean process design easily meets the Sarbanes requirements of ensuring the reliability and integrity of financial reporting. The chapter discusses how this greater purpose actually allows lean enterprises to meet not only the financial reporting objectives necessary to comply with Sarbanes, but all the other Committee of Sponsoring Organizations of the Treadway Commission objectives as well.

CHAPTER 11 EXECUTIVE SUMMARY

"Collective System Design to Enhance and Sustain Lean as a Tool to Rethink Lean Accounting," by David S. Cochran, PhD

Chapter 11 brings this book full circle by articulating a practical, systematic way for accountants to contribute to redesigning systems for the lean transformation. As a comprehensive, integrated approach to enterprise guidance and management, lean principles inevitably filter down to the system responsibilities of the management accountant in the traditional enterprise—accounting and performance management. What should an accountant do when the enterprise attempts to transform itself according to lean principles? What is the actionable role of the management accountant that makes accounting more relevant in the lean enterprise?

Chapter 11 captures all of the lean principles and perspectives from earlier chapters and articulates the pathway that management accountants need to understand to guide the emerging lean system design. Each preceding chapter has focused on the importance of cultural change and the ways that accounting language and communication methods support cultural change. This chapter addresses lean enterprise environment functional requirements and physical solutions that lead to the lean transformation by articulating the language that accountants use in successful, sustainable lean initiatives.

Lean is an ecosystem composed of many self-regulating, balanced, supportive subsystems. Accounting is but one of those subsystems, but it must conform to the overall system design and balance. As one of the most important articulations for the management accountant, this chapter demonstrates the many ways that lean principles map the correct directions for the accounting profession.

ABOUT THE CONTRIBUTING AUTHORS

Bruce Baggaley (Chapter 4) is senior partner and cofounder of BMA, Inc., a firm that specializes in assisting companies that have adopted lean manufacturing to implement lean accounting practices and tools. Mr. Baggaley is a frequent speaker and author on management control for lean companies and is coauthor of the book, *Practical Lean Accounting* (Portland, Ore.: Productivity Press, 2003). He can be reached at bbaggaley@maskell.com.

Peter C. Brewer (Chapter 5) is an associate professor in the Department of Accountancy at Miami University. His research interests include activity-based costing, theory of constraint-based performance measurement, balanced scorecard strategic performance measurement, and lean accounting. He has published numerous articles in a variety of journals, including *Management Accounting Research, Journal of Information Systems, Cost Management, Strategic Finance*, and *Journal of Accountancy*. He is a coauthor of two market-leading managerial accounting textbooks, *Managerial Accounting* (New York: McGraw-Hill/Irwin, 2004) and *Introduction to Managerial Accounting* (New York: McGraw-Hill/Irwin, 2006).

Dr. David S. Cochran (Chapter 11) is the founder of System Design, LLC. He was part of the mechanical engineering faculty at MIT from 1995 to 2003 as assistant and associate professor. He established the Production System Design (PSD) Laboratory at MIT and his company to advance the science of system design and integrated performance measurement, which provides a road map to sustain lean and the Toyota Production System and advance enterprises beyond these system designs. He is a two-time recipient of the Shingo Prize for manufacturing excellence for his work in the design of lean systems, and he received the Dudley Prize for best paper from the *International Journal of Production Research* in 2000 for his work to integrate system design theory.

Dr. Cochran facilitates system design change with major companies. His work is presently focused on the collective system design of enterprise, and integrated product design and delivery systems with the Missile Defense Agency, Lockheed Martin, and RAC Advanced Composites.

Dr. Cochran is a visiting professor at Meijo University in Nagoya, Japan, in the management-engineering program. He is a former board member of the Greater Boston Manufacturing Partnership and is affiliated with the Society of Organizational Learning founded at MIT. Dr. Cochran received his PhD in industrial and systems engineering from Auburn University and MSc in manufacturing systems engineering from Pennsylvania State University.

Jean Cunningham (Chapter 9) is a thirty-year financial professional with wide-ranging experience in public and private companies. Her lean accounting journey started while the chief financial officer and vice president of company services, responsible for accounting, human resources, information systems, and telecommunications at Lantech, LLC. From 1991 through 2004, Ms. Cunningham was a leader in Lantech's evolution from a small, family-owned business to a lean industry leader. She joined the continuous improvement effort at Lantech from their first Kaizen and took the revolution of lean from the manufacturing floor to the accounting department and throughout the business office.

Jean is coauthor of *Real Numbers: Management Accounting in a Lean Organization* (Durham, N.C.: Managing Times Press, 2003), a Shingo Prize–winning study of real-life applications of lean accounting. Another book is in prepublication on information systems in a lean organization. More recently, Jean has expanded her consulting activities into a full-time endeavor. She consults with clients throughout the United States on business strategy, process improvement, and growth and acquisition planning, and she regularly writes and lectures on lean accounting and operations management. Jean has a BS in accounting from Indiana University and an MBA from Northeastern University. Jean and her husband live in the Chicago area.

Orest (Orry) J. Fiume (Chapter 3) was vice president of finance and administration and a director of the Wiremold Company, West Hartford, Connecticut, which gained international recognition as a leader in lean business management in *Lean Thinking* (New York: Free Press, 2003), by James P. Womack and Daniel T. Jones. He was Wiremold's senior financial officer from 1978 until his retirement in 2002.

Mr. Fiume led Wiremold's conversion to lean accounting in 1991 and developed alternate accounting systems that supported the company's entire lean business efforts. He went on to install lean accounting at more than 20 Wiremold acquisitions. He has studied lean production in both the United States and Japan. In addition, he has taught courses on management accounting in a lean business at the Lean Enterprise Institute, the TBM Institute, the University of Dayton Center for Competitive Change, Manufacturing Extension Partnerships in five states, and numerous companies. He was a member of a delegation to China to discuss U.S. financial management practices.

Mr. Fiume is coauthor of the 2004 Shingo Prize–winning book, *Real Numbers: Management Accounting in a Lean Organization* (Durham, N.C.: Managing Times Press, 2003), and was inducted as a life member of the Shingo Prize Academy, which has been referred to by *BusinessWeek* as the Nobel Prize in manufacturing. He has a master's degree in management from Rensselaer Polytechnic Institute and a bachelor's degree in accounting from Fairfield University. He is a certified public accountant, a member of the American Institute of Certified Public Accountants, a member of Financial Executives International, and serves on the board of directors of several companies.

Frederick P. Garbinski (Chapter 10) is currently an assistant professor with Case Western Reserve University in Cleveland, Ohio, where he teaches financial management control systems and works with Brian Maskell Associates (BMA) assisting companies in implementing lean accounting methods. Before his retirement in 2005, he was with Parker Hannifin Corporation, a leading producer of motion-control components and systems. While with Parker, Mr. Garbinski led a number of financial initiatives including reengineering finance, lean accounting, and most recently Sarbanes-Oxley. Previously, he was responsible for financial reporting, manufacturing accounting, and government accounting and served as the director of internal audit.

A certified public accountant, Mr. Garbinski began his career at Deloitte & Touche after receiving his BS degree from Indiana University of Pennsylvania. He is a member of the American Institute of Certified Public Accountants and has served on a number of its committees. He is also a member of the Ohio Society of CPAs and the Financial Executive's Institute.

Lawrence Grasso (Chapter 8) is an associate professor of accounting at Central Connecticut State University in New Britain, Connecticut, where he teaches managerial and cost accounting and accounting information systems. After seven years in public accounting, he obtained a DBA from Boston University and entered academia. His research interests are performance measurement and accounting to support lean businesses. He can be reached at grassola@ccsu.edu.

Jim Huntzinger (Chapter 2 and Glossary) is the president of the Lean Accounting Summit, LLC, and Highland Path, a lean enterprise consulting group and research network in Pendleton, Indiana. He began his career as a manufacturing engineer with Aisin Seiki (a Toyota Group company) when they transplanted to North America to support Toyota. He also spent eight years at Briggs & Stratton in a range of engineering and management positions working to implement and evolve lean into its manufacturing operations and business practices.

Mr. Huntzinger has spent over eight years as a manufacturing consultant helping businesses, ranging from global corporations to small privately held companies, implement lean tools and strategies and has researched at length the evolution of manufacturing in the United States and with an emphasis on lean influences and development. Mr. Huntzinger holds a BS in mechanical engineering technology from Purdue University and a MS in engineering management from the Milwaukee School of Engineering. He can be reached at jim@leanaccountingsummit.com and 317-813-5415.

H. Thomas Johnson (Chapter 1), professor of business administration at Portland State University, was named one of the 200 leading management thinkers living today in a survey published by Harvard Business School Press in 2003. Mr. Johnson has an undergraduate degree in economics from Harvard, an MBA from Rutgers, and a PhD in economic history from the University of Wisconsin. Before entering an academic career, he was employed as a CPA by Arthur Andersen & Company. Johnson is an internationally noted authority on economic history, management accounting, and quality management, having published seven books and over 100 articles and reviews on these subjects. His coauthored book, *Profit Beyond Measure: Extraordinary Results through Attention to Work and People* (New York: Free Press, 2000), received the 2001 Shingo Prize for Excellence in Manufacturing Research. His best-selling *Rele-*

vance Lost: The Rise and Fall of Management Accounting (Boston: Harvard Business School Press, 1987, coauthored with Robert S. Kaplan, was named by *Harvard Business Review* in 1997 as one of the most influential management books published in the twentieth century. Johnson has spoken and consulted with scores of organizations on five continents. His current research focuses on the intersection of systems thinking, modern science, and sustainable operations management. He is exploring the application of natural living system principles to the design of ecologically focused local business operations that emulate and extend the scope of the Toyota Production System.

Frances Kennedy (Chapter 5) is an assistant professor at Clemson University and teaches undergraduate cost accounting and graduate controllership. Prior to teaching, Dr. Kennedy had 13 years of experience in public accounting and in industry. While at Rubbermaid, she worked as accounting manager in a manufacturing facility and as an analyst on a new product development team at the division's headquarters. Dr. Kennedy's research focuses on performance measurements and control systems in lean enterprises. She is the 2006 recipient of the Silver Lybrand Medal awarded by the Institute of Management Accounting and the 2006 Award of Merit from the International Federation of Accountants for her contributions to the field of management accounting. She has published in both academic and professional journals, including *Performance Measurement and Management Control*, *Journal of Business and Economic Perspectives*, *Accounting Education*, *Journal of Accounting Education*, *Advances in Interdisciplinary Studies*, *Cost Management*, *Strategic Finance*, *Journal of Corporate Accounting and Finance*, and *Target*.

Brian Maskell (Chapter 7) is the president of BMA Inc., a New Jersey consulting firm specializing in lean accounting and other management methods used by lean enterprises. Since 1992 he has worked with more than one hundred organizations pursuing the transformation to lean. He is the author or coauthor of six books related to lean and world-class manufacturing including *Performance Measurement for World Class Manufacturing* (Portland, Ore.: Productivity Press, 1991) and *Practical Lean Accounting* (Portland, Ore.: Productivity Press, 2003). Mr. Maskell can be reached by email at bmaskell@maskell.com or by phone 609-239-1080. The BMA Web site can be found at http://www.maskell.com/LeanAcctg.htm.

Dr. C. J. McNair's (Chapter 6) motivation to embrace lean thinking comes from many sources. For Dr. McNair, it came in the form of the book *Relevance Lost* (Boston: Harvard Business School Press, 1991) by Johnson and Kaplan. Since 1987, Dr. McNair has completed numerous studies of emerging management and accounting practices, authored eight books and many articles on these topics, including *The Profit Potential* (New York: John Wiley & Sons, 1995), which discusses various forms of organizational waste and how to develop measures that will lead to its elimination; *Benchmarking: Tool for Continuous Improvement* (New York: John Wiley & Sons, 1995) with Kathleen Leibfried; and *Total Capacity Management* (Boca Raton, Fla.: CRC Press, 1998), which was sponsored and published by the IMA, and worked with leading companies to identify and implement new cost management systems since 1987. Over the past six years, Dr. McNair has extended her work into the area of strategic cost management. Dr. McNair has developed a model and methodology that defines and develops cost management from the "outside in." The resulting Customer Value Management System (CVMS) has been researched, implemented, and tested in the United States, Canada, and Europe.

PART I
LEAN ESSENTIALS

1

LEAN DILEMMA: CHOOSE SYSTEM PRINCIPLES OR MANAGEMENT ACCOUNTING CONTROLS—NOT BOTH

H. THOMAS JOHNSON

1.1 LEAN CURE: SYMPTOM VERSUS ROOT CAUSE

Businesses everywhere have given enormous attention to "lean" management programs for over a decade. However, none emulates what Toyota, the creator of "lean," has achieved. To be sure, many businesses temporarily improve their performance, some greatly, by adopting Toyota practices. But none succeeds as Toyota has at continuously improving lead time, cost, productivity, quality, and overall financial performance year after year after year, for decades.

Failure to reach a desired goal despite repeated attempts often reflects a systemic pattern of problem solving in which people ameliorate symptoms of a problem without removing the problem's root cause. Because they find relief from its symptoms, if only for a while, businesses postpone looking for the problem's deeper root causes. The problem persists and continues to produce troubling symptoms that one temporary fix after another merely alleviates, without ever eradicating the core problem. Does this mode of problem solving characterize most "lean" initiatives? If it does, then such initiatives fit the popular definition of insanity: "doing the same thing over and over again while hoping for different results."

3

All businesses desire high and stable profitability, period after period for as long as possible. That surely is the goal of most performance improvement programs, including "lean" initiatives. However, such programs invariably boost profitability for only a while, followed by increasing instability and reduced performance until the cycle repeats and management once again rolls out another improvement program that boosts profitability for a while, followed by another disappointing downturn that leads to yet another improvement program, and so on. As a consequence of such improvement-initiative cycles, average results over the long term move in the opposite direction of the desired result, despite brief periods of improvement in the short run.

1.2 BUSINESS RESULTS: MECHANISM VERSUS LIFE SYSTEM

I believe this unintended consequence of improvement initiatives occurs in most businesses because management's view of what causes business results differs greatly from how the business system itself naturally produces those results. In virtually all businesses today, and for the past 50 years or more, management actions meant to improve financial performance reflect a mechanistic view of what causes financial results. In that view, financial results are a linear, additive sum of independent contributions from different parts of the business. In other words, managers believe that reducing an operation's annual cost by $1 million simply requires them to manipulate parts of the business that generate spending in the amount of $1 million each year, say by reducing employee compensation or payments to suppliers. Because managers assume that all parts of their operations make independent contributions to overall financial performance, like the parts of a machine, they would consider any or all of the following steps to be equally effective: lay off employees whose annual pay equals $1 million; reduce wages, salaries, or benefit payments by that amount; force suppliers to accept reduced prices for their goods or services; and outsource employment or contract purchases to less developed countries. It does not matter what steps are chosen, as long as they eliminate $1 million of annual spending.

Were managers to assume, however, that the financial performance of business operations results from a pattern of relationships among a community of interrelated parts, and is not merely the sum of individual contributions from a collection of independent parts, their approach to reducing costs could be entirely different. In that case, managers might attempt to reduce costs by improving the system of relationships that determines how the business consumes resources to meet customer requirements. This would suggest that they view "improvement" primarily in terms of a system of relationships—the human social system that is the business—and not simply in terms of an arithmetic sum of separate parts. More specifically, this would imply that they define and "measure" continuous improvement in terms of a long-term vision of how work should be conducted to best satisfy customer needs with the least consumption of resources. Viewing current operations through the lens of this vision would enable everyone in the organization to see the direction that change must take to move operations closer to that vision.

This is how managers might act if they viewed the operations of a business as part of a natural living system. As I have noted many times in the past two decades, it is not uncommon for scientists today to view human social systems, such as business organizations, as examples of self-organizing and self-identifying living systems.[1] However, such thinking has not yet influenced business education and practice. Indeed, the thinking and behavior of almost all managers in today's business world reflect a worldview grounded in the whole-equals-sum-of-parts and win-lose competitive principles of nineteenth-century mechanics and eighteenth-century classical physics, not the systemic, cooperative, and win-win symbiotic principles of twenty-first century cosmology and life science. In short, today's managers and business educators typically view the financial performance of a business as the sum of independent contributions from separate parts of a machine, not as the emergent outcome from complex interactions among the interrelated parts of a life system. That explains, I believe, why virtually all improvement initiatives, including so-called lean initiatives, inevitably generate long-run financial results that fall far short of what was intended by the initiatives' designers.

It all has to do with a "confusion of levels," a phrase writers often use to describe what the twentieth-century systems thinker Gregory Bateson called a type of epistemological error, an error in the nature of an organization's knowledge, its presuppositions and foundations, and its extent and validity. Bateson said that humans in any culture share certain premises about epistemology, that is, premises "about the nature of knowing and the nature of the universe in which we live and how we know about it."[2] Many of these premises, because they work at some levels and under certain circumstances, are misapplied to other levels. Problems occur when this happens.

People in Western cultures have premises for explaining or understanding the world at two main levels, referred to briefly above. At one level, call it the mechanical, all events are explained by the influence of external force or impact on independent objects. At the other level, call it the living, all events are explained by patterns of relationships connecting a world of self-organizing beings. The premises at the first level have been successfully used for nearly two centuries to study mechanical processes and to promote engineering technology. They are the basis for scientific and business education and practice in the Western world today. But problems have grown increasingly severe from the erroneous application of these premises to human practices with nature and in social organizations, such as businesses, that as networks of human relationship embody principles of living systems. For example, viewing reality through the premises of the mechanical level, a management accountant in modern business views a spreadsheet of financial results *as the company*. Oblivious to premises at the living level due to the embedded values of the business educational system and the professional organizations that promote these values, this person fails to see the system of human relationships that produces those financial results as the company. As a consequence, the person promotes policies to "improve financial results" by arbitrarily destroying relationships through layoffs or outsourcing, not by nurturing and reinforcing the features of those relationships that produce robust results. The long-term outcome, predictably, is less than expected.

1.3 CONFUSION OF LEVELS: LEAN PRACTICES VERSUS TOYOTA RESULTS

In their customary way of doing things in business, managers confuse linear cause-effect connections at the abstract quantitative level of financial results with the nonlinear, complex cause-effect connections that naturally exist at the concrete level of relationships among employees, suppliers, customers, owners, and community. Their business training and experience cause managers to believe that linear cause-effect connections at the abstract quantitative level apply everywhere in the world, including the level of real operations. Thus, they proceed to manipulate and control people and things at the complex and nonlinear operating level as though they behaved according to the linear principles that apply at the abstract quantitative level.

Therein lies what I refer to as a "confusion of levels"—failure to see that whereas in a mechanical system one-dimensional quantities can both *describe* results and *enable one to control* the linear process that produces those results, in a living system quantities can *only describe* results, but **cannot** *explain or enable one to control* the multidimensional interactions and feedback loops of the process that produces the results. As I discuss in more detail below, this "confusion of levels" invalidates all management accounting practices in which traditional businesses attempt to use financial quantities to explain and to control financial results. Those practices, which are endemic to American management but are not evident at Toyota, are the main reason why lean initiatives fail to have their desired impact on financial performance in American business.

An example of the damaging impact of this confusion is in a case I describe elsewhere that compares the financial (and other quantitative) results in two automobile bumper-making plants.[3] One is run by an American "Big Three" automaker whose managers continually manipulate separate parts of the plant's operations and arbitrarily increase output in order to achieve unit cost targets defined by an abstract financial cost equation. The other is run by Toyota, whose managers focus on nurturing systemic relationships in the plant according to a constant vision that has guided all operations in the company for many decades. The case demonstrates that the lowest cost and highest overall performance are achieved by Toyota, the company that does not confuse linear cause-effect connections at the abstract level of financial cost equations with the complex cause-effect connections at the concrete operating level of human relationships.

I believe it is because lean initiatives do not change the underlying mechanistic thinking that has guided management decisions in virtually all American businesses for the past half century or more that those initiatives fail to achieve results for American companies like the results observed at Toyota. Lean initiatives in non-Toyota companies invariably fail to embody the unique way of thinking about business and the fundamentally different approach to management in which Toyota's practices evolved. Thus, businesses transplant Toyota practices into a context of alien thinking that overpowers and dilutes the effectiveness of those practices. As a consequence, such companies can demonstrate Toyota-style management practices, but not Toyota performance results.

1.4 MANAGEMENT ACCOUNTING CONTROL SYSTEMS BLOCK LEAN

The prevalence of management accounting control systems in American business probably contributes more than any single thing to the confusion of levels that causes American managers to believe they can run operations mechanically by chasing financial targets, not by nurturing and improving the underlying system of human relationships from which such results emerge. It is significant, then, to note that where this confusion of levels is not present, as in Toyota, one sees virtually no use of management accounting targets (or "levers") to control or motivate operations. I argue that this is an important reason why Toyota's financial performance is unsurpassed in its industry.

People at Toyota place great importance in problem solving on *genchi genbutsu*, or "going to the place" where the problem occurs to see for yourself, firsthand. You don't rely on secondhand reports or tables and charts of data to get true understanding of root cause. Instead, you go to the place (*gemba*) where you can watch, observe, and "ask why five times." This attitude reflects, of course, no "confusion of levels." Instead, it shows a deep appreciation that results (and problems) ultimately emanate from and are explained by complex processes and concrete relationships, not by abstract quantitative relationships that describe results in simple, linear, additive terms.

It should not be surprising, then, to realize that managers in a Toyota plant, unlike their counterparts in American organizations, do not refer to accounting documents such as standard cost variance budgets to discuss the state of current operations. Indeed, as I was told in 1992 during my first of scores of trips to Toyota's Georgetown, Kentucky plant, Toyota views daily plant operations as a "black box" that the accounting system essentially does not enter.[4] Accountants, of course, record everything that goes into the plant and all the products that come out. But within the plant they don't track the flow between incoming resources and outgoing finished product. Everything one needs to know about the transformation that takes place inside the plant is inherent in the flow of the work itself. Indeed, a key feature of the Toyota Production System (TPS) is that the work itself provides the information needed to control its state. In other words, all the information needed to control operations is in the work.

Professor Kazuhiro Mishina introduced me to this aspect of the TPS in 1992, when he showed me a high-level "material and information flow map" for the Georgetown plant. He explained that the map is designed to show *material* flowing from left (raw material) to right (finished autos) and *information* flowing from right to left. Basically, there was only one line going from right to left—a line to represent the customers' orders entering the plant each day and going directly to the body welding operation.[5] Today, this type of map is familiar to anyone who has studied "value-stream mapping." But Kazuhiro pointed out to me that no lines representing information enter the plant from either the accounting system or the production control system. The work itself provides all the information that in non-Toyota plants customarily comes from computerized manufacturing resource planning (MRP) and standard cost variance reports.

While the value-stream mapping literature does an excellent job of showing how the TPS dispenses with the need for production controls (e.g., MRP) in daily operations, it is silent on how TPS also dispenses with the need for accounting controls in daily operations. This is an unfortunate lapse, in my opinion, because it has left the door open to the idea that "lean" manufacturing programs must include "lean" accounting controls, something that Toyota people, especially the late Taiichi Ohno, often referred to as *muda* (waste).

In Toyota plants, all information needed to control operations is in the work simply because all work flows continuously at a balanced rate through virtually every operation, from the beginning to the end of the manufacturing process. The work has been carefully designed so that one can "see" its current state quite literally. Is it on time to meet the day's orders? If not, how much additional time will be needed? Have defects or other errors occurred along the way? Are components to final assembly being replenished on a timely basis? Has any undue inventory accumulated anywhere? Are problems being identified and addressed according to standard procedures? Such questions, and hundreds more, can be answered every moment in every step of the process throughout the plant. No accounting system can alert managers as well or as fast if anticipated costs and revenues will not be achieved. Any "exceptions" that managers might need to address to keep financial results on track are visible in real time as the work is being done, not days, weeks, or months later in a report from the accounting department.

1.5 LEAN ACCOUNTING ANSWERS THE WRONG QUESTION

If traditional management accounting practices are the key problem preventing American businesses from emulating Toyota's performance, what should companies do? Many proponents of lean accounting suggest that companies should reform management accounting itself by doing things such as activity-based value-stream costing, direct costing, cash-flow accounting, value-add capacity analysis, and more. These proposals should cause a sense of *deja vu* among those who are old enough to recall some 20 years ago the proposals to gain better control over burgeoning overhead costs with activity-based cost (ABC) information. ABC seemed like a good idea at the time, but in retrospect it was a good answer to the wrong question. We see better today, when we understand more fully what Toyota does, that reducing manufacturing overhead costs requires a new way to organize work, not better cost information. The question that proponents of ABC should have been asking was how to organize work to eliminate the causes of overhead activity, not how to trace costs of overhead activities to products in more discriminating ways. Perhaps now is the time for companies interested in becoming "lean" to reframe the question that management accounting control systems are supposed to answer. It is time to recognize that management accounting controls are a good answer to a wrong question; that if the question were properly reframed, management accounting controls probably would not be a valid answer.

The question most companies ask now is how to control the financial results of business operations if financial results are a linear sum of individual contributions from separate parts of the business. Accounting control information seems the logical way to show how those contributions, and changes in those contributions, add up to the organization's overall financial results. But if we assume that financial results emerge from complex interactions and nonlinear feedback loops in the interrelated parts of a natural living system, then attempting to control those results with linear accounting information is not only erroneous, but possibly destructive to the system's operations in the long run. In this case, the new question is: how does one control, if at all, the financial results that emerge from operations that abide by the principles that govern a natural living system?

1.6 ANSWERS TO THE RIGHT QUESTION—FROM SHEWHART AND DEMING TO TOYOTA

An early answer to this question was provided in the 1930s and 1940s by Walter Shewhart and W. Edwards Deming, both trained in mathematical physics and both experienced in using state-of-the-art statistical tools in business and government. One of their lasting contributions was to devise a scientific way to estimate the "control limits" within which a business system's results would almost always fall until one of two steps were taken that altered the limits. One step was to ignore all but abnormal variation in results and work to improve the system itself, thereby narrowing the control limits and improving long-term performance. The other step, a less desirable but more common way of managing, was to try to improve long-term performance by intervening in the system every time results varied from a desired target. The inevitable consequence of the second step, Shewhart and Deming proved, is to widen the system's control limits and impair its long-term performance.[6]

In essence, Shewhart and Deming likened a well-designed business system to a living system in nature. Its results vary over time, but the range of variation has limits. However, in a human system such as the operations of a business, managers can improve performance by taking steps to reduce that range of variation. The key to performance improvement, then, is to nurture the system that produces results, not to drive the system to achieve targets that fall outside its normal performance limits. In his early work, Deming articulated 14 principles (or points) that defined what he meant by nurturing the system. Those principles included things such as create constancy of purpose, constantly improve systems by reducing variation, cease dependence on inspection, do not base purchases on price alone, do not reward individual performance, institute training, eliminate management by objectives, and more.

This is precisely the approach that Toyota takes to manage its operations. Toyota lives by a set of deep underlying system principles that, after observing their system on many study missions to their plants in the 1990s, I tried to sum up in my own words with the concept "managing by means." As I outlined it in my book *Profit Beyond Measure* (New York: Free Press, 2000), the essence of that concept, which compares Toyota's system to a living system, is that satisfactory business results follow from nurturing the company's system (the "means"), not from manipulating and wrenching its processes in order to achieve predetermined financial results (a mechanistic strategy popularly known as "managing by results").[7] In his own recent and excellent synthesis of Toyota's system principles, Jeffrey Liker articulates the same concept in his book *The Toyota Way* (New York: McGraw-Hill, 2003) with the phrase "creating the right process will produce the right results."[8]

This sentiment is central to the Toyota organization's deep-seated belief that one cannot improve financial performance by intervening in the system and forcing operations people to achieve results targets. Instead, they emphasize the importance of defining the properties their operating system should manifest and of having everyone in the organization work assiduously to continuously move the system toward those properties. Frequently, one hears Toyota people refer to those properties as "True North." True North in Toyota's system includes properties such as safety (for employees and for customers), moving work always in a continuous flow, one order at a time on time, with no defects, with all steps adding value, and with the lowest consumption of resources possible. The assumption is that the more that every process in the system manifests the properties of True North, the better will be the company's long-term performance.

These three approaches to managing operations—the Shewhart-Deming approach, managing by means (MBM), and the Toyota way—suggest how different it is to nurture the system that produces a company's financial results than it is to arbitrarily intervene in and wrench the system in an attempt to force it to produce a desired result beyond its current capabilities. The latter strategy is, of course, followed by virtually all large companies in the United States today, especially the large publicly traded companies whose top managers are pressured to deliver results demanded by financial markets and other outside interests. It seems unbelievable, but many of those companies are pursuing lean initiatives in the expectation of achieving performance like Toyota's. The fact that they will not or cannot forego pressure to drive operations with management accounting "levers of control" makes the likelihood of their realizing such expectations nearly zero.

1.7 MANAGEMENT ACCOUNTING CONTROLS OR SYSTEM PRINCIPLES: PICK ONE, NOT BOTH

If managers look primarily at financial information to judge the performance of a business, then they are certain to be working in the dark, unless I am mistaken and the operations they manage do in fact behave according to mechanistic principles. But anyone who is aware of modern life science can never again view a human social organization, such as a business, as anything but a natural living system. That being the case, it stands to reason that the key to favorable long-term financial performance is to design and run operations according to the principles that guide living systems. Such principles resemble Deming's, 14 points, the principles of managing by means (MBM), and those that Toyota refers to today as The Toyota Way or True North. Only if a company can describe its operating system in terms of such principles can it know whether or not the system is improving.

Financial quantities cannot reveal if a system is improving or not. To assume otherwise is to fall prey to "confusion of levels." If a company requires cost information to show the "savings" from "going lean," it is lost and will never get there. Requiring cost information to justify taking the steps that are necessary to become lean discourages people from continuously removing sources of delay and error that stand in the way of moving closer to achieving system principles such as those underlying living systems or Toyota's True North. Instead, they will create work-arounds such as rework loops, forks, and inventory to keep work moving (even if it is not continuously flowing) in the hope of eliminating unfavorable unit cost variances. In other words, the demand to justify operational decisions with cost information confuses levels, causing people to forego root-cause problem solving and, instead, to build "cost-effective" work-arounds that violate system principles. Eventually, the system principles are forgotten and managers spend increasing amounts of time working to improve the efficiency of the work-arounds.

No company that talks about improving performance can know what it is doing if its primary window on results is financial information and not system principles. No amount of financial manipulation will ever improve long-term results. Performance in the long run will improve only if managers ensure that the system from which the performance emerges adheres more and more closely to principles resembling those that guide the operations of a living system. The dilemma facing all companies that intend to become "lean" is that they can follow a truly systemic path to lean or they can continue to use management accounting "levers of control." They can't do both.

1.8 EPILOGUE: LEAN AND THE QUESTION OF SUSTAINABILITY

Management accounting controls impose a curse on lean management programs; they cause managers to believe that addressing the imperative of growth is compatible with the possibility of systemic well-being.[9] Abstract quantities by themselves can, of course, grow without limit. However, the universe has never allowed any real, concrete system within it to grow endlessly. Such attempts to grow endlessly inevitably fail. Had it been otherwise the universe by now would be only one thing—the system that never stopped growing until it became everything, and nothing.

Nevertheless, all businesses that chase accounting targets for revenue, cost, profit, or return on investment somehow believe they are an exception to this universal pattern. They "confuse levels" and are deaf to the primordial message being delivered every time their real operations fail to deliver the long-term performance that their abstract equations and their occasionally favorable short-term returns seem to promise. They fail to see that the pursuit of endless growth is incompatible with the long-term survival of the system.

This message applies to the entire human economy as well as to individual businesses in the economy. Even if every company in the world were to become as "lean" as Toyota, today's economy in which they operate is not sustainable. Forces drive it to focus on quantitative goals, hence, on extensive growth. Government tax, spending, and monetary policies promote more and more production and consumption, to grow gross domestic product (GDP) endlessly. Financial markets drive companies, including Toyota, to play in the same game. But an economy that lives on steroids is no more sustainable than any growth-driven organization operating within it. Until they can escape the curse of endless growth, both the economy and all its members are doomed to collapse and die.

Our Earth and its life-sustaining biosystem, as well as all systems in the entire universe from which Earth emerged, reflect the existence of continuously open fields of possibility. The most fundamental and most pervasive process in the universe, and especially on our Earth, is the constant emergence of newness out of what went before. Nothing ever constrained the flourishing of possibility in that process until humans introduced the idea of quantitative choice to the system. Quantity automatically limits possibility and emergence to outcomes that can be measured. Quantum physicists have suggested that undisturbed systems in the universe naturally stay in multiple states simultaneously, unless someone intervenes with a measurement device. Then all states except the one being measured collapse. Perhaps what you measure is what you get. More likely, what you measure is *all* you get. What you don't (or can't) measure is lost.

By using quantitative targets to manage results without regard to the effect our actions have on the underlying system from which the results emerge we close fields of possibility and limit ourselves to what our measures will produce. In effect, that describes existence inside a machine, not life. Life implies flourishing in fields of continuously renewing possibility. Mechanistic existence suggests a repetitive, homogeneous system running down to death, without hope of renewal or new possibility. Our worship of quantity virtually guarantees that the economy we inhabit today and the businesses within it are life-denying, not life-enhancing.

Businesses, like any living systems, should grow to be what they are supposed to be, not more. Ants grow to be ants, elephants grow to be elephants, and humans grow to be humans. Each in its context flourishes in life, in being—not in growing, accumulating, or having. Sustainability, as my colleague John Ehrenfeld has said, is *the possibility that humans and other life flourish on the Earth forever*.[10] Nurturing that possibility is the challenge that companies, citizens and the communities we inhabit must accept in the name of sustainability. "Lean" management in the sense of running companies according to living system principles is an important first step in meeting this challenge. Then comes the hard part: conducting our economic activities within the limits of Earth's regenerative processes. To fail at that will make all the lean initiatives irrelevant. But we can succeed, as long as we choose to live according to the principles of living systems and not according to the imperative of quantitative growth.

NOTES

1. H. Thomas Johnson, "Using Performance Measurement to Improve Results: A Life-System Perspective," *International Journal of Strategic Cost Management*, Vol. 1, No. 1 (Summer 1998), pp. 1–6; H. Thomas Johnson and Anders Broms, *Profit Beyond Measure: Extraordinary Results through Attention to Work and People* (New York: Free Press, 2000), pp. ix–xvi, 1–9, and 33–42; Fritjof Capra, *The Hidden Connections: A Science for Sustainable Living* (New York: Doubleday, 2002), Ch. 4; Elisabet Sahtouris, "The Biology of Business: New Laws of Nature Reveal a Better Way for Business," *World Business Academy Perspectives*, Part 1 in Vol. 19, No. 3 (September 15, 2005) and Part II in Vol. 19, No. 4 (September 22, 2005).
2. Gregory Bateson, *Steps to an Ecology of Mind* (New York: Ballantine Books, 1972), p. 478.
3. H. Thomas Johnson, "Lean Accounting: To Become Lean, Shed Accounting," *Cost Management*, January/February 2006, pp. 3–17.
4. H. Thomas Johnson and Anders Broms, *Profit Beyond Measure: Extraordinary Results through Attention to Work and People* (New York: Free Press, 2000), pp. 103–110.
5. See note 4, p. 82, Figure 3-1 for a version of the material and information flow map.
6. A succinct and excellent introduction to Deming's (and Shewhart's) thinking, including applications of statistical process control tools, is in Brian L. Joiner and Marie A. Gaudard, "Variation, Management, and W. Edwards Deming," *Quality Progress*, December 1990, pp. 29–37.
7. See note 4.

8. Jeffrey K. Liker, *The Toyota Way: 14 Management Principles from the World's Greatest Manufacturer* (New York: McGraw-Hill, 2004), Section II.

9. H. Thomas Johnson, "Confronting the Tyranny of Management by Numbers: How Business Can Deliver the Results We Care About Most," *Reflections: The SoL Journal on Knowledge, Learning, and Change*, Vol. 5 Compilation (2004), No. 4, pp. 51–61; "Sustainability and Lean Operations," *Cost Management*, March/April 2006, pp. 40–45.

10. John Ehrenfeld, "Searching for Sustainability: No Quick Fix," *Reflections: The SoL Journal on Knowledge, Learning, and Change*, Vol. 5 Compilation (2004), No. 8, pp. 137–149; "Beyond Sustainability: Why an All-Consuming Campaign to Reduce Unsustainability Fails," 2006, http://www.changethis.com/25.03 .BeyondSustain.

2

LIMITED PRODUCTION PRINCIPLES: RIGHT-SIZING FOR EFFECTIVE LEAN OPERATIONS AND COST MANAGEMENT

JIM HUNTZINGER

Of the many business concepts that mislead managers, economy-of-scale thinking almost universally leads to poor operational design and accounting practices in manufacturing. This chapter explains how lean principles and methods create systems designed for more effective production processes. While lean can be applied to manufacturing and service enterprises, this chapter introduces lean principles from a manufacturing perspective because this sector has the most mature lean practitioners.

Flow principles and techniques are the key concepts behind designing and executing an effective operation for any product- or service-focused lean enterprise. Flow applications that use right-designed systems, processes, and machines demonstrate the many shortcomings and inefficiencies of economy-of-scale manufacturing practices. Enterprises that learn and practice lean principles in the production designs of their products and services engage in true cost management rather than basic cost accounting.

The design of lean manufacturing systems and equipment incorporates the essential principles that guide successful lean organizations. Lean system and equipment designs are based on key elements of right-sizing and right fit. Accountants lead right-sizing activities in emerging lean environments because lean designs reduce costs and determine cost management methods. Consequently, lean accountants must understand how right-sizing and lean design facilitates work flow and the limited production applications that replace traditional economy-of-scale accounting practices.

Mastering the applications of lean principles is a lifelong learning process, and the people of Toyota Motor Corporation have been perfecting their production system since before World War II. This chapter discusses some of the key elements of lean production design to demonstrate how *operational* design leads accounting practices at Toyota and other proficient lean organizations. The glossary at the end of this book defines essential lean accounting and manufacturing terms used throughout this discussion. Important lean terms appear in italics each time they first appear in this book.

2.1 LIMITED PRODUCTION VERSUS ECONOMIES OF SCALE

Economies of scale are characterized by falling costs per unit as the speed and volume of output increase. This twentieth-century manufacturing definition continues to be the mantra of today's manufacturing industry and, more recently, service industries as well. The economy-of-scale approach succeeds as long as the market can continue to consume output growth, but as soon as the market becomes too slow, levels off, or declines, scale economies begin to fail. Two obstacles stand against enterprises that attempt to respond to their threatened economy-of-scale practices. First, managers apply economy-of-scale remedies and close plants, discontinue services, or lay people off because they are not trained to deal with threatening market changes. Second, by design, economy-of-scale production systems cannot adjust to changes in demand that come with slowing or shrinking markets.

The scale economies mind-set leads managers to focus on cost reduction at point locations rather than overall system improvements. Cost reductions are not the issue in a lean, limited production environment—establishing continuously flowing (one-piece flow) value streams is the path to be pursued. At Toyota's Georgetown facility "no cost system traces or calculates the flow of those items inside the plant."[1] Imagine any other major manufacturing enterprise without a standard cost accounting system to manage, control, or track product flow or costs in its operations. "Toyota does maintain cost systems for pricing and project purposes, but never to drive operations. In any event, the cost systems maintained reflect actual—not standard—costs, and they compile costs only as needed."[2] A cost-based focus on point location improvements may seem to make sense at the microdepartment level, but it reinforces the mentality for ever-increasing volume, which is the crux of failure for economies of scale—the inability to smoothly adapt to changing market environments.

In contrast to the limited production, made-to-order design of a lean system, economies of scale rely on batch production. Managers push output through their local areas or departments and create an environment of speed and volume to maintain favorable costs. The economy-of-scale system drives managers to increase output because more product "absorbs" overhead, creating the illusion of reduced costs. This thinking can be so ingrained that it creeps into organizations attempting lean transformations. Even when product is being produced in a cellular value stream flow operation, managers new to lean still plead with their people to bring down costs. "We need more cost-reduction projects!"

This pressure to produce as a means of decreasing costs creates a vicious cycle that confuses and deflates operations employees. Economy-of-scale enterprises produce as much output as possible in every part of the organization as a universal strategy for achieving minimum total cost. As more product absorbs more overhead, managers seek to minimize the unit cost of output produced in every individual process, which creates the illusion of minimizing total cost. In other words, economy-of-scale organizations assume that the total cost is the sum of individual costs in all the parts. *Profit Beyond Measure* author H. Thomas Johnson explains that:

> Minimizing the cost per unit of output from every individual operation presumably ensures the lowest total cost for the products assembled from that output.
>
> An inevitable but usually overlooked consequence of this cost minimization strategy is that it requires a company to produce more output in every period. The usual rationalization for requiring more output to achieve lower unit costs is the concept of scale economies.[3]

(a) Limited Production: The Lean Alternative

Accountants working with lean principles must come to understand what triggers and regulates production in the lean enterprise before designing a compatible cost management system. Tom Johnson and Anders Bröms describe how Taiichi Ohno started and propagated the Toyota Production System (TPS) throughout Toyota and its supply base as a *limited production* system. Ohno wanted to avoid any work in excess of what it took to produce what could be sold.[4] This focus was driven by Toyota's cash-strapped financial status after

World War II. The company could not afford to invest in *anything* beyond the exact material, equipment, and labor that it needed to produce *only* what had been ordered.

He worked by trial and error over many years to develop a production system that would consume only the absolute minimum resources necessary to produce only and exactly what the customer requested. Although Ohno's directive was driven by circumstances, it fit very well into Toyota Motor Company founder Kiichiro Toyoda's vision of Toyota's just-in-time manufacturing scheme. Ohno achieved both with the development of his limited production system.

The limited production system within Toyota has continued to develop through the years and has been carried to the very top level at Toyota. In *The New Manufacturing Challenge*, Fujio Cho (Mr. Cho is the former President of Toyota and also worked directly for Taiichi Ohno and is currently Chairman) puts a fine point on the way limited production systems differ from economies of scale when he defines *waste* in the context of the limited use of all resources as "anything other than the minimum amount of equipment, material, parts, space, and worker's time, which are absolutely essential to add value to the product."[5] Cho's definition is entirely consistent with the concept of limited production, represents anti–economy-of-scale thinking, and supports the practices of Toyota and all other lean organizations.

Taiichi Ohno presciently stated that economy-of-scale systems were the greatest waste of all, "the waste of overproduction—our worst enemy—because it helps hide other wastes . . . this kind of waste is definitely the result of pursuing quantity and speed."[6] Overproduction is simply a waste manifestation of economies of *scale*.

Where nonlean companies run large-scale plants as fast and as full as possible to achieve the highest possible throughput for the existing level of costs, the lean enterprise sees its customers and workers as parts connected in a web of interrelationships. Toyota does not attempt to drive outcomes by forcing large-scale production because ". . . this thinking has led companies to optimize cost with economies of scale. We produce to order" according to a few basic principles.[7]

Dr. Johnson puts it this way: "Toyota does not view low cost as a consequence of producing more, only as a consequence of consuming just enough to meet each customer's expectations, and no more. In short, Toyota's approach to cost minimization stresses 'enough' not 'more,' and it focuses attention on resources consumed, not on output produced."[8] John Shook spent 11 years working for Toyota while the company established a presence in the United States, and he describes how Toyota's focus was not economies of scale but a completely different approach:

> Economies of scale need not be the goal of the production system. You can attain greater overall system efficiency through concerted efforts to eliminate waste thoroughly. Ohno's efforts focused on developing the ability to survive and even thrive in low growth.[9]

The concept of right-designing systems and machines for limited production is a key concept to becoming a lean enterprise and to successfully developing a lean cost management system. Since physical changes to the operation must first be applied to create a flow environment, and machines and processes must often first be constructed differently to facilitate flow, lean organizations work to understand and apply right-design as a required alternative to batch manufacturing. Without this different application, an operation remains in a perpetual Kaizen—trying to improve a poorly designed manufacturing system. This is the essence of Ohno's experiments during his days in Toyota's machine shop.

2.2 LEAN AND RIGHT-SIZING

One of the most important terms for understanding lean principles is *right-sizing*, defined by Womack and Jones in *Lean Thinking* as: "A design, scheduling, or production device that can be fitted directly into the flow of products within a product family so that production no longer requires unnecessary transport and waiting."[10] The terms *right-sizing*, *right-fit*, and *right-design* are often used interchangeably, but they communicate different elements of lean principles. *Right-size* denotes the physical properties of equipment or processes, *right-fit* refers to the placement of the equipment within the overall process, and *right-design* involves the art of bringing all right-sized and right-fitted components into the best possible configuration. See Exhibit 2.1 for a contrast between machines that have been right-fit into manufacturing and machines that are not right-fit.

Lean enterprises achieve right-size equipment by focusing on four goals:

1. Make operations as compact as possible.
2. Make operations as inexpensive as possible.

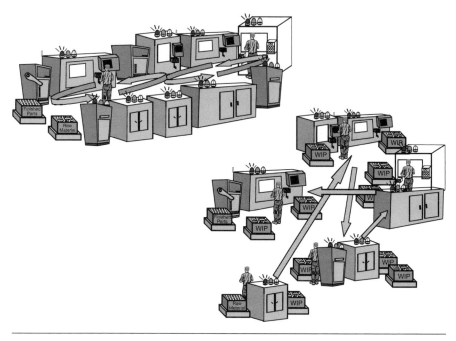

EXHIBIT 2.1   Lean Right-Fit versus Economy-of-Scale Design

3. Produce within the takt time.
4. Dedicate equipment to only one part or part-family in the overall manufacturing process.

This series of right-sizing goals reflects the philosophy of lean thinking: continuous improvement lies at the heart of all lean work. An ideal lean machine, process, or system:

- Is physically compact
- Utilizes one-piece flow (manufactures one piece at a time)
- Operates mixed model production or can be changed over in less than ten minutes with a goal of zero changeover time
- Moves as one contained unit rather than in separate units, i.e., machine base, hydraulic, unit or an electrical panel
- Operates within the designated *takt* time

- Is simple to repair, maintain, and operate
- Has built in *autonomation*
- Has *chaku-chaku* and *one touch start*
- Exemplifies the *5 Ss*[11]

These critical concepts help managers and accountants from traditional environments begin to understand the operational importance and implications of right-sized, -fitted, and -designed equipment or systems in terms of the role of the accounting system in a lean environment. While equipment sizing, fitting, and design most clearly demonstrate lean principles, right-sizing can also be applied to a number of applications other than production equipment, such as containers for part storage and transportation, technical support functions (engineering, accounting, ordering, shipping), and information systems (computer systems, documentation).

2.3 RIGHT-DESIGNING FOR FLOW

Manufacturing companies convert to lean principles by right-designing operations to replace batch-style manufacturing methods with *flow* manufacturing. Flow manufacturing or service delivery designs replace process-focused departments with product- or service-focused value streams. Flow is both a *mechanical means* that directly links customers to the fulfillment of their needs and a *philosophical means* that provides guidance for everyone involved in the value stream who builds, supports, and improves the link between customers and their needs—customer satisfaction. Lean enterprises vigorously apply flow for all product *and information*, including the customer and supply base. They establish flow where it does not exist, and immediately reestablish flow when and where it breaks down. Remember that most of the lean tools and methods are simply manifestations of ways to: (1) achieve flow where it does not currently exist, and (2) reestablish flow where and when it breaks down. And in situations where flow is not yet possible, establish *pull*.

Lean manufacturers and service providers develop and implement pull systems to precisely move small batches (the smaller the better) according to customer demand. As with flow, organizations must establish pull where it is needed and to resolve breakdowns in the pull system immediately when and where they happen. In this way, lean organizations deploy an infrastructure that thrives on *building, supporting, and improving the link between customers and their needs using flow and pull.*

Another familiar term for flow is *just-in-time* (JIT). JIT is often defined as supplying the customer, "just what they want, just when they want it, in just the amount they want." JIT practices at Toyota date back to the 1930s, when Kiichiro Toyoda, the founder of the Toyota Motor Company, had the JIT slogan hanging on the wall of his office and most adamantly believed that his company must achieve this capability. Kiichiro learned this concept from Henry Ford—whose engineers had vigorously applied the concept at their Highland Park Plant, the home of the Model T. Kiichiro visited the Ford Motor Company and continually studied Ford's book, *My Life and Work* (London: William Heinemann, 1931). This vision and quest remains embedded within Toyota to this day, since Kiichiro was the source of Taiichi Ohno's drive and inspiration as he worked his way from the supervisor of the machine shop to become recognized as the "father of lean."

(a) Right-Designing Flow with Value Streams

A production *value stream* can be defined as all operations, activities, and support functions required to produce a specific product or service from order to raw material to delivery of the finished product or service into the hands of the customer. Frequently, a value stream can contain smaller value streams; for example, manufacturing cells, like the machining cells illustrated in Exhibit 2.2, can be part of a larger engine manufacturing value stream. Right-designed value streams create the timely, focused flow of resources to a specific product or product family.

Traditional batch manufacturing depends on a complex, confusing network of product movement during production. Lean value streams and their related changes in physical design eliminate this complexity. The lean value stream not only focuses product or service flow and resources, it eliminates the large and unnecessary amount of information that batch manufacturing environment designs generate. Importantly, the limited operational information generated by the value stream design is directly focused on and around the product or service value stream so that it supports decision making at the operational level. The layout in Exhibit 2.2 is an example of an operation right-designed for flow utilizing linked manufacturing cells in a focus factory or factory-within-a-factory.

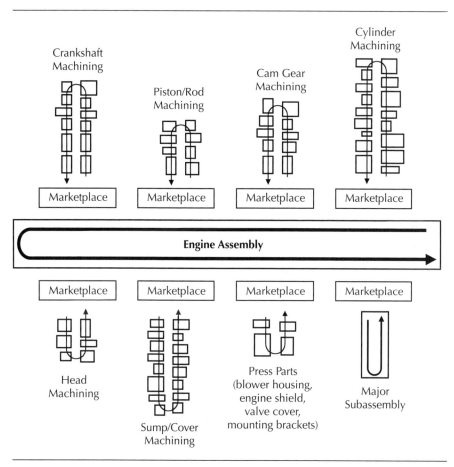

EXHIBIT 2.2 Value Stream Tributaries

2.4 ONE-PIECE FLOW

Flow is fundamental to understanding right-designed lean systems and the cost management systems that support them, because lean designs tie operations *directly* to customer's needs and demands. When effectively designed and implemented, operational flow creates an enterprise that uses the minimum amount of resources to satisfy customers' requirements. Toyota has achieved this customer connection and continues to refine it in the pursuit of operational perfection.

This pursuit of operational perfection has made the Toyota Production System (TPS) the world's most cost effective manufacturing environment. Unlike many traditional companies, Toyota does not drive cost reduction activities. While the company may promote point improvements, cost reduction approaches used by traditional organizations (often referred to as isolated "islands of improvement") do not address the comprehensive design issues necessary for establishing and enhancing effective workflow. Lean companies work to develop and establish value with continuous improvement of their value stream flow, not by cost reduction practices.

The pursuit of the perfect flow design seeks to comprehensively link all enterprise value stream product families into a one-piece, seamless system. All TPS principles and tools can be viewed as simply a means to this singular end—one-piece enterprise-wide flow. All available techniques and tools either become methods and functions to support flow, or they are eliminated (see Exhibit 2.3). Lean organizations use these techniques and tools to both establish flow and as countermeasures to resolve flow interruptions.

In his keynote address for the 1997 Lean Manufacturing Conference at the University of Kentucky, Mike Kitano, then President of Toyota Motor Manufacturing North America, described the secret of TPS: "one-by-one confirmation." One-by-one confirmation means *doing it right the first time*,[12] and one-piece flow is the physical manifestation of one-by-one confirmation.

One-piece flow is the goal in the pursuit of perfection for any lean enterprise. Toyota has its own term for the seamless one-piece flow goal that guides their pursuit of perfection: *True North*. Enterprises new to lean learn to pursue the perfect right-sized equipment, systems, and processes that support the lean one-piece objective from the moment the customer places the order to the time of delivery. In *Profit Beyond Measure*, Tom Johnson and Anders Bröms maintain that when "work links customer with customer in a balanced, continuous flow every step of the way, it satisfies every new customer demand with minimum resources. Toyota's 'produce to order' system, for example, balances resources at every stage to the amount needed to advance one customer's order one more step along the way to completion."[13]

(a) Contrasting Operational Methods and Costs

What are the practical, operational differences between economies of scale and flow-based limited production? Economies of scale can be defined by *costs per unit falling as the speed and volume of output rise*.

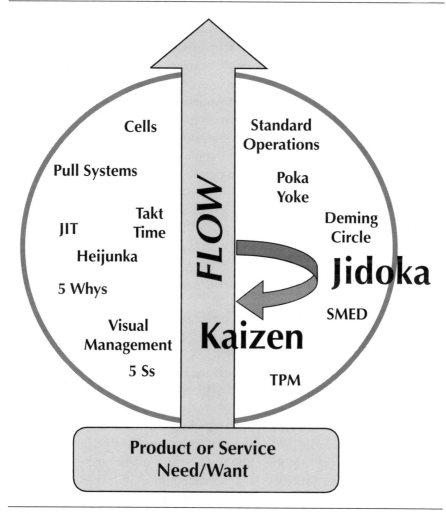

Cells

Standard Operations

Pull Systems

Poka Yoke

FLOW

JIT   Takt Time

Deming Circle

Heijunka

Jidoka

5 Whys

SMED

Visual Management

Kaizen

5 Ss

TPM

Product or Service Need/Want

EXHIBIT 2.3   Lean—It's All about FLOW

A simple comparison of scale economies and limited production methods illustrates the difference. In order to machine a casting, machining processes must be procured. The economy-of-scale choice is a large high-speed machining center that has the capability to completely process the part based on its tolerance requirements. This high-speed machining center can machine parts twice as fast at the same quality as older machines that the company currently uses for similar processing. The features of the part require drilling, milling, and reaming a variety of critical surfaces and holes. The price of the machine tool is $850,000 plus the multifixtured (six fixtures on each side of a two-pallet system) tombstone pallet system—24 total fixtures.

With this configuration, machining 12 parts (two sets of six on each side of the tombstone pallet) during each machine cycle takes a total of 23 minutes to complete a fully loaded tombstone (1.9-minute machining cycle time for each part). Therefore, the throughput time is 23 minutes. Management is pushing to find some more parts to run through this machine to help drive down the cost because of the capital outlay for the machine. But the process engineers are excited and confident that this will happen because the machine has so much capability.

The alternative flow scenario consists of a one-piece flow cell with six machine tools: three milling machines, two drilling machines, and one reaming machine. The reason for the multiple machine tools is twofold. First the takt time of four minutes drives each machine to complete its cycle to maintain the output needed to meet *actual customer demand*. Second, due to orientation requirements suitable for the features required for the part, the part needs to be reoriented again and again at the correct angle for drilling and reaming a variety of holes and milling surfaces. These machines are laid-out in a U-shaped manufacturing line (see Exhibits 2.1 and 2.2) utilizing one-piece flow through the cell. One operator walks to each machine manually loading and unloading each piece in a specific sequence (part of the established standard operations) within the takt time. In contrast to the high-speed machining center, the machine tools in this one-piece cell are simple—in most cases rebuilt existing machines that the company has used for many years. The total cost of putting the cell together (rebuilding the machines and fixtures and moving the equipment in place) was just under $100,000. The throughput time of the cell is just a few seconds under the takt time of four minutes. Both scenarios use one operator.

Exhibit 2.4 shows a comparison of the two scenarios. Which situation better satisfies the customer at the least cost? From the standpoint of machine efficiency, the new machine is easily *twice as efficient* as the older, rebuilt machines. Recall that the machining center can output a part every 1.9 minutes compared to the cell, which outputs a part in just less than 4 minutes. While the improved efficiencies of a variety of parts can be gained by running them through the machining center (and, of course, improved efficiencies in traditional accounting translates to improved costs), from the standpoint of the customer, the machining cell provides a much quicker lead time. It also is a capital outlay of nine times less.

	Machining Center	Machining Cell
Cost	$900,000	$100,000
Throughput Time	23 minutes	<4 minutes
Machine Efficiency	2X	1X
Number of Operators	1	1

EXHIBIT 2.4 Comparing Economies of Scale and Lean Flow

(b) Maximum Flexibility and Minimum Risk for a Changing Environment

In time, even the most ideal external environments for economy-of-scale methods change (e.g., Detroit), leaving managers with either (1) economy-of-scale remedies like plant closures and layoffs or (2) rigid, inflexible systems that were not designed to adjust to changes in demand—especially a shrinking market. The machine center/machine cell comparison demonstrates other important differences between economies of scale and limited production methods.

The machining center can continue to take in capacity until it is running 24 hours on all three shifts. Thereafter, machine capacity increases only if the machining cycles can be reduced. If the market shrinks, the machine goes unutilized and its cost is amortized over fewer parts, thus appearing to increase costs. The organization is stuck with $900,000 of an underutilized asset.

A look at the machining cell shows sharp capacity contrasts from the machining center. If more capacity is needed, another operator can be added to the machining cell to increase production output. Increased demand can be absorbed until the cycle time of the first bottleneck machine is reached (the machine with the cycle time closest to the takt time). Once demand reaches a bottleneck machine's cycle time, the cell's capacity can be increased by either improving the machines cycle time (like the machining center) or by adding another machine to the cell and further split processing time between the two machines. The addition of another machine does, of course, add costs, but it is added at a small incremental rate—recall that the costs of these simple machines were only around $15,000 to $25,000 each. If volume demand were to increase significantly—even double—a *duplicate cell* can be added at the incremental cost of $100,000. Within the machining cell, which utilizes lean flow production principles, volume increases can be added incrementally in smaller chunks, and with significantly less cost.

If volume decreases in the machining cell scenario, since the initial investment was less (nine times less), the cell has the capability to remove a machine or several machines and deploy the machines elsewhere. Also, as volume decreases, the initial sunk cost also remains significantly less than the machining center option. The machining cell design results in less risk and more flexibility with both increases or decreases in customer demand.

2.5 BEGINNING THE JOURNEY: EXECUTING RIGHT-DESIGN

It's good to have a reliable map before beginning any journey as transformative as the one from scale economies to limited production and lean. Three lean principles help chart the goal of this journey. First, and perhaps most accessible, is the customer dimension. Most managers, executives, and engineers familiar with work in an economy-of-scale environment have no context to understand the underlying lean and customer-facing principles of the TPS before they pick up the tools and attempt to apply them.

As a remedy for this unreadiness, people need a much deeper understanding of what right-designing for the lean enterprise really strives to accomplish— properly designing the *complete system* to give the customer just what they want, exactly when they want it, while maintaining superior quality at a minimum price. In lean, the minimum price means both an acceptable customer or market price and a cost to support acceptable margins. Although removing waste from current systems is always an improvement, the entire enterprise system needs to be completely redesigned so that it can deliver customer value from the larger, long-term lean perspective.

The second lean principle that helps define the destination of the lean journey is the premise that all component parts should cost the same at any production volume runs parallel with the concepts of just-in-time and flow in the lean organization. The ultimate goal of eliminating economy-of-scale influences is having all component parts cost the same at all volumes. Lean companies furthest along its path are still not perfect, but they move closer to this goal every working day. Lean enterprises make this same effort for the cost of products, and right-sizing and right-designing practices push them in this direction.

The third lean principle that guides execution of the lean transformation, *zero inventory*, results as the lean enterprise moves closer and closer to seamless one-piece flow. This means a manufacturing system without any inventory where all products move one by one through every process continuously at the pace of takt time—the epitome of lean. It is the result of what Womack and Jones call "perfection" and Toyota refers to as reaching "True North." It is the *ideal* manufacturing situation—the objective of the journey, but also the journey itself.

Enterprises that understand how to implement flow realize that this journey is a long one, and right-design is the path that makes the journey possible because all the goals depend on the execution of right-design. The approach to zero inventory is not a method. Zero inventory results from the application and practice of many actions and principles that must be implemented by trial and error. The actions and principles include *quick changeovers, pull systems,* U-shaped cells, and preventative maintenance to name a few (see glossary for definitions). Lean environments emerge only when a manufacturing enterprise commits to properly execute these three right-designed lean principles with an understanding of the underlying philosophy they represent by actually applying the changes to manufacturing operations.

The application of four concrete activities that reflect lean principles allow the enterprise to begin transforming its operations.

1. Create value streams by reconfiguring processes into one-piece flow cells.
2. Implement preventative maintenance on these lines to reduce downtime.
3. Apply quick-change techniques to the line so that it has the ability to run small batches and can be rapidly changed over to run subsequent small batches in accordance with customer demand.
4. Teach employees these methods and principles by embedding them in problem-solving skills applied each and every day to their work.

The only way to understand the deeper meaning of lean principles and methods is to apply them daily, learning how and why to apply them and how the many techniques are interrelated. Constant application of lean principles and methods in operations leads to deeper knowledge and experience, and the ability to understand how to right-size and why to right-size becomes clearer with each application. Persistence and patience are needed to develop a clear vision and understanding. The next section examines a few of the essential steps people in an organization must take to start and follow through on execution of the lean transformation.

(a) Takt Time: The Right-Design Reference Point

Economy-of-scale companies create waste by pushing overproduction because their equipment, facilities, personnel, and other resources are not integrated into a design that effectively delivers products or services to customer order. *Takt time* is a key lean concept for achieving equal cost at all volumes and the other elements of lean operational design that give the customer just what they want, exactly when they want it, while maintaining superior quality at a minimum price. Takt time ties manufacturing production to customer demand and is calculated by dividing the amount of time available in a given work period (e.g., a shift) by the rate of customer demand during that period. It is also *the first lean concept that companies must employ in lean design* because the calculation of takt time sets the company's operational standard for the production design of individual products and families of products.

The lean enterprise designs and integrates all machines, operators, and support functions based on takt time. This brief introduction to takt time underscores why economies of scale create waste by pushing overproduction. Machines, operators, and support functions in those environments are not designed with production checks and balances to market demand.

(b) Right-Designing a Machining Line

Machining lines are one of the most critical portions of the value stream in any lean manufacturing enterprise, and the transformation to lean manufacturing focuses heavily on right-designing machining lines to reflect lean principles. This section walks through a concrete example to show the steps in the redesign of an engine seal machining line to incorporate takt time and other lean principles.

When an engine seal produced in a lean environment needs to be machined at four different volumes, increasing each year over a four-year period (204,000, 516,000, 614,000, and 828,000), the cost of this part remains constant through all the volumes when the process is right-designed. Designers begin by looking at the components that make up the cost of the part: capital equipment, material, labor (operators), and support functions. Capital equipment normally includes equipment to manufacture the part or add value to the part. As a manufacturing enterprise takes the time to develop right-designed machinery, it chooses small pieces of equipment with just enough capacity to accomplish its particular assignment to meet the takt time. Designers also arrange each piece of right-sized equipment in an efficient, cellular-one-piece-flow configuration to achieve right-fit for optimum efficiency.

Next, lean system designers load and balance labor to meet the takt time by assigning the minimum number of operators to manufacture the part. Designers then right-size support functions including utilities, supervision, maintenance, engineering, and work facilities. Techniques should be used to minimize the supervision needed for lean manufacturing, but any supervisory cost should be assigned directly to a single part. Consider the supervision needed to manage engine seal manufacturing. Since the supervisor of engine seal manufacturing supervises *only* this product, the supervisory cost is easily assigned to the part. In this way, right-sizing supervision does not require accounting techniques, allocation percentages, or cost tracking. This is the very role the team leader and group leader hierarchy plays at Toyota. These positions are embedded functions of leadership and problem solving within the value stream.

Maintenance right-sizing presents more challenges because it encompasses many factors that depend on subjective judgment: equipment quantity, reliability, and technology; training/education requirements and timing; and execution procedures. With time and experience, designers who right-size allow costs to be assigned directly to the product family either (1) by assigning maintenance personnel to the product, cell, or focus factory or (2) by means of product-line supervisor "contracts" for maintenance services. Implementing a total productive maintenance (TPM) system is a more comprehensive alternative for right-sizing maintenance as designers become more familiar with its performance elements. Manufacturing-line operators accomplish a large bulk of maintenance activities when companies use TPM consistently. Maintenance costs directly follow parts without the need for cost allocation tracking other resources.

2.6 RIGHT-DESIGNING COST MANAGEMENT

Business operations shape how the business is managed and how companies design and use their systems for operating and managing. Consequently, lean enterprises focus on understanding and managing the *incidences* of cost (cost management) where *operational design precedes cost accounting design* versus traditional accounting (cost management accounting) where accounting designs lead operational designs.

W. Edwards Deming put it this way: "A system can only deliver what a system is designed to achieve." A manufacturing system designed for batch operation works to achieve economies of scale, and all attempts to superimpose improvements or Kaizen events still leaves a compromised system when markets dwindle. Enterprises in transformation to lean that try to manage a system designed for batch production with lean flow methods face inevitable difficulties and confusion, especially when pressures to manage using the traditional accounting measures remain active (i.e., overhead absorption and labor hour variances).

How does the focus on right-designing value stream work flow impact enterprise cost management? Yasuhiro Monden is a professor of managerial accounting and operations management at the University of Tsukuba Institute of Socio-Economic Planning in Japan. His research across a wide variety of accounting and cost management issues, including Toyota's methods in accounting and production systems, discloses a significant point for people interested in learning to apply lean principles: *The accounting system must be a subservient system to the production system.*

In other words, development of enterprise cost management accounting follows the development and implementation of a lean manufacturing system or physical operation system. Professor Monden emphasizes that the design and operation of the production system are more important than managing the design of the cost system. "There is an increasing tendency to believe that applying accounting controls is impractical or even redundant. What is important, however, is to control the physical elements of production that can influence cost standards. Cost control in this sense implies workplace reforms."[14]

Corroborating these insights, Glenn Uminger is currently the general manager of production control and logistics for Toyota Motor Manufacturing in North America and was the architect of the management accounting system for Toyota's Georgetown, Kentucky, manufacturing facility. He emphasizes that the goal of the management accounting system must be to right-size and right-fit the needs of the operation.[15] *The accounting system must serve operations.* Uminger learned this lesson firsthand by spending six months in Toyota plants working in *manufacturing* before developing the Georgetown operation's accounting system.

His intimate, firsthand experiences allowed him to depart from cumbersome, complex traditional systems so that he could design and implement a more elegant cost management system that supported the needs of the lean manufacturing system.[16] Uminger works to right-size an accounting system by directly applying the lean principles that support the nine attributes of a right-sized piece of equipment listed in the first section of this chapter. In the end, it becomes increasingly clear why accountant Glenn Uminger spent six months in the Toyota plant learning the business *on the shop floor*. He had to understand *what happened* in the operation and *why it happened* the way it did. Like everyone else, he could *learn lean only by doing*. One begins to wonder how six months was enough time. In the end, Uminger's experiences echo Deming's words, "The best way to eliminate *muda* (waste) is not to create it in the first place."[17] Design the operational, information, *and* cost systems for flow by utilizing right-design and right-fit concepts. Designing for flow with these precepts and methods embeds control and functionality into the lean operational system where they belong.

2.7 ALL PARTS AT EQUAL COST

As an enterprise begins to implement and continuously practice lean concepts, progress in achieving all parts at an equal cost at any volume moves ever nearer to its destination, but it often develops in ways that disturb new lean accountants. The right-designed environment takes a while to achieve as companies gradually learn to transform their equipment, facilities, and resources. Over the course of this transformation, the costs of parts per volume develop a "sawtooth" dynamic that flattens out over time as practice approaches lean perfection (see Exhibit 2.5).

Early cost-per-volume fluctuations follow a sawtooth pattern because cost naturally drops slightly as volume increases due to typical mass production economy-of-scale changes—costing the number of parts produced over the equipment and resources used to manufacture them. Since the objective of the lean transformation is to implement capacity incrementally, costs are added incrementally as well. This equates to costs being added to the numerator of the value stream cost equation while incremental volume is added to the denominator (see Chapter 7 on value stream costing).

Product Cost (within a product family or value stream) =
Value Stream Costs/Volume of Output

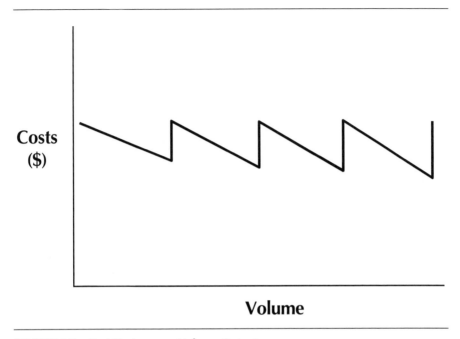

Costs
($)

Volume

EXHIBIT 2.5   Part Costs versus Volume Output

Right-designing is the foundation for implementing lean production. It incorporates other lean principles and corrects the volume-related drop in cost back to original levels. Two main factors contribute to this correction in a lean environment: equipment and operators. Accountants do not like the cost upswings in the early days of the lean transformation, but accountants new to lean have a hard time trusting the change dynamics of lean: Economies of scale are at the mercy of the marketplace; lean limited production enterprises are at the mercy of engaged, empowered employees who continuously add value to the production processes. Lean companies focus on low capital cost and leveraging human capital—they depend on their people to continually develop and evolve the system. Following the success of the Toyota model, virtually all lean enterprises demonstrate *respect for people* (see how lean enterprises demonstrate respect and empower employees in Chapters 3 and 5).

(a) People and Cost/Volume Fluctuations

Operators and material handling can be adjusted to keep a nearly even productivity level at any volume in a properly designed and regulated lean environment. All well-designed lean systems use good cell design and balancing workers to takt time to make these adjustments according to changes in customer orders and flow. When production is designed to meet the takt time, then labor is added or subtracted according to demand—customer orders—while maintaining *equal costs per output*. The design adjusts the number of operators and material handlers on any type of line—machining, welding, fabrication, or assembly. Lean enterprises achieve nearly equal costs per volume when operators and material handlers are loaded and balanced to the takt time.

The lean workplace accomplishes these ever-changing adjustments to demand by seeing people as integers, not fractions. Balancing to takt time is always critical. Consider the example of the necessity of changing from 4 to 5.8 line operators. Since a 0.8 person does not exist, lean systems supply the line with six operators. This "whole employee" lean principle contributes to the sawtooth pattern of the cost-per-volume graph over time, but the impact of fractions becomes greatly diminished as a company becomes more skilled and experienced in applying lean principles to achieve continuous operational improvement.

(b) Equipment Management and Cost/Volume Fluctuations

Equipment costs often have the largest impact on cost/volume fluctuations in the early stages of lean transformation. Lean principles lessen the cost of machines and equipment when comprehensively implemented. Precision chip-cutting machines for producing critical components and assembly conveyor systems for moving large products like automobiles can be very expensive, and these costs significantly impact the cost of the product. When production lines that deploy expensive equipment are designed to lean principles such as takt time; U-shaped, right-sized machines; and work flow, employees develop strategies to lessen the x-axis. For example, if product volume is projected to increase, lines can be added as needed to meet customer demand.

Consistent application of lean principles to equipment management has many advantages besides equal costs per volume. It becomes much easier to invest capital incrementally as volume increases with right-designed equipment, instead of risking a large, single capital outlay in the hope of covering the not always realized final volume estimates of a long-term projection. Incremental investments in capital equipment by purchasing right-sized equipment saves capital if estimated volumes are not reached due to changes in the actual market demand. Similarly, the lean enterprise has fewer sunk costs if market demand fails to reach the estimated projections. Lean equipment management techniques dissipate the losses inherent to the economy-of-scale mentality.

Lean pioneer Mark DeLuzio, former vice president and corporate officer of Danaher Corporation, knows the value of understanding, developing, and implementing right-designed systems and machines to achieve the smooth integration of capacity and capital:

> Many companies think of manufacturing in terms of buying large increments of capacity. But if you think of lean in a machine design sense, you are purchasing small increments of capacity that is flexible and can be quickly changed over. It can be easily adaptable to new designs, and can be easily movable within your plants so you can add an extra 10 percent of capacity without any problem. Your investment is small—you're not adding another $500,000 machine to add just 10 percent more capacity.[18]

2.8 THE JOURNEY TO THE PROMISED LAND—PERFECTION

Economies of scale may never become totally extinct like dinosaurs and other inappropriately oversized experiments of nature and humanity, but this chapter stresses the ways that organizations on the road to a lean transformation must systematically purge all remnants of economies of scale thinking. Learning to be lean requires a commitment to system wide changes in operations and supportive cost management practices that focuses on the work, not the financials. Lean environments are designed for people as much as for profit, and lean environments manage costs by evolving work flow to ever-greater levels of effectiveness. Perfection? Almost everyone enjoys a personal version of the pursuit of perfection in its tangible forms—the perfect french fry, the perfect partner, or in the case of lean principles, the perfect workplace that makes the perfect product. Economies of scale ask people to chase the lowest cost (how inspiring), perhaps the most important reason to begin writing their epitaph.

Lean looks to the future of the management accounting professional. Most accountants work in an operational system designed to leverage economies of scale. Although this is simply the world that most accountants live in, even when constrained by the issues of traditional environments, flow methods and thinking can be successfully applied. With the knowledge and learning derived from applying flow thinking to the operation, successful change can begin anytime the accountants choose to learn the operations. Accountants are an inevitable part of this transformation—in fact, they need to take on much of the leadership role of this change.

Chapter 3 explains the leadership roles of the chief financial officeer (CFO) and accounting staff on this new frontier in more detail. Once begun, the lean journey is exciting and challenging, but it exposes accountants to many new perspectives, roles, and ways of thinking. One accountant who played a leading role in his firm's transformation actually learned and applied single minute exchange of dies (SMED) techniques to a press, reducing the changeover time from 1.5 hours down to under 10 minutes in less than a week. This same accountant was actually doing the changeovers himself in the new standard of less than 7 minutes. One of his cost analyst coworkers commented, "This was the most excited I've ever seen him!"

The message for the accountant is simple: *go learn*! Follow Glenn Uminger's example: Learn as you go, look for ways to apply lean to your operation, think of ways to apply flow in your situation, and then actually apply them. Learn how to do more by doing less, and the rewards will be both personal and business-wide.

2.9 WHAT THE CFO NEEDS TO UNDERSTAND AND COMMUNICATE DURING A LEAN TRANSFORMATION

So what is the CFO to do? First, a summary of the key points offers some guidance:

- *Right-sizing and right fit as methods of cost management.* Understanding and applying right-sizing and right-fit promotes changes that mitigate the need for many of the transactional tasks currently required in traditional accounting. This helps to free up some time and resources to begin the learning process of applying and understanding what lean is about and its impact on the accounting function.
- *Right-sizing as an attribute for flow implementation.* Learn what the pursuit of "perfection" or "True North" means from a physical change and implementation standpoint for your enterprise. The CFO can actively engage with operational employees to learn firsthand the *what* and *why* of the changes being made in the lean transformation. In this way, the CFO both learns about lean operations firsthand and gives the operational people support from a financial decision-making perspective.

- *Apply limited production versus economies of scale.* As the cross-functional lean implementation team (financial and operational membership) works and learns together during the implementation process, the difference in philosophy between economies of scale and limited production become tangible instead of abstract. Together, everyone can begin to give actual examples of how *and why* they applied one-piece flow as a means of limited production, and what that means in running the business in a more competitive manner versus competitors still utilizing economies of scale.

- *Right-size thinking and applications reduce costs.* With their financial experience and knowledge, CFOs can help the cross-functional implementation team articulate the saving they can achieve through their application of right-sizing the operational, information, and support system. The reality of cost improvements can be understood and articulated in connection with the changes and activities being applied.

- *Accountants as leaders in right-size deployment.* Through *applied learning* in conjunction with others in the organization, the CFO not only understands the business reasons—that is, the dollar savings—for the right-sizing efforts, but now can thoroughly articulate them in terms everyone can understand. The CFO now feels comfortable and confident enough to chat with an operator on the shop floor and express what is happening in terms that the operator will understand. These valuable insights give the CFO the understanding and communication skills to speak to anyone in the organization about what the business is doing and why.

NOTES

1. H. Thomas Johnson and Anders Bröms, *Profit Beyond Measure: Extraordinary Results through Attention to Work and People* (New York: Free Press, 2000), p. 107.
2. See note 1, p. 240.
3. H. Thomas Johnson, "A Recovering Cost Accountant Reminisces," August 15, 2002 draft, p. 3.
4. See note 1, pp. 101–102.
5. Kiyoshi Suzaki, *The New Manufacturing Challenge: Techniques for Continuous Improvement* (New York: Free Press, 1987), p. 8.
6. Taiichi Ohno, *Toyota Production System: Beyond Large-Scale Production* (Portland, Ore.: Productivity Press, 1988), pp. 59, 109. *Toyota Seisan Hoshiki*, the Japanese edition, was originally published in 1978.

7. See note 1, p. 4.

8. See note 3, p. 5.

9. John Y. Shook, "Bringing the Toyota Production System to the United States: A Personal Perspective," in Jeffrey K. Liker, (ed.), *Becoming Lean: Inside Stories of U.S. Manufacturers* (Portland, Ore.: Productivity Press, 1997), p. 49.

10. James P. Womack and Daniel T. Jones, *Lean Thinking: Banish Waste and Create Wealth in Your Corporation* (New York: Simon & Schuster, 1996), p. 309.

11. The 5 Ss are five Japanese terms that define how a manufacturing facility should be clean and organized. Originally based on five Japanese words: *seiri* (sort), *seiton* (straighten), *seiso* (scrub), *seiketsu* (systematize), *shitsuke* (standardize).

12. Mikio "Mike" Kitano, "Toyota Production System: One-by-One Confirmation," University of Kentucky, Lean Manufacturing Conference May 14–16, 1997 (May 15, 1997): keynote address.

13. See note 1, p. 183.

14. Yasuhiro Monden and Michiharu Sakurai (eds.), *Japanese Management Accounting: A World Class Approach to Profit Management* (Portland, Ore.: Productivity Press, 1989), p. 37; and Yasuhiro Monden, *Cost Management in the New Manufacturing Age: Innovations in the Japanese Automotive Industry* (Portland, Ore.: Productivity Press, 1992), p. 68.

15. Glenn Uminger, "Lean: An Enterprise Wide Perspective," Presentation at the Ninth Annual Lean Manufacturing Conference by the Japan Technology Management Program at the University of Michigan–Ann Arbor, Ypsilanti, Michigan, May 6, 2003.

16. Jeffrey K. Liker, *The Toyota Way: 14 Management Principles from the World's Greatest Manufacturer* (New York: McGraw-Hill, 2004), p. 287.

17. Glenn Uminger from his presentation at the 2003 University of Michigan's Lean Manufacturing Conference. Uminger is referencing the ability to design a manufacturing system correctly or without waste in it in the first place.

18. Mark DeLuzio, "Danaher Is a Paragon of Lean Success," Interviewed by Richard McCormack, in Richard McCormack (ed.), *Manufacturing News*, June 29, 2001, p. 11.

3

LEAN STRATEGY AND ACCOUNTING: THE ROLES OF THE CEO AND CFO

OREST FIUME

Before any meaningful discussion of the roles of the chief executive officer (CEO) and chief financial officer (CFO) in a lean business can take place, we need to come to a common understanding about what lean "is." Lean is not a manufacturing tactic. Lean is not a cost-reduction program. Lean is a business strategy. The reason for focusing most of the initial attention on manufacturing processes is that is where most of value-added activities that need to be liberated take place. Cost savings are achieved over time, but that takes place in the context of implementing lean as a business strategy. A simple example of two companies illustrates this.

Company A is the industry leader and makes its products on standard equipment purchased from traditional machine vendors. It takes one hour to do a changeover from one product to another on its machines. Company B makes the same products on the same machines, purchased from the same machine vendors. However, B has improved the setup process so that it takes only one minute to change over from one product to another. Both A and B operate one shift with seven hours devoted to production time and one hour to change-over time. With this profile, Company A can produce two different products each day, for example, make product X first, do a changeover, and then make product Y. But with this same one-shift production schedule, Company B can make 60 products in a day, each consuming only one minute of setup time. Thus, Company B has greater flexibility in responding to changing customer demand, and customer demand is *always* changing.

The standard delivery lead time in this industry is between four and six weeks, but Company B begins to advertise a 72-hour lead time. How might Company A respond? It might add inventory in an attempt to duplicate the shorter lead time. It might not even attempt to shorten lead times, but may choose to reduce its selling prices in order to offset Company B's delivery advantage. Either way, Company A will end up with less profit than Company B because of either lower relative revenue or higher inventory carrying costs. Thus, this "small" process improvement in the factory has significant strategic implications when applied properly to the market.

The strategy in this example is often referred to as a *time-based strategy*. In other words, how do we reduce the amount of time that it takes to do everything we do? Not just make products, but take orders, pay bills, develop new products, and sort the mail. Because when a company focuses on reducing time, it recognizes that it can achieve this by eliminating non-value-added activities—in other words, waste. When companies properly apply these improved abilities to the marketplace, they can gain competitive advantage, which is what strategy is all about. Toyota remains the best example of a lean company. Toyota doesn't "do" lean and in addition they have some grand strategy over it. Lean *is* their strategy—even if they don't call it "lean"—a term created in this country more than 40 years after Toyota began "doing" it. And Toyota is on the threshold of becoming the largest automobile company in the world by diligently pursuing, over many decades, its strategy of creating sustainable competitive advantage through operational excellence.

3.1 LEAN STRATEGY RESULTS

Exhibit 3.1 shows the results in certain key measurement areas before Wiremold adopted its lean strategy, and ten years later. Looking at the company from the shareholders' perspective, lean results in extraordinary growth in value. In 1990, Wiremold had an enterprise value of about $30 million. In 2000, the company was sold for $770 million. The total return to shareholders during this period was about double the Standard and Poor's (S&P) 500. Toyota's market capitalization today is greater than the combined value of the next seven largest automotive companies in the world. Lean creates value. And it does that by creating competitive advantages that better satisfy the customer.

EXHIBIT 3.1   Wiremold Before and After Lean

	1990	2000
Assessed Value	$30 million	$770 million
West Hartford:		
Gross profit	38%	51%
Sales per employee	90,000	240,000
Throughput time	4–6 weeks	2 hours–2 days
Product development time	2–3 years	3–6 months
Number of suppliers	320	43
Inventory turns	3.4	17.0
Working cap % sales*	21.8%	6.7%

* W/C = A/R + Inv – Trade Payables

3.2 EASY TO AGREE WITH, HARD TO DO

If lean is that good, why doesn't everyone do it? Even though the benefits of lean are extraordinary and the basic concept simple, lean is actually very hard to do because many of the things that have to be done successfully to follow a lean strategy run counter to what most people have been taught and what they practice. In addition, managers are continually looking for that one solution that will solve all their problems—the "silver bullet" solution: "We're going to put in a new computer system, and that's going to solve all of our problems." "We're going to automate and get people out of the process, because they're the problem." "We're going to install the latest and greatest version of manufacturing resource planning (MRP) or enterprise resource planning (ERP), and that's going to solve all of our problems." "We're going to designate Six Sigma as our 'umbrella program' to reduce costs, and that's going to solve all of our problems."

Six Sigma is a very good problem-solving tool for some problems, but to apply it as "the" problem-solving tool is a waste of money. Remember the old saying, "If the only tool that you have is a hammer, everything looks like a nail." That's the problem with Six Sigma—it ignores the fact that there are many other problem-solving tools that are more appropriate for most problems. After chasing all of these programs in the hope that one of them will solve all of our problems, everyone becomes disappointed when they don't find the panacea. Companies end up with what employees call the "program of the month" syndrome.

Experience shows that approaching lean as a manufacturing tactic rather than an enterprise strategy is the most common reason for companies to fail at their lean implementations. When viewed as a tactic, responsibility gets delegated to the operations people and none of the *barriers* are removed.

When asked, only a small percentage of companies see themselves as a "make the month" company. However, when asked how much product they ship in the last week of a typical four-week month, the response is generally a guilty laugh. Many companies ship as much as 60 to 70 percent of their month's volume in the last week. Organizations that try to put this much activity through 25 percent of the available time experience an inordinate waste of resources. And they are "make the month" companies.

The list of barriers goes on and on. Companies continue to use MRP (push scheduling) in spite of the fact that one of the principles of lean is pull scheduling. They continue to maintain that they are "different" from those companies that have successfully implemented lean and, therefore, not everything (usually the hard stuff) applies to them. They allow policies and procedures to exist in virtually every function outside of manufacturing that work against lean principles and cause internal conflicts. They continue to use standard cost-absorption accounting (more on this later), and they continue to use metrics that drive nonlean behaviors (more on this later, too). See Chapter 8 for more obstacles to lean.

3.3 WHAT DOES IT TAKE TO IMPLEMENT A LEAN STRATEGY?

Much has been written about Toyota and the principles, practices, and tools of lean. However, very little has been written about the pillar of its strategy that Toyota considers most important. It has been expressed as "respect for people" and it recognizes that, in the end, it's all about the people. At its core, any company is just a collection of people trying to satisfy another collection of people (the customer) better than those other collections of people (the competitors). And in the end, the best, most motivated, and focused collection of people wins. Therefore, successfully implementing a lean strategy requires that people change the culture of their companies so that they think and behave lean. How is this accomplished? In fact, what is culture? There have been different ways of defining culture, but the one that makes the most sense to me is this:

The people in our company hold a set of values and beliefs that causes them to behave in certain ways. When they behave in accordance with their values and beliefs and get the results they expect, they reinforce the validity of those values and beliefs in their minds. This self-reinforcing cycle of values and beliefs driving behavior, behavior yielding expected results, and results driving values and beliefs is what we call *culture*.

How do people change the culture of their company? Some companies attempt to force a new set of values and beliefs on people with such mandates as, "We are now going to be customer focused." If the company has always been internally focused, this statement will have little effect because leadership cannot externally impose new values and beliefs on people. That is an internal, personal change process. The alternative? The key to changing values and beliefs, and thereby culture, is to require people to behave differently so that they can experience a set of results that are better than what they have experienced in the past. As this happens over and over again, they evolve to a new set of values and beliefs (thinking lean) that drives new behaviors (acting lean) yielding better results (being lean).

Who is responsible for changing culture? There is only one correct answer. The CEO. Since implementing strategy is the primary responsibility of the CEO, since lean is a strategy, and since implementing this lean strategy requires a change in culture, the CEO must take personal responsibility for this cultural change. The Association for Manufacturing Excellence (AME) recognizes this principle. In its "Cultural Leadership Program," it states that the CEO must "lead the change to a new culture." How does the CEO do this? Part 3.4 of this chapter describes the major areas in which the CEO must provide leadership.

3.4 THE ROLE OF THE CEO

CEOs must be concerned with many things in the performance of their jobs, but the CEO of a lean company must also focus on ensuring that lean thinking and behaviors are practiced throughout the organization. This section discusses 12 critical aspects of the transformation process that the CEO must lead if the company is to successfully implement a lean business strategy.

(a) Learn Lean Thinking

The days when CEOs could be just good visionaries are over. Today, CEOs must be both good visionaries and good implementers. In order to be a good implementer, one has to know one's subject, and know it as well or better than anyone else in the organization. When most companies embark on implementing a lean strategy, they find that there are a small percentage of their people that understand it quickly, like it, and want to run with it. At the other end of the spectrum, a small percentage of people do not like it, feel threatened by it, and try to kill it at every opportunity. Everyone else in the middle is watching to see who will win.

Within the group that is trying to kill lean strategy are some very bright, very articulate people that continually try to explain why the company should not or cannot take some of the critical steps necessary to make the lean strategy work. Unless the CEO really has a deep understanding of lean (the "how" *and* the "why"), there is a high probability that these naysayers will sway the CEO from making some fundamental changes critical to a successful transformation. Lean is not only an institutional transformation but also a personal one. Art Byrne, Wiremold's CEO during its lean transformation, has said, "If the CEO doesn't know lean and how to do it, you're not going to be successful at implementing it in that company."[1]

(b) Out Front—Hands On—Do Not Delegate

Jim Womack, coauthor of *Lean Thinking*, said, "Lean Thinking . . . is an entire business model that must be run by the CEO."[2] Art Byrne is even more direct: "If you can't get the CEO to lead this, then don't start because you are wasting your time." It is this author's opinion that learning lean is about 20 percent intellectual and 80 percent experiential. There is a lot of material for the CEO to read, and a lot of seminars for learning about the basic principles, practices, and tools of lean. But true learning comes from actually doing it.

There is nothing more powerful than participating in a five-day Kaizen and personally creating significant improvement, such as a 95 percent reduction in setup time. It is in the process of "try-storming" (as opposed to "brainstorming") that one really learns what works and what doesn't for a particular situation. Once this kind of knowledge has been internalized, people cannot be talked out of believing that it works.

The other benefit of the hands-on approach is that by working side by side with the other members of the team (but never as the team leader), the CEO publicly recognizes that all work is honorable. Even though the organization wants to eliminate nonvalue activities, the culture that the CEO builds communicates that there is no such thing as work that is beneath someone's status. It reflects a mind-set that human relations have nothing to do with rank, and are only about people.

(c) Many Leaps of Faith

As stated earlier, many of the changes that companies have to make to successfully implement a lean strategy are counter to what most people have been taught and what they have practiced. Some of those changes are dramatically different and can make a CEO hesitate for fear of being wrong and doing significant damage. It is important to understand that whenever a person makes a decision, be it in one's business life or personal life, two factors always play a role. First, there is never enough time or money to collect all of the information one needs to make an absolutely risk-free decision. Some risks are unrecognizable because they are so small. In contrast, other risks seem to be so great that people decide against whatever change is under consideration.

The second decision-making factor is that every decision one makes is a prediction of the future. We chose option X over option Y because we predict that X will give us the desired results better than Y can. Because the lean transformation requires fundamental change in the way people operate, it is important that the CEO leading his or her first transformation get a sensei—someone who has successfully led one before and can support the first-timer through those inevitable leap-of-faith moments. (A note of caution: there are lots of fake senseis out there today.)

An additional way for the CEO to deal with the leap-of-faith issue is to visit some companies that are very advanced in their lean transformation (e.g., Toyota tier-one suppliers). It is very easy to read about the improvements that are possible, but to actually see them in operation creates a much higher level of understanding and acceptance that they are possible.

(d) Change Metrics

Why are metrics important? There is an old saying: "You get what you measure." Metrics send a message to employees as to what management thinks is important (with a secondary message that it ought to get better). Employees want to appear to be doing what management wants them to do. Thus, metrics shape behavior, and changing behavior changes culture. When should the CEO address the subject of changing metrics? *At the beginning of the lean transformation.*

As discussed earlier, leadership intent on changing company culture has to intervene with ways that cause people to behave differently so that they can experience better results. Changing metrics is the primary way of accomplishing this change in behavior (see Chapter 4 for a discussion of lean metric implementation methods). Almost every lean transformation begins with the management statement, "We are adopting lean," and then management leaves all of the old metrics in place. Effectively, they send conflicting messages that confuse people: We want you to behave differently (i.e., lean), but we will measure you the same way we always have. In the end, the metric message wins out over the verbal message, especially if some of those metrics are embedded in compensation formulas. In order to have employees understand that they have to behave differently, the metrics must change.

(e) Use Process-Oriented Rather than Results-Oriented Metrics

Rowan Gibson observed that, "Leaders may be judged by the numbers they deliver, but that's not the way they should run the company."[3] Art Byrne, again in his direct manner, says, "The winners will be those companies that focus on their processes, not their results." This certainly is one of those leaps of faith. It promotes the belief that the desired results will come if people focus on doing the right thing. This concept is more fully explained in the CFO section discussion about productivity.

(f) Set Stretch Goals

Stretch goals make people realize that they can't reach the goal by just doing what they are already doing but working just a little bit better. The stretch goal forces them to realize they actually have to do things differently. The argument against setting stretch goals goes something like this: If you set a goal so high that people don't believe they can achieve it, they won't even try. This author doesn't subscribe to that way of thinking. Whether people try or not depends on how management reacts when they don't reach the goal—and if it is truly a stretch goal they will rarely, if ever, achieve it. What should management do if the goal is to improve productivity by 20 percent but the company achieves "only" 15 percent? Celebrate! It is still more than five times better than the national average. Companies that punish people because they miss stretch goals subsequently have a big problem with how hard people even try.

(g) Create an Environment Where It Is Okay to Fail

There is a world of difference between making a mistake and failing. Making a mistake means knowing how to do something but doing it wrong (e.g., not following standard work). No new learning comes from this. Failing means trying something new that doesn't work out as predicted. People expand their knowledge by trying new things and sometimes failing. At a minimum, we discover what doesn't work. It is here that the CEO needs to provide "air cover" for early adopters so that they can try new things, sometimes fail, and not be punished for failing. This sends a strong message about the culture you are trying to create. In a traditional culture, people who try new things and fail generally find their careers in jeopardy. In the lean culture, people who do not fail often enough are probably not stretching enough to discover better ways of doing things. Naturally, there is a right way and a wrong way to try new things. We don't want the "failure" to be a fatal one to the company. If the new thing being tried is easily reversible, then "just do it." If it doesn't yield the expected results then you can just reverse it. However, if the new method requires destruction of the old method and is not easily reversible, or contains significant risk, then the "trying" should be in a simulation mode. Once its effectiveness is demonstrated it can be implemented live.

(h) Eliminate Concrete Heads

There are generally two types of people within that small group at the end of the spectrum who are trying to kill the transformation process. Initially, they look alike, but given the opportunity, they separate into two groups. The first group contains those who will never accept the lean strategy as a good thing and will continually try to undermine it: the concrete heads—solid concrete from ear to ear with never a new idea to enter. The second group contains people who initially look like concrete heads but actually only have concrete shells. With the proper guidance, these people come to understand lean and can become some of its staunchest supporters.

There is only one way to handle the true concrete heads. Eliminate them from the organization. Do not take the approach of putting them in a job "where they won't do any harm." They will always do harm. They must go. But because they often are longer-term employees, be very careful how they are eliminated because the rest of the organization is watching. Be very generous (good severance, extended medical coverage, etc.), give them sufficient outplacement assistance so that they can find another job where they can carry on their work as concrete heads, but they must go.

(i) Institute a "No Layoff" Policy

One of the things we discovered early in the transformation process is that the people doing the work have a good sense of where the problems are and have some pretty good ideas about solutions. Double-digit productivity gains are more possible when the employees become fully invested in the improvement process. However, if the company begins the lean transformation by achieving those gains and then laying off the "excess" people, the willingness of the employees to participate in future improvement efforts is effectively killed.

People will not work themselves, their family members, or their friends out of a job. Even if the layoffs are separated from the improvement event by months, jobs are jobs, and people are smart enough to connect the dots. In order to successfully implement a lean strategy, the CEO must give a guarantee that no one will lose employment as a result of productivity gains. This does not mean that people's jobs will not change. They will, and sometimes significantly. This does not mean that if the economy tanks and the company has to reduce the workforce that it can't. Most people recognize this as an external event that may be required for the company's survival. Importantly, the layoff policy does not mean that people cannot lose their employment due to poor performance. They can, and most people understand and support the difference between firing the poorly performing employee and losing employment due to productivity gains.

(j) Organize around Value Streams

Traditional organization structures hide problems. First, each layer acts as a filter of information as it moves both up and down the organization. The information that gets filtered out as it flows up to management is the negative kind, so that management rarely gets an accurate picture of the problems that exist at the working levels. Second, companies organized around functions (i.e., vertically) defy the way processes work. Most processes are cross-functional. They operate horizontally, not vertically, through the organization. As a result, it is rare that anyone has a complete view of the process and functions in a functionally structured organization because everyone attempts to improve their piece of the process, which suboptimizes flow. In addition, when the customer is disappointed, functional structures give people the ability to blame someone else.

In order to really understand what is going on in the company and reduce the time it takes to perform work by eliminating nonvalue activities, leadership must work to flatten the organization and then organize around value streams. Value streams have a customer orientation and lean organizations give the value stream team leader as many of the resources as possible to satisfy the customer. This reduces everyone's ability to pass the buck when the customer is disappointed.

(k) Change Compensation Systems that Do Not Support Lean

Nothing affects behavior more that the compensation systems linked to performance metrics. The basis on which companies pay people drives them to do whatever is necessary to increase their personal earnings under that particular system. The discussion about the need to address metrics at the beginning of the transformation process applies to compensation plans also. How can companies expect to become lean if their compensation plans drive anti-lean behavior?

In the past, most compensation systems were designed to drive people to improve their individual performance on the assumption that if each individual improves his or her performance, the performance of the company will improve. In most cases, however, there was no coordination among compensation plans to ensure that people did not do things that benefited them personally, and actually had a negative effect somewhere else in the organization. Some examples illustrate this dynamic throughout the organization.

Factory: Piecework incentives drive production employees to make more product in order to increase their take-home pay, regardless of whether that product is needed. The end result is unnecessary inventory. In addition, narrowly defined job classifications, and many pay grades based on them, don't enhance flexibility. Lean environments with production cells that require people to be multiskilled require only a few, broadly defined pay grades.

Middle Management: Bonus plans that contain individual performance objectives drive each person to achieve their objectives. When the objectives across the organization are not coordinated, there is a risk that people's objectives may actually conflict with each other. And since the objective is driven by a results-oriented mentality, people are rarely concerned about how the results are achieved. This can lead to bonuses being paid even though the results were achieved by dysfunctional behavior.

Sales: Bonuses based on achieving a periodic sales quota (e.g., quarterly) can result in artificial demand toward the end of the period so that the salespeople can get their bonuses. This surge in orders rarely results in an increase in overall sales; it normally is just a mechanism for pulling future orders into the current period, but still results in bonuses being paid.

Senior Management: Most compensation plans for senior managers contain several elements: a fixed, salary element; a short-term incentive element; and a long-term incentive element. When the short-term element is based on achieving individual or functionally oriented objectives, companies see the same type of behavior as when middle management plans are structured that way. This type of behavior can be even more disruptive at the senior management level than at the middle management level. The best incentive plans for senior managers contain performance criteria for the company as a whole to emphasize that the senior management group must truly act as a team to achieve the desired level of compensation. Swim together or sink together.

(l) Plan to Answer the Question "What's in It for Me?"

At some point, employees understand what lean is about and the benefits that are being achieved, and ask different versions of the same question: "What's in it for me?" or "I used to run one machine and can now perform every operation in the cell—what's in it for me?" Wiremold's answer to that question is a profit-sharing plan that is paid quarterly in cash. The plan was a strong part of its culture as it had been instituted by the company's founder, D. Hayes Murphy, in 1916. If we did not have the plan, we would have created one.

The plan is quite simple. Each quarter, Wiremold pays profit-sharing equal to 15 percent of earnings before income taxes, shared by everyone from the president to the janitor, on a pro rata basis. In the early days it was called a "Profit Sharing Dividend Plan" because Mr. Murphy believed that the company's "human capital" should share in the company's success along with the "financial capital." The formula was set up so that the total dollars paid to employees in profit sharing was about equal to the total dollars paid to shareholders in the form of dividends. Brilliant!

In fact, why just "plan" to answer the question? Why not preempt the question and institute profit sharing as a proactive initiative, not just a reactive response?

Certainly, there are many other things that CEOs must be concerned with in the performance of their jobs. However, the 12 areas discussed in this section are critical points of concentration if the company is to successfully implement a lean business strategy.

3.5 LEAN AFFECTS ACCOUNTING

Since lean is a business strategy, it affects everything the company does, including accounting. In their 1987 book, *Relevance Lost: The Rise and Fall of Management Accounting*, Tom Johnson and Bob Kaplan state that "corporate management accounting systems are inadequate for today's environment."[4] Brian Maskell has done work in the area of accounting in a lean business environment, and he makes the observation that all of the essentials of modern management accounting were established by 1930, without any significant change since then. What are Maskell, Johnson, and Kaplan talking about?

In the early part of the twentieth century, the typical American manufacturer had a product cost structure of about 30 percent material content, about 60 percent touch labor content, and about 10 percent overhead content. Today, the typical American manufacturer has a product cost structure of about 60 percent material content, about 10 percent touch labor content, and about 30 percent overhead content. The standard cost accounting system that we use today was created to support the "yesterday" environment when a small amount of overhead was allocated to products on the basis of their touch labor. That environment doesn't exist anymore, but we are still using its accounting system. Companies beginning to implement a lean strategy often complain that they do good things in operations, such as increase productivity and reduce inventory, but it shows up as a negative in the company's financial statements. To borrow a medical term, this phenomenon is a *false negative* and is the result of the mechanics of the standard cost-absorption accounting model.

Many accountants have been frustrated by the meaningless information generated by a standard cost system, but their efforts to change to something more meaningful are thwarted by many obstacles. One of those obstacles is the complexity of our existing systems driven by the incredible number of transactions that companies process in an attempt to capture data at the smallest increment possible.

I have occasionally supervised a series of manufacturing simulations that illustrate the benefits of lean production methods versus batch and queue methods. During those 20-minute simulations, the participants produce two products through six operations. In addition to making the products, participants have to complete all of the transactions normally found in a Class A, MRP environment such as purchase orders, move tickets, and labor tickets. Usually, between 200 and 220 transactions are generated during the simulations. Extrapolate that to a real-world company with thousands of products, hundreds or thousands of operations, and thousands of minutes in a week.

Companies are processing millions of transactions through their business systems. Since those transactions are a significant source of information for the financial statements, accountants want to ensure that they are processed in a way that is complete (we have them all) and accurate. That many transactions cannot be processed with those objectives without the use of very complex processes. All of this is driven by the combination of MRP systems and standard cost accounting systems. The end result? Standard cost/variance profit-and-loss statements that are virtually unusable.

The other significant obstacle is the traditional emphasis within the accounting community on compliance rather than improvement. While one of the major responsibilities of the accountant is to make sure that proper internal control exists and is being followed, the way that accountants go about fulfilling that responsibility has put them at odds with the rest of the organization. A number of years ago, Financial Executives International's research arm, the Financial Executives Research Foundation, did a study on what operating people thought about their financial peers. More than 50 percent of the respondents described them in what could loosely be called "corporate cops." If my peers perceive me this way, how willing are they going to be to seek my help solving their problems?

This situation has been exacerbated by the compliance requirements of Sarbanes-Oxley. Like many laws, it started off with good intentions (addressing accounting abuses), but it got lost along its way to implementation. Let's face it—accountants have been given a nuclear weapon, figuratively speaking. We can stop any change that we do not like in its tracks just by invoking the phrase "Sarbanes-Oxley" or "the auditors won't sign off on that." If we use it this way, we are guilty of misusing our professional authority.

3.6 THE ROLE OF THE CFO

So what is the CFO's role in implementing a lean business strategy? Naturally, the CFO is responsible for all of the traditional accounting, financial, and treasury activities of the company. But the role is bigger that this. Someone once described the CFO as the CEO's copilot. In this way, the CFO must be concerned with all of the things that the CEO is concerned with, plus more.

(a) Learn Lean by Doing Lean

As previously discussed, most of the real learning about lean comes from hands-on implementation. Accordingly, CFOs and their professional staffs must participate in lean improvement events (Kaizens). This has several benefits. First, it provides firsthand knowledge of the magnitude of the gains that can be achieved. Second, it frustrates them that they personally create these gains but can't find them in the current financial reports. And third, they learn that the principles and problem-solving tools of lean are transferable when they start working on improving the business systems. It is easier to learn these principles and tools in a production environment, where everything is more physical, than in a business process, where the output is represented by pieces of paper or information on a computer screen.

(b) Change Metrics

Since accounting is generally the "keeper of the keys" when it come to performance measurement, accounting must be the primary source of information for the CEO in determining which metrics to change. The CFO must have a clear understanding of the behavior required for the new culture. The CEO and CFO must lead an analysis of company metrics to determine which ones should be discontinued, which should be modified, and which new ones should be introduced.

There has been considerable discussion recently about using the "Balanced Scorecard" as a tool to drive improvement. But the Balanced Scorecard is only

as good as the metrics it contains. If it contains metrics that drive anti-lean behavior, what good is it?

(c) Understand the Difference between Efficiency and Productivity

The very first slide of the very first presentation that Art Byrne gave to Wiremold's employees when he joined the company in September 1991 was:

Productivity = Wealth

This simple concept became one of the cornerstones of our philosophy. At
a recent conference, one of the presenters stated, "I've been at my company
for 20 years, and if we had achieved all of the productivity gains that we said
we had, we would have no employees left." After a chuckle from the audience,
and upon reflection, it became obvious that this speaker's company did not
know how to measure productivity properly. If it did measure productivity
properly, one could not come to this conclusion, since the company still had
thousands of employees.

Productivity is the relationship between the quantity of output versus the
quantity of resources consumed in creating that output. People get confused
about how to measure productivity because they are trained to think in terms of
dollars, whereas productivity deals only with quantities. But every time we see
a dollar amount, we can break it down into its elements of quantity and price:

Sales \$ = Quantity × Price
Material \$ = Quantity × Price
Labor \$ = Quantity × Price
Overhead \$ = Quantity × Price

It is the relationship of the "Qs" that represents productivity. No amount of
financial engineering will ever create one iota of productivity gain. Productivity measures must focus on the *quantities* being consumed versus the output being achieved, and if people want to improve productivity, they must
focus on improving that relationship. Furthermore, productivity improvement
does not come without physical change. Some of the physical changes we made
at Wiremold were to:

- Physically group product by value stream
- Physically change process layout to facilitate flow

- Physically eliminate work in process storage
- Physically store inventory at point of use
- Physically reduce set up time at least 95 percent
- Physically co-locate marketing and product development functions
- Physically combine production control and purchasing, move to operations
- Physically co-locate credit and customer service, while maintaining internal control

Because productivity is a physical concept, most lean metrics must be nonfinancial and process oriented. These metrics help ensure that when a company focuses on doing the right thing, the desired results will come—that leap of faith discussed earlier.

This discussion does not mean to imply that the "Ps" in the equation are unimportant. They are important, but are called "price recovery." For example, if material prices increase, can we get it back in selling prices? If not, we have to offset that increase by a productivity gain or price reductions of other resources consumed; otherwise, profit will suffer. The number of people in any organization who can affect the "Ps" is small compared to those who can affect the "Qs." Everyone affects the "Qs."

Efficiency is the relationship between two inputs, usually standard and actual. Therefore, labor efficiency is the relationship between the standard labor hours "required" to produce something and the number of hours actually incurred. The problem with the efficiency metric is that it presumes that the standard is correct. What is the incentive to improve if a unit happens to achieve 100 percent efficiency? The way to ensure continuous improvement is to focus on productivity because it always deals with actual results compared over time.

(d) Make Business Processes Lean

Because lean is not confined to manufacturing operations, but affects everything a company does, apply lean principles to the business support processes. As companies reorganize around value streams, they need to change business processes to reflect the simplicity that is being created. Most companies find that more that 90 percent of the time it takes to do anything in its business processes is non-value-added time. Eliminating that time drives the lean transformation forward even faster.

(e) Provide Information that Non-accountants Can Use

Most people (and probably most accountants) don't understand a standard cost profit and loss financial statement (P&L). It starts with the presumption that standard costs are accurate and calculates arcane variances from those standards. But, let us look at how standards are derived. Below is a description of the method used to set material, labor, and overhead standard costs. The words in *italics* represent estimates:

Material: Quantity × Unit Cost:
  Quantity based on engineering standard, *modified for yield*
  Unit Cost based on *current average, quotes, or ???*
Labor: Hours × Hourly Labor Rate:
  Labor Hours based on engineering *studies*
  Labor Rates based on *average rate for the department or plant*
Overhead: Labor Hours × Overhead Rate per Hour:
  Labor Hours based on engineering *studies*
  Overhead Rate based on *Budgeted Overhead* divided by *Budgeted Labor Hours*

So this thing called "standard cost," which is usually calculated out to three or four decimal places and is given an enormous degree of credibility, is really made up of a series of estimates and assumptions.

Exhibit 3.2 represents a standard cost P&L for a company that has just embarked on a lean transformation. Even though sales are up, gross profit in dollars is flat and, as a percentage of sales, is actually down. In attempting to explain what has happened, the standard cost statement gives no meaningful information. We could go line by line, but would have no better understanding when we finished than before we started. This is the position that most accountants are in when they sit at the monthly management meeting and try to explain what happened. We revert to speaking accountese, everyone else thinks "I'm glad *someone* understands" and eyes glaze over.

In the example given in Exhibit 3.2, the normal management reaction when implementation of lean has been delegated as a manufacturing thing would be, "I don't know what you are doing with this lean stuff, but stop it—it's killing us." Even though operations management knows that they have achieved some good results, the financial performance information does not support that conclusion.

EXHIBIT 3.2 Standard Cost Example

	This Year	Last Year
Net Sales	100,000	90,000
Cost of Sales		
Standard costs	48,000	45,000
Purchase price variance	(3,000)	10,000
Material usage variance	(2,000)	5,000
Labor efficiency variance	7,000	(8,000)
Labor rate variance	(2,000)	9,000
Overhead volume variance	2,000	2,000
Overhead spend variance	(2,000)	8,000
Overhead efficiency variance	16,000	(17,000)
Total cost of sales	64,000	54,000
Gross profit	36,000	36,000
Gross profit %	36.0%	40.0%

USELESS MANAGEMENT INFORMATION

In a lean business, one of the responsibilities of the accounting function is to provide financial information that reflects reality and can be understood by those who do not have degrees in accounting (which happens to be most of the other people in the company). Exhibit 3.3, often referred to as the "Plain-English P&L," was developed at Wiremold during the early years of its transformation. It reflects the sales, costs, and profits for the same company in Exhibit 3.2, but does so in a way that is understandable. Even nonaccountants can see where there has been improvement (e.g., material consumption, factory wages, services and supplies, and scrap) and where there are problems (e.g., benefits). It also clearly shows why the company has not reported any improvement in profit.

Accountants have been taught that inventory is an asset. This is only partially true because it is really two things. It is part asset (raw materials and the material content of work-in-process and finished goods) and part deferred costs. These deferred costs represent the labor and overhead "capitalized" in inventory, because under the matching principle of generally accepted accounting principles (GAAP), when we make a product but don't sell it (i.e., create inventory), we have to defer the cost of making that product to that future period when we actually do sell it. In the example, last year the company was building inventory (and capitalizing labor and overhead through a noncash credit to the P&L), and this year the company reduced inventory (i.e., improved inventory turns) resulting in a noncash charge to income. Therefore, the current

EXHIBIT 3.3   Plain-English P&L

	This Year	Last Year	+(–)%
Net Sales	100,000	90,000	11.1
Costs of Sales			
Purchases	28,100	34,900	
Inventory (Inc) Dec: Material Content	3,600	(6,000)	
Total Materials	31,700	28,900	9.7
Processing Costs			
Factory wages	11,400	11,500	(0.9)
Factory salaries	2,100	2,000	5.0
Factory benefits	7,000	5,000	40.0
Services and support	2,400	2,500	(8.0)
Equipment depreciation	2,000	1,900	5.3
Scrap	2,600	4,000	(35.0)
Total Processing Costs	27,500	26,900	2.2
Occupancy Costs			
Building depreciation	200	200	0.0
Building services	2,200	2,000	10.0
Total Occupancy Costs	2,400	2,200	9.1
Total Mfg. Costs	61,600	58,000	6.2
Manufacturing Gross Profit	38,400	32,000	20.0
Inv Incr (Dec): Labor, Overhead content	(2,400)	4,000	
GAAP Gross Profit	36,000	36,000	0.0
	36.0%	40.0%	

year's P&L is being charged for both current operating costs and prior years' operating costs that are coming off of the balance sheet due to the reduction in inventory.

The bottom line is that the company actually did some good things in terms of reduced current operating costs and reduced inventories but could not see this in the standard cost P&L. The Plain-English P&L rectifies this inability to clearly see what is happening.

(f) Avoid the Two Big Surprises

The phenomenon just described is a natural result of GAAP. Though it always comes as a surprise, it is totally predictable. Ask the operations people how much they are going to reduce inventory and over what periods of time, and one can calculate how much the P&L is going to suffer because of this. Management needs to understand this to properly assess what is happening. Accountants somehow make them understand the positive cash flow results of reducing inventory but not the negative P&L results, which always comes as a surprise and in a standard cost environment is generally explained as unabsorbed overhead due to insufficient "earned" labor hours. This in turn puts pressure on operations to increase earned labor hours, thereby increasing inventory and defeating the lean efforts.

The second surprise reflects an even more fundamental lack of understanding about lean. Although people do Kaizens week after week and talk about achieving double-digit productivity gains at the wrap-up meetings, when the financial statements are issued and management doesn't see an increase in profit, they say, "Where's the money?" It's always a surprise that Kaizen results do not translate into immediate profit improvement. This reflects the misunderstanding that lean is a cost-reduction program and sometimes even manifests through a new management requirement that the "benefit" of each Kaizen event be calculated and "delivered."

When people do Kaizen, reduce the number of people needed in a particular area, but reassign the excess people to other areas of the operation (because of the no-layoff policy), they create a productivity gain without an immediate profitability improvement. This productivity gain will not result in future profitability until it is actualized. How does a company actualize productivity gains? The best way is to sell more products because it can do so without adding people. In effect, the productivity gain represents improved capacity. In most cases, the added cost of those additional sales is just the material content because the company already has the people, machines, and support staff. The profit leverage that this represents is significant.

Since most companies can create productivity gains greater and faster than they can increase sales, there are other things that can be done to actualize those gains, such as reduce overtime. Make it very difficult to incur overtime. As productivity increases, hold on to attrition. Even though companies give people the assurance that they will not lose employment as a result of productivity gains, they do not guarantee a fixed level of employment. Make it virtually impossible to replace people who leave for any reason. Look for in-sourcing opportunities. If the company sends something to a vendor that it is capable of doing in-house, in-sourcing represents a wonderful opportunity to improve profitability by transferring that value added from the vendor's P&L back into the company's.

Whose responsibility is it to actualize productivity gains? Again, there is only one answer: management. Employees create productivity gains, and it is management's responsibility to convert those gains into improved profits.

(g) Don't Forget Control, but in the Context of Lean Processes

The earlier discussion of the obstacles to implementing lean accounting addressed the compliance mentality and Sarbanes-Oxley. Unfortunately, the big accounting firms charged with reporting on a company's internal control systems have taken a "belt and suspenders" approach to compliance. This is unfortunate and has caused companies to spend millions of dollars needlessly. And so people ask, "How can I implement lean accounting and comply with Sarbanes-Oxley?" This question implies that controls disappear as lean is implemented. Nothing could be further from the truth, as lean actually enhances the ability to have good controls.

The intent of Sarbanes-Oxley is to ensure that CEOs and CFOs know that their company policies and procedures are being followed. In effect, they have to know what is happening and can't use the excuse "I didn't know" when something significant goes wrong. The application of lean principles to business processes makes them simpler and more transparent. When processes are simpler and more transparent, they are easier to control. Therefore, adopting a lean strategy actually enhances a company's ability to comply with both the spirit and letter of Sarbanes-Oxley.

(h) Communicate, Communicate, Communicate

It is generally accepted that people are afraid of change. In reality, people are afraid of the unknown. People are not afraid of change if they understand and believe that the change will benefit them. When this happens, they adopt change so fast that it can make one's head spin. Once again, the problem lies not with the people but with management. Managers are often lousy communicators in terms of explaining how the lean transformation process will benefit any of the company's stakeholders. The art of being a good manager is not being able to "motivate" people to do what you want, but to lead them in doing it. People follow leaders voluntarily because they believe it benefits them to do so, not because they have to. Each of the company's stakeholders (shareholders, boards of directors, employees at all levels, unions, banks, auditors, suppliers, and customers) need to have a communication plan to help them understand how they will benefit from a lean business strategy. The CFO is in a perfect spot to help shape these communication plans and to help lead the company in its lean transformation.

Many books have been written over the years about the latest management fad. Many programs, some with sophisticated names, have come and gone. Many CEOs have been touted as having discovered the magic formula for success. But ask anyone about the fad, program, or CEO that was at the top of the list five years ago and you will probably get a blank stare. Then ask anyone who has been the most successful automobile company consistently at the top of the customer satisfaction surveys for the past three or more decades and you will probably get "Toyota" as an answer.

Toyota has not achieved this status by following the latest management fad. It has relentlessly pursued a business strategy that we have come to know as *lean*. Whatever we call it, it is a way of doing business that increases customer satisfaction by leading everyone in the company to focus on creating value for the customer, which in turn creates value for its stakeholders. Other very different companies, like Wiremold, that have emulated the lean way of doing business, have demonstrated that lean successes are not unique to Toyota. They apply to any business endeavor that chooses to adopt and truly integrate lean principles. But adopting and integrating lean principles is not easy because it requires people to "unlearn" many bad habits, and that happens only through a true understanding of lean, and leadership from the company's principal strategic leaders: the CEO and the CFO.

NOTES

1. All quotations by Arthur P. Byrne are used with his permission.
2. James P. Womack, "Manufacturing: Lean Thinking Starts with CEO," *Automotive News*, August 5, 2002, p. 8.
3. Rowan Gibson, "Leadership Agenda," *Financial Executive*, July/August 2003, p. 11.
4. H. Thomas Johnson and Robert S. Kaplan, *Relevance Lost: The Rise and Fall of Management Accounting* (Boston: Harvard Business School Press, 1987), p. 18.

PART II

PERFORMANCE MANAGEMENT

4

CREATING A NEW FRAMEWORK FOR PERFORMANCE MEASUREMENT OF LEAN SYSTEMS

BRUCE BAGGALEY

Successful lean manufacturing implementations often fail over the long term. Initial reductions in lead time and inventory levels achieved in the early days of the lean effort have evaporated on return visits three years later. A common theme in these situations is that companies continue to measure and evaluate their operations based on traditional assumptions of what constitutes value. In short, lean manufacturing cannot be sustained over the longer term without replacing these traditional measurements.

This chapter examines the problems that traditional measures of value impose on performance management in a lean enterprise. It explores the application of systems thinking in the development of performance measures for the lean company, and it describes the characteristics of measures that support lean. With this as background, it develops a set of measures that embody these characteristics. The chapter concludes with a method that companies ready to adopt lean principles can use to develop a set of performance measures that sustain lean enterprises.

Companies increasingly apply the frameworks developed by system thinkers such as Margaret Wheatley.[1] These new frameworks force companies to rethink the assumptions on which their traditional measures have been based. At the same time, systems thinking frameworks point to new opportunities for performance management consistent with lean thinking. Margaret Wheatley is a leader in the application of system thinking for managing in times of chaos. Her work questions the validity of traditional management approaches in light of the findings of the "new sciences" of chaos theory and quantum physics. These comprehensive systems for describing the ways our universe behaves challenge the validity of laws of Newtonian physics, a mechanistic version of behavior that underlies a central premise of Western culture—nature and human behavior can be properly controlled once they are completely understood.

In contrast, system sciences strive to include Newtonian and all more advanced perspectives on the ways we understand the universe and find order in nature derived not from predefined rules of cause and effect but from seemingly chaotic processes that lead to order through continuous interaction among system components. Ms. Wheatley describes how the structures and processes of different kinds of human organization parallel natural systems—that the marketplace and business environment are inherently systems of chaos and constant change. She concludes that just as the traditional methods fail to comprehensively explain how life emerged from the mechanical world of Newtonian physics, management systems that rely on static forms of thinking to justify use of command-and-control methods to achieve order will also fail.

At the same time, findings of the new sciences create pathways for thinking about managing and measuring the enterprise that are entirely consistent with lean principles. Lean thinking is a management approach that emphasizes creating a culture of continuous improvement and adaptation at the local level. As such, it provides a systems approach, suited to the need for continuous adaptation to a changing business environment. The interrelation between the findings of the new sciences about how change happens and the management of change in the lean system is an important goal of the chapter, but first, an examination of how traditional approaches create performance problems during a lean transformation.

4.1 THE PROBLEMS WITH TRADITIONAL PERFORMANCE MEASURES

Traditional measures fail in the lean environment for the same reason that manufacturers in the United States have a poor track record in implementing lean manufacturing. Lean managers must start with an understanding of what is wrong with the traditional measurement methods and the value systems that underlie them. Exhibit 4.1 provides an outline of ways that traditional value notions depart from lean thinking. The next section examines the ways that traditional measurement processes lead to the destruction of the enterprise's ability to change and adapt, which is the critical ingredient to attaining lean status.

(a) Shareholder Value versus Customer Value

People beginning to design a lean workplace commonly use two competing notions of value to explain the primary purpose of the enterprise. First, the traditional model says that the enterprise exists to create value for shareholders and owners. Under this rubric, the most important job of senior management is to maximize the market value of the firm. The theory states that when shareholder value is maximized, resources are more effectively employed in the economy as investors reward the company with a higher share price and resulting low cost of capital, making it cheaper to raise money for expansion and growth. Furthermore, society as a whole is better off because of the rate of improvement in the overall standard of living. Companies employ more people directly, and they indirectly support employment in supplier companies through increases in purchases of raw materials and capital equipment. Adam Smith's "invisible hand" is at work to translate private gain into societal well-being.

This traditional view of value has caused a focus on meeting security analyst expectations of quarterly sales and earnings and drives choices that may ignore the long-term welfare of customers and employees. Scorecards and other "driver-based" performance measurement systems that view shareholder value as the ultimate source of value inevitably assess all business processes (operations, product development, sales, and marketing) by their impact on revenue and growth, cost reduction, and return on assets. Everyone in the company is thereby evaluated on how his/her job contributes to these goals.

EXHIBIT 4.1 Lean Measures for Learning and Problem Solving

Traditional Use	Lean Use
• Shareholder value	• Customer value
• Results orientation	• Improvement feedback orientation
• Top-down authority	• Adaptation and sustainability
• Focus on control of people	• Focus on creativity and problem solving
• Sub-optimization of system	• System effectiveness

Lean thinking does not reject the need for financial results, but it does use a different focus as the primary goal of the enterprise. It focuses on an alternative view of value—"Value to Customers"—as the reason for the firm's existence. In this view, businesses exist to deliver value to customers. This leads to alignment of the whole organization around the process of delivering value to its customers despite occasional short-term financial losses. Such alignment leads to an evaluation of every person and every function against the standard of providing value for customers. With this as the vision, lean enterprises encourage employees to identify existing methods and work practices that do not lead to customer value and fix them permanently. A corollary of the drive to delivering customer value is to discover what it is that customers value and to design these features and characteristics into the product. Followers of this theory of value believe that superior long-term financial results are due to a focus on customer value.

Successful lean practitioners increasingly argue that long-term customer value cannot be attained so long as the primary goal of the company is shareholder value. Those wishing to learn more are encouraged to read *Rebirth of American Industry: A Study of Lean Management* by William H. Waddell and Norman Bodek.[2]

(b) Results versus Improvement Feedback Orientation

A second problem with traditional measurement systems is their extreme focus on results. It is very difficult to obtain targeted strategic goals by measuring results. Exhibit 4.2 depicts the traditional measurement focus and the change in focus that lean practices provide. Most financial and operating measurements compare a period's operating results to budgeted amounts or goals. They seek to explain why results achieved were greater or less than expected, leading to two problems. First, result measures are historical. They measure the effects of past operations generally defined for operations by senior management. Often, events that affect current results measured occurred days or weeks before the date of the measurement. Second, result measures are aggregations of operations data. This is particularly true of financial measurements. These two factors make result measures poor tools for managing change programs. Particularly useless is the attempt to derive meaning from aggregations and averages, which actually hide decision-making information about change program problems.

Faced with the mandate from management to "improve results," operations people have one option—work harder. But results follow from improvements in the way work is done. So if organizations want measures that are useful in guiding change, they must understand what factors lead to the results they want and measure them. As shown in Exhibit 4.2, these factors are *causal, predictive* measures.

This is particularly important for lean manufacturing. Lean change programs rely on those people leading the change to create hypotheses (to predict) concerning the effectiveness of change programs in terms of the factors that cause changes and lead to the desired results. In their *Harvard Business Review* article, Stephen Spear and H. Kent Bowen identify this method, creating hypotheses about the effects of change and then testing them, as one of the keys to the success of the Toyota Production System (TPS).[3] The hypothesis is that if "we implement this specific change program to modify the causal factors by a specified amount, this will result in the desired change in results." Implementing the planned program to change the causal factors and comparing the results against the predicted values tests this hypothesis. The distinctive feature in this method is that the measures and hypotheses are designed by the people making the

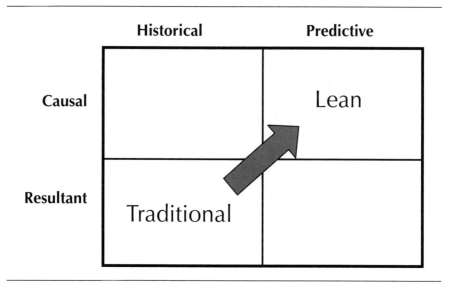

EXHIBIT 4.2 Lean Monitors Causal and Predictive Factors

change to monitor their own programs, not by senior management. Here, measurements provide feedback concerning the effectiveness of changes made to operations, not to measure the results of operations themselves. This use of performance measures to identify problems and assist in framing hypotheses for problem solving and improvement is at the heart of the lean method.

(c) Top-Down Authority Oriented versus Adaptation and Sustainability

One of the reasons why the TPS works so well is that Toyota relies on a culture of continuous improvement and learning that enables adaptive employees to solve problems and address changes in the environment. To this end, every person at Toyota is taught to be responsible for identifying and solving problems and defining new and better methods for getting the work done. A "problem" is anything that does not conform to standard ways of doing work, or 100 percent quality demanded by customers, or prescribed times to complete tasks. For the most part, management casts the vision to create value for customers, and the employees themselves figure out how to achieve this vision.

The problem-solving culture adopted by Toyota makes for a very adaptive organization well suited to survival in the twenty-first century environment of increasing uncertainty and radical change. In such a business climate, most managers are finding that they are increasingly unable to predict the future with any accuracy. For example, who would have predicted the 9/11 catastrophe? This occurred right in the middle of budgeting season for most companies, and any forecasts for the year 2002 and beyond were immediately invalidated by that event. Our only certainty is that there will be uncertainty, and our organizations must be capable of learning and adapting to change if they are to be sustained. Top-down management makes decisions too slowly and is less and less effective in this kind of environment. The only hope is to develop learning and change cultures like Toyota's, in which the systems themselves have the ability to change *themselves* in response to changes in their environments as part of their core competence.

What does this say about management-by-objectives programs and scorecards developed from strategies set in the annual planning cycle? In her book on simplified organization design, *Finding Our Way: Leadership for an Uncertain Time*, Margaret Wheatley quotes a statement by the chief financial officer of Oracle Corporation in June 2002 as reported in the *Wall Street Journal:* "We are hoping for a revenue recovery in the second half of the year. But I said that same thing six months ago, and I have lost confidence in my ability to predict the future."[4] The CFO's peers in other companies could have made this statement. The reality is that we have lost our ability to plan operations based on a forecast of business conditions six months or a year out.

Strategies and targets for performance set once a year by senior management for implementation by employees are too brittle and inflexible to work in a high-change environment. They assume that the causal relationships built into the plans remain the same, so that once defined, plans can be executed based on these relationships. However, common sense and system sciences demonstrate that causal relationships do not remain fixed. They are constantly changing in response to conditions both outside and inside the company. In this environment, planning systems must incorporate continuous feedback mechanisms to adapt to continuous change in the environment and the critical factors for success in adapting to this change. What is called for is creation of a flexible, adaptive lean culture and system embedded in the operations themselves.

The central role of management is the creation of management systems, including performance measures and standards, that embody the principles of adaptive culture and interrelated enterprise systems that are in continuous dialogue with the environment as well as with the network of internal relationships. For their part, employees learn how to use measures to identify problems, create workable solutions, and test their effectiveness on a daily basis. Managers learn the art of ongoing dialogue with their employees to discover together how changes in the world and in the business environment (customers, markets, competition, technology) affect their day-to-day work.

To be useful in today's world, planning processes must be continuous, dynamic dialogues among all participants in the system where all aspects of the system are open to modification. A top-down approach that cascades strategy through lower organization plans and goals lacks the continuous feedback and adaptation required in a period of rapid change. Exhibit 4.3 depicts a program that is more suited to the continuous adaptation required of the modern business.

Here, the development of strategy for the value stream is fed by weekly operational value stream results, progress toward continuous improvement goals, and projections of capacity expected to be freed up by lean. The value stream strategy is developed in the monthly sales and operations planning process. In this process, 18-month rolling forecasts of sales, new product development, and capacity plans are continuously updated and related to known opportunities to improve customer value and address threats in the business environment.

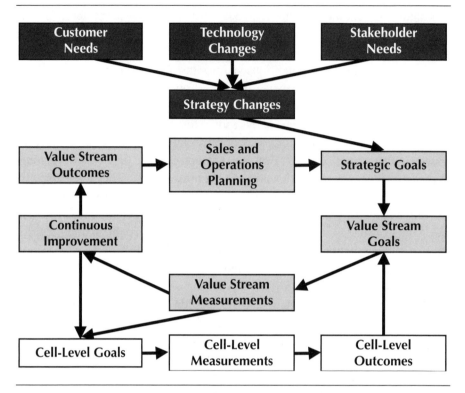

EXHIBIT 4.3   Continuous Value Stream Planning Drives Continuous Adaptation

This continuous dialogue results in an ongoing modification to a rolling 18-month financial plan for the value stream and continuous value stream and cell adaptation to changes in the business environment. Value stream strategy is continuously affected both by conditions at the cell that limit or reinforce its achievement and by conditions external to the value stream that shape the direction in which the value stream must change. These forces in turn determine and change the cell conditions that reinforce or limit the achievement of the value stream goals. Thus, strategy development is embedded in the continuous learning and change processes built into the lean management system itself.

(d) Focus on Control of People versus Creativity and Problem Solving

Related to the first three problems of using traditional performance measures in a lean environment, the use of measurements to control people is based on the belief that measurements, goals, and targets are needed to motivate people to align their goals with that of the organization. The belief system underlying most employee incentive systems and performance measures suggests that (1) people are motivated by fear, greed, and self interest; (2) promoting competitiveness and individual initiative leads to organizational goal achievement; and (3) left to their own devices, employees will not work as hard.

Control-minded organizations pit managers against each other and establish bonuses, raises, and promotions based on the ability to reach stretch financial goals. The game is called "Gotcha," and it goes something like this: Every year at budget time, middle and senior managers engage in the same dance. Senior management tries to get middle managers to agree to impossible targets—which can be achieved only by extraordinary effort on the part of their employees. Middle managers try to lower the targets. All the players expect that well-negotiated targets and rewards will motivate the exceptional effort required. When the goals are not achieved, individual managers get the blame. They obviously did not work hard enough or were not smart enough. And so the game continues. . . .

But it has been known for a long time that people are not motivated by financial rewards or stretch goals and targets beyond fulfillment of the basic necessities of life. They are motivated by work that uses their inherent creative capacity. In his classic *Harvard Business Review* article "One More Time, How Do You Motivate Employees?," Frederick Herzberg, makes the point that people are not motivated by targets, rewards, or negative reinforcement. The article states, "Forget praise. Forget punishment. Forget cash. You need to make their jobs more interesting."[5] In other words, organizations motivate their employees by drawing on the inherent creativity that resides within each worker. But traditional performance measures are based on traditional notions about motivating manufacturing work that stem from the belief fostered by Frederick Taylor and others in the scientific management school that only management can do the creative thinking; employees are only capable of executing unthinkingly. These beliefs have been proven to be false, but they are hard to dispel because they underlie the way American businesses organize and reward. Importantly, they stifle the employee creativity required to operate a problem-solving culture. None of the traditional motivational techniques provide the flexible, adaptive behavior required to sustain a lean organization. So the challenge for the lean company is to design measurement and management processes that channel the creative energies of all employees and managers into solving the problems that come up on a daily basis.

(e) Suboptimization versus System Effectiveness

The preceding problems demonstrate that existing performance measurements drive organizations in the wrong directions. Traditional performance measures are based on (1) antiquated, sometimes wrong-headed notions of value; (2) measurement of results rather than the causes of success; (3) systems designed to measure top-down strategies and goals rather than promote flexible and adaptive processes; and (4) misguided notions of how people are motivated. The final problem of traditional performance measures is one of the most damaging—all traditional performance measures are designed to improve accounting results based on philosophies of success that support mass production, not lean methods.

This returns us to the question that begins this chapter: Why do apparently successful lean manufacturing implementations become unsustainable over the long term? Initial reductions in lead-time and inventory levels that these companies achieve in the early days of the lean effort are no longer present three years later. A common theme in these situations is that the companies continued to measure and evaluate operations based on their achievement of unit cost targets built into their standard costing systems, providing evidence that lean manufacturing cannot be sustained over the longer term without replacing these standard costing measurements.

Standard costing measures do not work in a lean company because they were created to support mass production. Mass production was created to achieve lowest unit product cost through long production runs at each operation. Under this theory, the lowest unit cost for the product can be achieved when the unit cost produced by each operation is minimized. Using this measurement scheme, individual operations are given incentive to produce as many parts as possible per unit of time. Parts produced in excess of amount demanded by customer orders are stored in work-in-process storerooms and used to support future demand.

Conversely, lean manufacturing stresses making products one at a time, thereby eliminating the production of large work-in-process inventories, but leaving the operations with large amounts of unused machine and labor capacity as production volumes are reduced to support only those amounts needed to fill current customer orders. The basic conflict created by using mass-production measures to support lean now becomes very evident: mass-production measures reward maximum production and large work-in-process inventories while penalizing the creation of unused capacity. If a company continues to use traditional performance measures, it will not be able to sustain lean manufacturing because the measurements "push back" against the changes implemented by lean program principles.

4.2 SOLUTION TO THE PROBLEMS

The solution to these problems gets result and cost measures off of the shop floor entirely and replaces them with measures designed to support the causes of cost and performance consistent with lean thinking. These new measures should thoroughly reflect *operationally informed* lean business strategies and goals at all levels. Operationally informed means that the organization embeds the strategies and goals it creates in the operating systems *themselves*, using a process such as the one depicted in Exhibit 4.3. Rather than being imposed by senior management, the system itself decides what it needs to adapt to changing customer value propositions and to demands of perfection in quality and flow. The system is guided by a vision—a set of principles that directs the way the system adapts. This set of principles shapes how the system provides value to customers, employees, and communities and guides fulfillment of the business purpose. As people seek to adapt existing methods to achieve greater customer satisfaction, quality, and flow, they achieve the higher business purpose of providing value to customers.

(a) Characteristics of Effective Lean Performance Measures

Just what should the new performance measures look like to support this kind of business? How does an organization establish these goals and measures? The answers to these questions lie in the organization's goals and performance measures, and effective lean performance measures follow a sequence of four characteristics that encompass lean goals:

1. Reflect the principles of lean thinking.
2. Provide feedback about the effectiveness of improvements on overall system results.
3. Provide feedback about adherence to lean process standards.
4. Link lean processes and the system effectiveness to operationally informed lean business strategies and goals.

We have already described their characteristics in an earlier section. We now want to make them more explicit. This section makes these characteristics more explicit. Using the terms *system* and *process* to refer to "value" stream and "cell," these characteristics become the *defining principles of lean performance measurement.* Individually and as a whole, they represent a radical departure from traditional methods and merit careful analysis.

(i) Lean Measures Must Reflect Lean Principles Lean performance measures must measure an organization's progress toward its desired lean state. In short, they embody the principles of lean thinking. Exhibit 4.4 presents these lean thinking principles as set forth by James Womack and Daniel Jones in their seminal book, *Lean Thinking.*[6]

Value to Customers. The purpose of a lean enterprise is to provide value for customers. This means that every process must be evaluated on the extent to which it provides value to customers. Lean performance measures must measure the extent to which the process supports the enterprise in providing value to customers. From the point of view of the end customer, value includes the notions of quality, service responsiveness, and how well the features and characteristics of the product or service meets the needs of each customer. From the point of view of the process, measures illustrate how well the upstream process satisfies the needs of the downstream process in terms of quality and timeliness. This notion of value represents a significant departure from the "shareholder value" principle that drives the traditional performance measurement model. In this model the enterprise exists to provide value to shareholders, which leads to a formulation of value based upon financial results.

Value Stream. This is the relevant "system." As discussed in Chapter 7, lean operates in the context of a value stream—the set of interconnected processes through which customer value is delivered. This notion of interconnectedness is what defines a system—be it a living system or a man-made system, and the defining characteristic of the lean system is the interconnectedness of its elements. Interconnectedness means that changes in a system component like a business process must be evaluated in terms of the impact on the total system. Lean defines the effectiveness of the system in terms of value stream performance.

The value stream sits at the center of any discussion of lean performance measurement, where a value stream is simply all the processes performed to transform a customer order into a delivered product or service. Therefore, lean performance measures must operate in this context. To be useful, the interconnections between two processes must be clearly defined and unambiguous. Products must flow along a predefined path, and every person who works in the value stream must be linked to the product through a predefined role in its production. In this way, far from being a "logical" view of the organization, the value stream is really a physical portrayal of how production flows. This *process* view of the organization represents the way the organization operates—a radical departure from the traditional "departmental" view that undergirds traditional performance reporting.

Flow and Pull. Lean operates in a just-in-time framework. Womack and Jones call this *flow*, and flow is key to the achievement of lean. Although people usually think of flow in terms of a liquid or certain process industries, lean uses this concept as it applies to discrete materials that pass through the manufacturing process. The image is of material that moves through the process at a constant rate without stopping, and the lean company strives to attain perfect, uninterrupted flow of its product from order to delivery. Lean also embodies the notion of pull, and that means that the rate of flow is determined by the rate at which customers "pull" (or demand) products. Lean performance measures help calibrate the extent to which the processes make products at this pull rate.

Perfection. The standard for lean is very stern indeed. It is not budget or performance within some statistical precision of the value, but the flow and rate at which the customer wants the product or service. This means that lean measurement processes must be very good at measuring all instances of "nonvalue" and "nonflow" or "nonpull." They must also provide information that can be used to identify the causes of these conditions, so that these causes can be remedied rapidly. Embodied in this is the Toyota concept of *Jidoka*, a Japanese term that means to provide workers and machines the ability to detect an abnormal condition (one that does not conform to the "standard" as defined by the customer) and immediately stop work to fix it. This enables identification of the causes of problems because work stops immediately. It also allows continuous improvement to be built into the operating processes.

Empowered People. Performance at this level requires people who can see when the process is not operating at perfection and who know what to do to correct the causes of problems as they occur. In a lean process, which operates with very low inventory buffers, there is no time to get permission from management to fix problems. People who know what is wrong and how to ensure that the problems do not recur must fix them immediately. The lean method of fixing problems involves the continuous engagement of the creative energies of the people who work in manufacturing to identify problems, get at the root causes, create and test hypotheses for solutions, and then update existing methods and standards accordingly.

(ii) Lean Measures Provide Feedback about the Effectiveness of Value Stream Improvements Financial measures show operational results that occurred in the past. As derivatives of operating data, they are very difficult to interpret. At face value, financial measures show how results of operations differ from expectations, but they provide no insight as to why this is so or what needs to be done to fix the problems that have caused the discrepancy. Consequently, they serve as a poor guide for decision making.

Lean companies cannot be managed by looking in the rearview mirror. They need the kind of measurement that helps manage the changing causes of desired results. To achieve performance goals for a value stream (lower lead times, greater productivity), lean organizations must undertake a program focusing on the changing factors that lead to goal achievement and then measure the extent to which the desired results have been attained as a result of lean programs to manage these factors. Sustainable lean organizations measure the

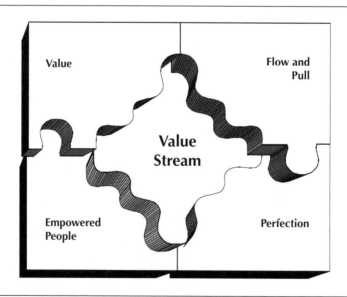

EXHIBIT 4.4   The Lean Thinking Principles Framework

achievement of these causal factors at the cell level in real time (hourly, daily), checking periodically whether the desired levels of value stream performance results have been achieved. When measures fall short of expectations, lean organizations work to discern how programs are insufficient and modify them accordingly. This process creates a program of continuous learning in which causal and result measures are linked to continuous program improvement.

The interplay among the desired value stream results, the continuous improvement program to establish new standards for critical factors for achieving those results, and the monitoring of those critical factors constitutes the lean performance measurement process that leads to continuous learning and desired results.

(iii) Lean Measures Provide Feedback about Adherence to Standards in the Lean Cells First, a lean cell is a set of interconnected operations employed in manufacturing or servicing. The measures at the cell assist the cell workers in identifying abnormal conditions so that cell operations adapt accordingly. In this role, lean performance measures identify when the cell starts performing contrary to the standards set for the cell and trigger a process to get the cell back into alignment. This process can be likened to a thermostat that regulates room temperature. This process is shown in Exhibit 4.5.

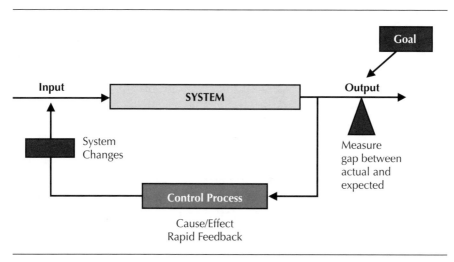

EXHIBIT 4.5   Lean Measures Achieve Effective Regulation

Note that the important characteristics of this regulation process includes a rapid feedback response to the system's performance outside set limits for the critical factor and a configuration such that the regulatory mechanism is related to the causal factor it maintains for the process. In the case of the furnace, the response is automatic and immediate. In the case of a lean cell, performance measures alert the cell team that there is a problem. The team responds immediately to the problem so that cell function and efficiency returns to goal-oriented performance as soon as possible. This may mean stopping cell work to fix the problem.

(iv) Lean Measures Link Cell and Value Streams to Operationally Informed Business Strategies and Goals Business strategy is logically related to value stream and cell operations so that the continuous improvement program is set with an eye to what is critical to achieving its goals at every level. Exhibit 4.6 depicts the measurement framework for establishing such a set of goals and measures. The diagram depicts a set of interconnected goals and measures between the lean business goals that affect the value stream as a system for delivering these goals where the value stream critical success factors embody the five principles of lean:

1. Delivering value to the customer is the primary goal.
2. Define the value stream that delivers customer value.
3. Design flow at the rate of customer pull (just-in-time production).
4. Work to maintain perfection in flow and quality (stop and fix).
5. Empower employees (continuous improvement and learning).

As can be seen, the goals for the value stream define what is meant to achieve these critical success factors in terms of the value stream performance. Performance measures are established to calibrate the attainment of these critical success factors and goals.

At the cell level, the activities in the Critical Success Factors column define the improvement initiative required to achieve the value stream goal. The result of the overall improvement initiative is measured by attainment of the goal at the level of the cell. It is important to note that each level has a feedback loop that works in real time to provide information about changing conditions, enabling cell members to modify their goals and critical success factors according to what is happening in the cell. By means of this continuous feed-

Strategic Objective	Strategic Measures	Value Stream Critical Success Factors (CSFs)	Value Stream Objective	Value Stream Measure	Cell Critical Success Factors (CSFs)	Cell Objective	Cell Measure
Specific corporate targets; specific time for achievement Guide value stream direction Refine product/ market goals Refine financial goals	Measure the attainment of specific corporate objectives/ targets	What must be done well at the value stream if the strategic goals are to be achieved?	Specific targets for the value stream to achieve the value stream CSFs Specific time for achievement	Measures the attainment of specific value stream objectives/ targets	What must be done well at the cell level if the value stream objectives are to be achieved?	Specific targets for the cell to achieve the cell CSFs Specific time for achievement	Measures the attainment of specific cell objectives/ targets

EXHIBIT 4.6   Performance Measurement Framework

back, conditions at the cell level adapt to critical value stream goals, and cell conditions may cause the value stream goals themselves to be redefined, as when a cell improvement changes the capability of the value stream. Similarly, changes in business strategy affect what is important for both the value stream and the cell, and changing value stream capabilities create new strategic possibilities. The lean system is in a state of continuous dialogue both internally and externally as it adapts to its changing environment. Furthermore, because every company is different, each should employ such a framework to design a unique set of performance measures to achieve its strategy and goals within its own need for adaptation and change. Exhibit 4.6 provides an example of how the critical success factors, goals, and measures link from strategy to value stream to cell.

In this way, lean organizations design performance measures to achieve operationally informed lean business strategy goals and enhance the performance of lean in both the value stream and at its component cells by serving to guide the design of improvement projects and providing feedback as to their effectiveness.

4.3 A STARTER SET OF LEAN PERFORMANCE MEASUREMENTS

Organizations can design a set of lean performance measures derived from lean principles that address the strategic needs of many, if not most lean manufacturers.

(a) Starter Set Overview

Exhibit 4.7 shows the starter set measures. Value stream and cell measures derive from the operationally informed lean business strategy and its targets. For example, if strategic customer value delivery goals dictate a 25 percent increase in sales and cash flow, the resulting strategic measures include both sales growth and cash flow from operations. For these gains to materialize at the strategic level, sales per person will have to increase by 25 percent at the value stream level. This happens due to lean improvement events that increase throughput of the value stream without increasing value stream resources.

For sales per person at the value stream to increase by 25 percent, the standard work and cycle time in the bottleneck cell/process must enable the increase in productivity measured by the day-by-the-hour report at that cell, showing the extent to which the cell is able operate at that increased rate. This lean mea-

STRATEGIC GOALS	STRATEGIC MEASURES	VALUE STREAM MEASURES	CELL/PROCESS MEASURES
Increase cash flow	Sales growth	Sales per person	Day-by-the-hour production
Increase sales and market share	Sales per employee	On-time delivery	WIP-to-SWIP
Continuous improvement culture	Cash flow from operations	Dock-to-dock time	First time through
	Inventory days	First time through	Operational equipment effectiveness
	On-time delivery	Average cost per unit	
	Customer satisfaction	AR days outstanding	

EXHIBIT 4.7   Lean Performance Measurement Starter Set

surement framework visibly demonstrates that if the bottleneck cell cannot increase its productivity to enable the 25 percent improvement in throughput, then the strategic business plans and budgets cannot be achieved. By linking the structure of goals, measures, and improvement projects at the cell level, the financial and business results will "take care of themselves." Without this kind of linked structure, no amount of managerial browbeating can achieve the desired results, but the performance measurement framework and starter set enable the achievement of operationally informed lean business strategy in most manufacturing companies.

(b) Value Stream Starter Set Measures

Value stream measures assess ongoing achievement of the performance targets derived from the operationally informed lean business strategy. Lean organization continuous improvement teams collect and analyze these measures weekly as "result" measures in terms of making lean progress. Value stream measures serve as a means of calibrating the effectiveness of ongoing continuous improvement activities and of designing future improvement initiatives. Six measures make up the value stream's starter set:

1. *Sales per person* measures the productivity and throughput of the value stream for the prior week, calculated by dividing the sales (or units) shipped from the value stream during the past week by the number of people in the value stream.

2. *On-time delivery* measures how well the value stream makes product to schedule at the rate of customer demand as a measure of the ability to deliver customer value. Remember to use the amounts and terms requested by the customer, not those that they settled for because the company couldn't give them what they really wanted.

3. *Dock-to-dock time* measures the material flow through the value stream in terms of the time it takes for material to flow from the receiving dock or order entry point to the shipping dock. As a measure of the ability to deliver on time, it is generally a good indicator of the effectiveness of lean initiatives to improve the lean flow. Lean organizations compute this measure from the number of days of average customer demand contained in all inventories (raw materials, work in process, and finished goods). It reliably indicates the extent to which inventories are being reduced and cash flow improved.

4. *First-time-through quality* measures the percentage of total parts that are completed the first time without rework or scrap for the value stream of the product the first time through at the cells. It demonstrates how capable the value stream is as a system for making good parts.

5. *Average cost per unit* measures the total cost of all the resources used by the value stream during the week, divided by the number of units shipped, where resources include production labor, engineering and operational support, supplies, outside processing, facilities, machine depreciation, and raw materials at their actual cost. The aim is to eliminate allocations so that true costs are measured. Lean organizations manage this measure as lean improvements facilitate throughput.

6. *Accounts receivable days outstanding* also measures the cash flow improvement of the value stream by showing the extent to which account collection improves as sales and throughput increase.

These measures are on display for improvement team meetings in the value stream team area. The team uses this performance information to discuss progress toward lean goals and design improvement initiatives to move lean progress forward. The format for a measurement display showing trends, root cause analyses, improvement projects, and other analytical data is shown in Exhibit 4.8.

(c) Cell Starter Set Measures

Cell level measures enable the cell team to finish all the work that must be completed each shift. The cell team's job is to make to takt (the rate of demand dictated by the customers) using prescribed standard work methods while adhering to the *kanban* signals that dictate work to be performed and work timelines. Cell measures identify problems that obstruct these cell work goals so that the attention of the value stream team can be focused to fix the problem immediately and to apply temporary countermeasures.

1. *Day-by-the-hour report* appears on a measurement board at the cell showing (1) the volumes and products that need to be made each hour, (2) a running tally of how much has been made that hour, (3) problems encountered, and (4) countermeasures employed. Report information allows the cell team and supervisory management to get the cell the help it needs to fix problems and get back on track.

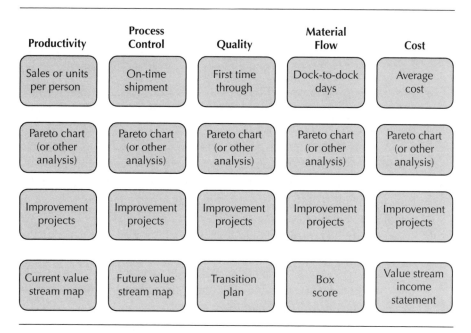

Productivity	Process Control	Quality	Material Flow	Cost
Sales or units per person	On-time shipment	First time through	Dock-to-dock days	Average cost
Pareto chart (or other analysis)	Pareto chart (or other analysis)	Pareto chart (or other analysis)	Pareto chart (or other analysis)	Pareto chart (or other analysis)
Improvement projects	Improvement projects	Improvement projects	Improvement projects	Improvement projects
Current value stream map	Future value stream map	Transition plan	Box score	Value stream income statement

EXHIBIT 4.8   Value Stream Continuous Improvement Team Board

2. *Work-in-process to standard work-in-process* shows the extent to which the amount of inventory at the cell equals the inventory levels specified when the cell was designed. It shows how well the cell follows the kanban signals. When the cell follows the signal perfectly, the ratio is 1. Ratios greater than one signal that the cell is making products without getting a kanban signal. For example, a cell might make product ahead of schedule when a machine goes down in a downstream work center when the temptation to make product in violation of the kanban signals undermines lean flow. More importantly, it prevents the team from fixing the problem. The lean way is to stop and fix the problem so that it will not recur before proceeding with the production. This measure serves to enforce the lean discipline of the cell teams.

3. *First-time-through quality* measures the cell's capability to make quality parts with the ratio of parts made correctly the first time (without rework or scrap) to total parts made that hour. Lean measures flag processes that start to make low-quality parts and signal cell teams to stop work and fix the problem immediately. Quality problems reveal

deviations from work standards or when the value stream needs a new standard. First, fix the problem; then, develop a new standard for implementation in the cell. In this way, cells continually identify problems and enhance value stream quality.

4. *Operational equipment effectiveness* identifies opportunities for machine capacity improvement, generally used for a bottleneck machine that has to operate at close to full capacity. The measure helps cell teams identify the highest-priority initiatives so that they can improve machine capacity. Operational equipment effectiveness is calculated by multiplying the ratio of availability of the machine (time up) to total time by the ratio of the actual run rate (actual parts per hour) to design (ideal) rate by the first-time-through ratio for that machine.

   For example, consider a bottleneck machine was up for six of the eight shift hours (75 percent) due to one hour down for repairs and one for changeover. It was designed to make 100 parts per hour, but it made only 80 (80 percent), and first-time-through quality was 80 percent. In this case, the operational equipment effectiveness measure ($0.75 \times 0.8 \times 0.8$) is 0.48. This machine operated at only 48 percent of its potential capacity.

The cell team leader manually posts these measures on prominent cell work area displays so that all who walk by can see them. The team leader reviews cell performance during the proceeding and upcoming shift, identifies problems that need to be fixed, and assigns the problems to team members for further study and improvement at the beginning and end of each shift. Displays capture key problems and countermeasures and submit them to the value stream continuous improvement team.

Standard problem-solving methodologies at both the value stream and the cell systematically discover the causes of problems, develop hypotheses concerning the effects of improvement programs to correct the problems, test the hypotheses, and develop new methods to change the system and eliminate the causes of the problems found uncovered by the measurement framework. An example of this process is depicted in Exhibit 4.9. This problem-solving method linked with causal-based measures gives the lean business system its ability to change and adapt methods, strategies, and goals continuously in response to changes in the business environment and customer value propositions. It indeed is the heart of the dynamic process called "lean."

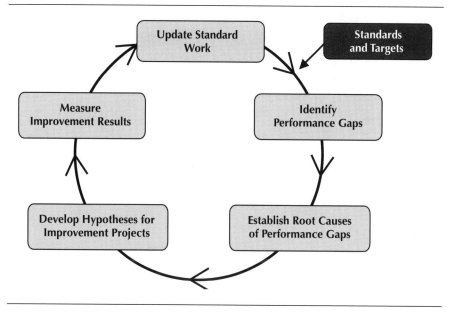

EXHIBIT 4.9 Lean Problem-Solving Process

4.4 SUGGESTIONS FOR IMPLEMENTATION

Organizations new to lean performance measurement can prepare by following a few preliminary steps. First, pick a location in a plant that has installed a lean value stream. Then, follow the problem-solving method and create a hypothesis that the lean system will operate better with the new measures than with the old. The purpose at this point is to create new lean value stream and cell measures and test them to confirm that the hypothesis is true. If it is true, then implement them on a broader basis. If not, modify the measures and perform the experiment again to test the new set.

Follow seven steps in a work plan process to implement these new measures. It enables lean measure development and testing by the people who will actually use them. This implementation method allows lean managers to iron out problems in the measures before deploying them across the entire organization.

1. Pilot the measures on value stream and one cell.
2. Decide whether or not to tailor the measures in the starter set.

3. Teach everyone in the organization about the new measurements and measurement philosophy.

4. Design the lean measures, measurement boards, data collection methods, and improvement methods.

5. Introduce the new measures and method to the pilot value stream and cell.

6. Run the value stream and cell for one month using the new methods, discontinuing all other performance measures for those areas. Remember that the purpose of the measures is to provide feedback concerning the effectiveness of improvement. So there must be improvement and problem solving integrated with the measures.

7. At the end of the month, review the pilot results, modify the measures, and retest the modifications before moving the lean measures and method to other value streams and cells.

To summarize this chapter, traditional performance measures actually work against lean progress in a lean factory. Sustainable lean organizations need measures that motivate adherence to the principles of lean thinking, serve to drive continuous improvement and assure adherence to standards in the cells, and link cell and value stream performance to operationally informed lean business strategy. The starter set gives organizations new to lean performance measurement a leg up in the implementation steps as way to get going. Now is the time to start implementation. Best of luck!

NOTES

1. Margaret J. Wheatley, *Leadership and the New Science: Discovering Order in a Chaotic World*, 2nd ed. (San Francisco: Berrett-Koehler Publishers, 1999).
2. William H. Waddell and Norman Bodek, *Rebirth of American Industry: A Study of Lean Management* (Vancouver, Wash.: PCS Press, 2005).
3. Stephen Spear and Kent H. Bowen, "Decoding the DNA of the Toyota Production System," *Harvard Business Review*, September–October 1999, pp. 97–106.
4. Margaret J. Wheatley, *Finding Our Way: Leadership for an Uncertain Time* (San Francisco: Berrett-Koehler Publishers, 2005).
5. Frederick Hertzberg, "One More Time: How Do You Motivate Employees?" *Harvard Business Review*, January 2003.
6. James P. Womack and Daniel T. Jones, *Lean Thinking: Banish Waste and Create Wealth for Your Corporation* (New York: Simon & Schuster, 1996), pp. 15–26.

5

MOTIVATING EMPLOYEE PERFORMANCE IN LEAN ENVIRONMENTS: RESPECT, EMPOWER, SUPPORT

FRANCES KENNEDY AND PETER BREWER

The U.S. Bureau of Labor Statistics forecasts a shortfall of 10 million workers by 2010; moreover, 40 percent of middle to top executives could retire in a few years.[1] These startling statistics suggest that managers should begin to think long and hard about answering one question: If you were in danger of losing valuable employees, how would you seek to retain them? Would you offer higher salaries? Promotions? Better working hours? These are all generous concessions, but they ultimately fail to help organizations promote high performance or retain high-performing employees because they overlook the root cause of employee defections and dissatisfaction. Cultural transformation is all-important to lean initiatives, and members of any culture communicate and contribute to cultural advancement with their language. Successful lean enterprises learn to use a new language when referring to traditional practices, including employee guidance and motivation. Rather than enticing employees with extrinsic motivators such as money, job titles, and working hours, research suggests shifting retention policies to three practices that are the essence of intrinsic performance motivation and inherent in lean systems: respect, empower, *and* support.

5.1 ENTERPRISE EXCELLENCE AND PEOPLE

Most people agree that human assets provide their organization's competitive edge. This is how companies differentiate themselves from competitors. When thinking about managing human (or intellectual) assets, it helps to consider a framework like the one proposed by Karl Sveiby of Skandia Corporation.[2] He first defines capital assets as either tangible or intangible. Tangible assets, such as equipment, buildings, and vehicles, are the assets typically considered when allocating investment dollars. Accounting is all about tangible assets. But given similar financial resources, these types of assets can be purchased by any company. Tangible assets provide organizations with a basic, off-the-shelf capability or platform for competing against other organizations.

Intangible assets such as systems, software, processes, training programs, and research and development (R&D) represent investments that provide future value regardless of accounting reporting convention. Sveiby pays particular attention to an intangible asset called *employee competence*. Employee competence is a combination of tacit knowledge and performance skills that grows through job experience and training. In this chapter, *human assets* mean the collection of talents and ingenuity employees possess and can apply to their work if given the opportunity. Enterprises lose these competence assets when employees retire or transition to another employer.

Why focus on employee competence in a discussion of lean performance? A good example is the transformation of Sears, Roebuck and Co.[3] Plagued by huge losses in the 1990s, the company took a second look at its strategy and determined that Sears needed to be a compelling place to work before it could become a compelling place to shop. To achieve this, it focused on developing a set of required employee competencies and created Sears University. The result was a significant financial turnaround. With higher levels of competence, employees were able to channel their work efforts more effectively, resulting in improved customer relations and smoother work processes.

Lean excellence directly depends on employee competence and committed participation in quality and performance improvements. Local work cell ownership, value stream quality responsibilities, and the five principles of lean thinking[4] are all about leveraging employee competence and performance. Employees use their knowledge, skills, and experience to redefine value from the point of view of the customer and extend these competencies to value stream management and product development. Employees define value streams as they work to continuously improve the flow of goods and services, which includes development of customer and supplier relationships.

A trademark of lean organizations is a reduced supplier base. In many cases, the number of suppliers has been reduced by as much as 70 percent. One implication of this change is that the enterprise avoids many costs of maintaining a large supplier base. Additionally, there is an advantage in developing closer relationships with suppliers, even including them in critical product planning and development on value stream teams. Competent employees are the key in fostering the supplier network that helps the enterprise gain competitive advantage from flexibility and new material developments. In this way, competence (or human capital) builds value in two directions—internally toward work processes, and externally toward customer and supplier relationships.

In their article, "Capitalizing on Capabilities," Dave Ulrich and Norm Smallwood offer a list of 11 organizational competencies demonstrated by well-managed companies and organizes them into three categories that interact to strengthen enterprise performance.[5] The first category embodies hiring, developing, and retaining talented people who understand that high performance is expected. These competent employees provide the creative ideas necessary to manage waste and innovate both products and processes in the lean environment. The second category focuses on process management—a critical element of lean. This means motivating people to collaborate to work quickly and efficiently. The third category promotes connectedness with external relationships such as customers and suppliers by fostering a consistent positive mind-set and employee experience in these relationships. These three categories of enterprise competencies—employee development, process management, and external relationship management—are entirely consistent with lean principles and help develop employee competence and improved performance in a variety of areas.

Exhibit 5.1 illustrates the mechanism through which employee competence impacts enterprise performance—especially a lean enterprise. As employees develop competence, their knowledge, skills, and experience are channeled into improving the value stream performance. The value stream embodies two other intangible intellectual capitals: internal process capital and external relationship capital. As internal processes are strengthened, the enterprise begins to reap the benefits of lean improvements. As relationships with customers and suppliers are nurtured and fortified, external processes are also improved. The enterprise achieves organizational excellence only as internal and external

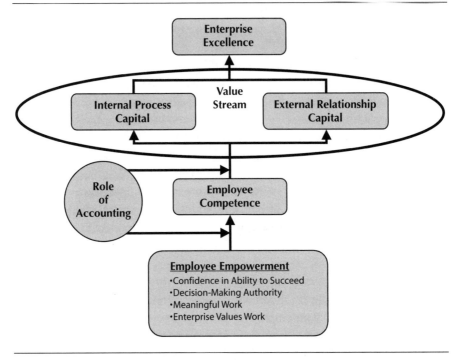

EXHIBIT 5.1   Promoting Empowerment, Employee Competence, and Intellectual Capital

processes improve, and improvements generally happen as the result of new, creative ideas—or *innovations*—especially in lean organizations.

5.2 INNOVATION AND PEOPLE

"What do we want to motivate our people to do?" The answer to this question depends on core enterprise performance management principles. The traditional enterprise responds, "To work harder, of course!" In a lean enterprise, the answer is as clear as it is different, "We want our people to innovate and continuously improve our products and services." This means that lean enterprises want employees to creatively find ways to eliminate all waste and develop new and better ways of delivering value to customers. Lean enterprises energize employees and motivate collaborative innovation.

Innovation is the implementation of a creative idea, whether that idea is applied to a new or existing product or service. Lean organizations motivate employees to innovate by tapping into their individual creative processes. As with any process, the environment can either encourage and optimize or repress and inhibit human creativity, and lean managers need a clear understanding of these factors to build and maintain an environment conducive to creative innovation. Four environmental conditions motivate employees to innovate.[6]

(a) Lean Goals and Performance Evaluations

First, lean enterprises encourage creativity through goals and performance evaluation methods. Employees are more likely to engage in idea generation and risk taking when these are explicit performance responsibilities. Employees who expect fair performance evaluations are more positively motivated to actively offer new ideas. However, performance evaluations held in threatening environments turn out employees who comply with the status quo, fear making mistakes, and seldom volunteer information.

Providing employees an environment in which they can make mistakes and learn from these experiences creates a comfort zone that allows them to press the lean "perfection experiment" onward. Chapter 3 highlights the need for a "no-layoff" policy as an example of the way lean environments provide the willingness to risk innovative thinking. People working in lean cells have the best sense of where the problems are and some of the best ideas to solve them. Performance evaluations mean jobs. When people feel threatened or distrust their manager's word, they are unlikely to participate creatively for fear of losing their own job or causing someone else to lose theirs.

(b) Ownership over Decisions and Processes

Ownership over decisions and processes encourages employees to seek information and make improvement decisions for their process performance. Lean operations are designed to provide this kind of ownership. Autonomy encourages employees to try new approaches, monitor outcomes, and make changes. This feeling of autonomy is repressed to the extent that employees perceive limited access to necessary process information or when their recommendations and ideas are not valued by the organization. Creativity is also repressed when decision-making authority is centralized. Dispersion of power and decision-making authority facilitates innovations and increases awareness and involvement.

Traditionally managed organizations compartmentalize responsibility so that employees have access to only the information they need to accomplish their local job responsibilities. In a lean organization, where the value stream dictates the flow of goods and information in its entirety from supplier through to the customer and the goal is to continuously improve that flow, information is tailored to freely provide critical performance indicators to whoever needs it. The ownership of information and decisions enables value stream and cell team members to make better decisions and generate more creative solutions.

(c) Resource Allocation Acknowledges Employees' Valuable Contributions

The allocation of necessary resources tells the value stream team that its efforts are valued and that its contributions are valuable to the entire enterprise. Creativity increases when employees believe that enterprise resources support personal ingenuity. On the flip side, when resources are continually withheld, employees develop the perception that new, creative ideas do not really matter. As employees become convinced that their ideas are not valued, why generate any new ideas at all?

While most people acknowledge the need to back up innovations with resources, they may not be as aware of what happens when they do not. In a classic example, data analysis revealed to a team of machine operators charged with reducing scrap at their work stations that one very manageable source of scrap occurred when the wrong label was applied to the product. The team recommended a more lean configuration of the work station to reduce the likelihood of an operator's grabbing the wrong label. Their simple solution involved painting floor stripes and markers in designated areas to ensure separation of material. Management accepted the recommendation and acknowledged the team for its achievement. In the meantime, the market heated up, and painting the stripes was put on the back burner for a while—six months to be exact! Acknowledgment means nothing to employees without timely management follow-through with appropriate resource allocations.

(d) Pressures that Enhance or Inhibit Creativity

Lean organizations manage organizational pressures that can either enhance or inhibit creativity. Excessive workload pressures force employees to reduce their available time for creative innovations. Downsizing choices almost always leave the remaining employees burdened with additional responsibilities. On one hand, this encourages them to come up with alternative ways of accomplishing tasks more efficiently. On the other hand, the environment after a layoff is demoralizing, and the extra work is unwanted—far from ideal conditions for motivating innovation.

The second way that workload pressures impact creativity is the method the enterprise uses to establish stretch goals. Decades of research on goal-setting generally conclude that the process of setting appropriate goals can lead to successful attainment. Stretch goals should hit a happy medium—not too easy and not too hard. They are attainable but only with ingenuity and work. Employees will use their creative resources to achieve a stretch goal if they believe it is within their reach and that the accomplishment will be appreciated.

Cell and value stream teams engage in setting their goals and monitoring their own performance. This participatory process promotes buy-in from the employees and enhances a sense of ownership in the outcomes. Metric boards at both the cell and value stream levels are usually maintained by the teams themselves and supply visible performance information for daily operational decision making. There is a real sense of ownership because employees are involved in generating and monitoring their own process.

5.3 THE POWER OF RESPECT

The first element in the practice of intrinsic motivation is to respect employees for their competencies and performance. They are the bedrock of competitive advantage. The challenge is to understand how to energize employees and maintain an environment that allows them the freedom to generate creative ideas and implement their best innovations. Managers can unlock unlimited employee ingenuity by fostering a sense of ownership and job security while providing resources and direction.

A good example of a company that rose to such heights from a very low bottom is the Hickory Chair Company in North Carolina.[7] The furniture industry faces large-scale importing competition, and Hickory Chair is no exception. Competitors now look at this company and wonder what could account for their success. Sales and profits have increased dramatically (without a price increase for four years), delivery times have decreased from six to eight weeks to two to three weeks, and inventory is half of what it used to be. How can competitors *not* notice?

Competitors are not the only ones who have noticed—so have their customers. The company invites furniture dealers to the manufacturing plant for lessons from "Hickory Chair University," where they see how quality is built into each chair and listen to employees who ask them what they need to double their sales. Using this information, Hickory Chair not only provides dealers with better sales tools like product videos and samples, but also adjusts their product mix to provide the dealers with the product their customers want.

Company employees participate in EDGE—Employees Dedicated to Growth and Excellence. EDGE originally began as a continuous improvement program designed for teams to identify and analyze problems and propose solutions. Over time, EDGE has become more. It now represents a culture of respect and trust that strives to continuously improve the performance of every process in the company. Through teams and continuous improvement initiatives, lean-thinking employees are reducing waste and increasing customer satisfaction. Employees note increasing levels of interest and involvement from people who had been skeptical about the changes. The impact on employee retention has been remarkable—turnover has dropped to half the industry average.

Hickory president Jay Reardon takes little of the credit but prefers to credit his more than 400 employees. The foundation of Hickory's employee engagement in the company's well-being is built on a "people-based culture—respect, responsibility for problem identification and solving, and total integration into the methods of improvements."[8] Yes, the teams use lean tools and techniques. But it was not until employees felt fully empowered and supported that improvements soared. Reardon argues that creativity cannot be controlled into existence, but that respect must be present throughout the organization. The chief lesson learned at Hickory Chair Company is that the potential of employee performance is limitless, and they are the company's most valuable competitive asset.

Virtually all of the literature about the lean enterprise emphasizes the importance of leveraging employee competence. The story of how the Hickory Chair Company employees turned their company into an example of a high performer in the furniture industry demonstrates the importance of respecting employee potential and allowing them to be in charge of their own processes in a lean environment. Respect truly empowers employees to take ownership of performance at both the personal and enterprise levels. But what does it mean to "truly empower" employees?

5.4 TWO VIEWS OF PERFORMANCE MOTIVATION

Along with human resources, accounting systems are part of an organization's management control systems. To get a better handle on this, one can start with the traditional description of *Levers of Control* author Robert Simons, "Management control systems are the formal, information-based routines and procedures managers use to maintain or alter patterns in organizational activities."[9] These systems develop to reflect and complement prevailing management philosophy. The transformation from traditional, vertically managed organizations to those embracing lean thinking has caused the prevailing management philosophy concerning employees to evolve dramatically from the Simons description. There are now two very distinct views of managing and motivating employees.

The ellipse at the bottom left of Exhibit 5.2 summarizes the key points of the traditional employee management mind-set. The management control system surrounding a traditionally managed organization is one of command and control. Decisions are reserved for management because employees are not trusted to make the right decision. Basically, employees are considered to be

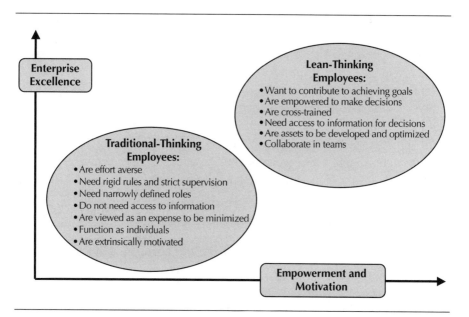

EXHIBIT 5.2   Alternative Motivational Philosophies

effort-averse people who work only the minimum necessary to stay out of trouble and still be paid. Because of this trait, it is believed they need to be strictly supervised to prevent loafing.

In traditional systems, employees have narrowly defined roles that rarely include any decision making and, consequently, little or no access to decision support information. When decisions are required, there are strict rules that govern how to make those choices. Employees receive direction and work assignments directly from their supervisors and are not allowed any discretion in how they perform their jobs. Because supervisors assign tasks to individuals, there is no need for teamwork or collaboration. There is only individual accountability. Finally, because roles are so narrowly defined and largely tied to fluctuating volume, employees are considered an expense to be minimized.

The ellipse at the top right-hand side of Exhibit 5.2 summarizes the key elements of lean thinking about employees. The overriding assumption of lean thinking is that employees are a resource—a human asset—that contributes to the organization in an abundance of ways. Employee competence is the bedrock on which lean enterprises build. They provide crossed-trained workers access to pertinent information employees need for decision making to leverage one of the most important forms of human intellectual capital in the lean enterprise: *process knowledge*. Resources are pumped into training, recognition, facilities, and other areas to develop employee competence and encourage collaborating in teams.

The bottom line is that traditional management practices do not empower workers and have little respect for them as hardworking assets. Therefore, traditional managers dangerously rely almost exclusively on extrinsic means to motivate employee performance, such as pay, bonuses, and benefits. The problem with using only extrinsic motivation is that employees perceive a limited set of signals regarding the value of their work and begin using that as a yardstick for determining how much effort to expend. They perform a mental calculation that says, "Well, if they are going to pay this much, then I will put in only this much effort." In other words, instead of motivating higher performance, extrinsic rewards actually put limits on what employees want to do and what they judge to be "fair."

This hardly means that extrinsic motivation is abandoned in a lean organization, but it certainly is not the only means nor is it the most important. Once employees feel they receive fair remuneration for their efforts, then intrinsic motivation kicks in and becomes the catalyst for higher performance. The difference is that the traditional view relies too heavily on the paycheck as the means for aligning an employee's self-interest with the company's interest. The lean view relies heavily on dignifying and empowering employees as a means of aligning their self-interests with the company's goals. Employees choose to perform at their highest level, not because they are being coaxed by a paycheck, but because they derive intrinsic satisfaction from being a member of a team that is continuously striving to raise the bar that defines world-class performance. Exhibit 5.2 illustrates that as companies move from the traditional view of controlling employees with extrinsic means to one of empowerment and intrinsic motivation, the organization reaps the benefits of increasing employee competence and tapping into their ingenuity, achieving organizational excellence.

Chapter 8, "Obstacles to Lean Accountancy," discusses the challenges that need to be met before a lean management culture can dominate in more detail. As it pertains to motivation, it describes how managers must abandon their role as commanders and controllers and embrace their new role as enablers. By the same token, accountants need to move from delivering financial reports that target managers to supporting empowered workers in their efforts to build and use appropriate information systems.

5.5 EMPOWERMENT AND PERCEPTIONS

Most companies embarking on the lean journey undergo major transformations in structure. They reorganize from departmental silos into value stream teams; they physically reconfigure operations from functional processes manned by skilled technicians to work cells run by cross-trained teams; they institute a new set of performance measurements. These organizations do whatever possible to provide training that unequivocally demonstrates the ways employees are empowered to make proactive changes consistent with lean principles.

Once again, it is important for organizations first embarking on the lean journey to look beyond gratuitous granting of decision-making authority to the value stream and cell level and discover what it means to really empower people in a way that sets them up for success. There are many definitions of empowerment. Examples include:

- "A means of giving the authority to make decisions to that level of people in the organization which, by virtue of available knowledge and closeness to the activity concerned, is most able to make a correct, quick, and effective decision."[10]

- "Have responsibility, a sense of ownership, satisfaction in accomplishments, power over what and how things are done, recognition for their ideas, and the knowledge that they are important to the organization."[11]

Taken together, these definitions offer a very complex view of empowerment and its impact on employee performance. Beyond giving employees the authority to make decisions, their decision must be made with forewarning of the likely outcomes, and employees must feel that their informed decisions will benefit the entire enterprise. This means that the employees must feel satisfied that they are consistently instrumental in making decisions that impact the success of the whole enterprise. Empowering employees suddenly looks more and more like a very big job! But let's break it down. Bradley Kirkman and Benson Rosen[12] do just that. They offer a framework for considering the complexities of the empowerment process and a definition of empowerment with four key dimensions.

(a) Employees Who Believe in Their Competencies

First, employees need to believe that they can be effective in performing tasks and reaching their goals. The bottom line is that higher employee competence and skills lead to better decision processes and ultimately to decisions that move the enterprise forward. Employee competence and skills are inextricably tied to performance. When a team tackles a problem, team members consciously and unconsciously take inventory of each other's skills and experience to determine whether the team has the critical skill set to accomplish the job. Team member confidence increases when the team collectively perceives that it has all the necessary skills. However, confidence plummets if the team is missing crucial experience or a critical skill.

By the same token, team members also look outside the team for ways that the enterprise can support their perceived needs. Support may take the form of access to information, supervisory encouragement, resources, and (especially) training. Again, when the lean team believes that it either has the necessary support or can get it, confidence increases. However, when teams observe that valid requests have been denied by budgetary constraints, teams become more discouraged and lose confidence. The result, of course, is less effort, less participation by the people who mean most to lean success, less innovation, and poorer performance.

Two management practices get lean teams off on the right foot. First, assign projects to the right team. This means a deliberate evaluation of team members' prior experience, training, and accumulated knowledge before assigning them a project. Properly matching skills and experience with a project is of primary importance. A mismatch dooms a team to failure and the demoralization that undermines all lean enterprise efforts for transformation from conventional thinking and behaviors. When teams review their process and select their own project, many traditional companies on the transition to lean encourage teams to first tackle small projects that can be quickly accomplished.

The second way to increase employee confidence in their competencies is to consistently acknowledge an awareness of the resource needs of the value stream or cell team. Communicate. Comunicate. Communicate. Managers who frequently interact with their teams and offer assistance are better positioned to recognize resource needs, provide help as needed, and give sound, timely reasons when resources are not available.

(b) Employee Perceptions of Authority and Independence

Lean employees need to be given a clear degree of authority to make decisions and the freedom and independence in choosing their actions as those actions align with lean principles. Being *told* that you can make a decision is very different than being *allowed* to make a decision. The traditional control structure surrounding decisions and actions often becomes so burdensome and threatening that employees feel betrayed by financial goals as they make honest efforts to improve the operational processes that improve enterprise performance and lead to financial success. In these environments, the team does not have sufficient authority to carry out its enterprise-mandated mission, and members becomes unsure about the team's authentic authority to carry out the enterprise mission.

The pivotal understanding in any transformation from traditional cost accounting and performance management systems is that control is never easily relinquished. After all, management's traditional job is to steer the ship and preserve the future of the enterprise for all its stakeholders. It is difficult to do so without assurances that the people making these decisions are considering the best interests of the enterprise. How can a member of a small cell team really understand the import of their decisions? Is it really a matter of giving up control? Certainly not in a lean environment! But it is a matter of articulating a very clear structure of authority for decision making—a structure based on meeting customer demands, not on conformity to artificially contrived structures of organizational control designed to meet shareholder expectations.

In *The New Why Teams Don't Work*, Harry Robbins and Michael Finely describe these decision authority dilemmas between teams and managers in traditional organizations.[13] Redefining authority structures is very confusing and at times requires arbitration or at least some kind of negotiation. Traditional solutions propose that we think in terms of *boundary management*, which is a process of agreeing to a set of constraints or boundaries within which lean work teams are free to make decisions on their own. Susan Mohrman, coauthor of *Designing Team-Based Organizations*, agrees and calls the constraint a *results framework*.[14] This method provides the team with decision parameters, as well as an idea of available resources for potential solutions. The point is to communicate any parameters the lean work team needs up front so that there is no confusion or disappointment on the part of the team and so that management can rest easy knowing that the team understands applicable limits.

(c) Employee Perceptions of their Work Contributions

Employees must perceive their task as meaningful. People want their efforts to mean something. In a work environment, employee job satisfaction and commitment grows as they see the impact their work has on the success of the enterprise. Performance measurements play an important role in communicating this kind of value to employees. For example, a lean production work cell in a manufacturing facility uses carefully selected process measures visibly displayed on the cell's metric board. The cell team members themselves are responsible for updating the metrics throughout the day. As the cell team members make decisions, they can see how those decisions affect the metrics. This gives the team immediate feedback to validate prior actions or to institute changes.

(d) Employee Perceptions of Value to the Enterprise

One of the greatest lean performance challenges is to support employee perceptions of their value to the enterprise in service organizations. Employees must perceive that the organization values their work. This appreciation is communicated through recognition programs where employees are rewarded for their performance by either remuneration or public recognition. For example, Delphi uses a Web site version of a "Hall of Fame" to recognize accomplished inventors, and many companies use bulletin boards to highlight accomplishments.[15] Plante & Moran, a regional public accounting firm, instituted a philosophy of "rerecruiting" designed to continuously encourage and recognize employees with the purpose of making them feel valued by the company.[16] P & M can boast that their turnover rate is half the industry average. Remember what it felt like to be recruited for a new job? The prospective company went out of its way to make you feel valued, convince you that your contribution was valuable, and demonstrate that you had a future right alongside theirs. For many employees, this is the only time they feel quite so valuable and wanted.

The core philosophy at P & M is to "continuously rerecruit staff so they constantly feel important, valued, and part of a team."[17] The key to rerecruitment is frequent and consistent communication. The company regularly holds informal meetings and frequently inquires about employees' satisfaction with their career paths. It includes a buddy system that teams up a new employee with one who has three to five years' experience. The company also ensures that performance measures and rewards support enterprise objectives. Basically, P&M holds the philosophy that to keep valued employees, you must treat them as valuable. The result is not only higher retention, but higher morale leads to better teamwork and a better bottom line.

To summarize, employees feel truly empowered to perform when they (1) have confidence in their abilities to succeed; (2) are given a clear degree of authority to make decisions; (3) perceive their work as meaningful; and (4) perceive that the enterprise also values their work contributions. Employee empowerment is the trigger that nurtures the development of intellectual capital. Empowerment practices improve enterprise performance by increasing employee competence and commitment. Competent and committed employees channel their work effort into strengthening external relationships and improving processes. The more meaningful an employee perceives his or her contribution, the more satisfaction with the job that employee will experience. This in turn fosters a desire to excel and further motivates employees to improve their performance and processes. This is the intrinsic motivation that sets the stage for lean thinking and a smoother transformation.

The lean principle of respecting employees for their creative potential and for their collective ingenuity can launch many organizations into significantly higher levels of performance. Empowering employees unlocks their creativity and encourages them to continually reach for new and better ways of working.

Together, these first two principles encapsulate *why* employee motivation is so critical. Without complete awareness concerning what makes people work at their highest level, it would be easy to overlook critical aspects of the performance environment.

The third factor that motivates employee performance in the lean environment—support—supplies the *how*. The conditions necessary to foster creativity and truly empower people sound so logical and reasonable that just about everyone can identify with and buy into them. The difficult part is how to adapt the management system to nurture these conditions. This is where accounting can step up to the plate and help to develop the information systems that support a creative and empowered workforce.

5.6 MANAGEMENT CONTROL SYSTEMS AND LEAN REGULATORY SYSTEMS

In essence, *control* is the traditional word for enterprise-wide *guidance*—structures that help to ensure that members of an organization work toward a common preestablished goal. Whether an organization is structured and managed traditionally or has transformed to lean operations, it is desirable to have guidance systems in place that make sure that all the horses on the track are still heading in the right direction for the benefit of the organization as a whole.

Traditional control systems rely on punishment and incentives to guide behavior and decisions. Decisions are primarily made by a small group of managers. Periodic accounting reports are a main source of the information used to determine whether actions are appropriate. Traditional accounting information provided to management for control purposes includes departmental expense statements, manufacturing variances, and numerous other bits of financial and operational information. These reports are compiled using data that has been collected on the production floor and communicated to accounting, where it is aggregated and summarized in formats consistent with financial reporting. The unfortunate part of this information is that it is "too little too late" and the wrong type of information for decision making in lean organizations.

The need for current information in lean organizations means that relevant information needs to be generated from the bottom up on a real-time basis. As this bottom-up information is relied upon for operational decisions, less reliance is placed on traditional financial reports, making them not only irrelevant and *muda* in and of themselves, but they become insufficient as a management guidance system. Does this mean that lean organizations do not need guidance systems? Some may say that control systems are no longer necessary because once employees are fully trained and operating with lean principles they are guided by the process and intrinsically motivated to make the right decisions. In reality, there is still a guidance system in the lean enterprise made up of mechanisms to motivate behavior consistent with lean principles and operational standards.

There are three types of guidance systems in all organizations that interact and reinforce each other to increase the probability of attaining goals and objectives. The first of these guidance systems focuses on *output*. This system includes the reporting of historical information discussed previously and is often tied to incentive systems. Traditional organizations rely heavily on this type of system.

A second type of guidance system focuses on employee *behavior*. Simply put, these structures are traditionally policies and procedures that have been formally established and documented. In traditional environments, these manuals are usually located in manager offices and are typically used to troubleshoot when questions arise. Lean environments use standard operating procedures, or SOPs. SOPs document the steps in *operational processes* and can be observed posted in manufacturing cells as both pictures and text. These help to not only standardize work but also to establish boundaries and frameworks for decision making. SOPs are particularly useful in an environment where cell employees are extensively cross-trained. The distinction is important. Traditional managers use policy books to control employee behavior; lean enterprises use process standards to guide and regulate employee behavior.

The third type of system focuses on *social coordination*. These are informal structures that help ensure that behavior is both desired and aligned with organizational goals without the need for constant supervision, and they are most highly developed in the lean enterprise. Three social mechanisms combine and interact to produce reinforcing social coordination: training, visualization, and peer pressure. Training is an essential part of working in a cell, as is cross-training on other cell members' jobs. In addition to technical process training, lean employees are also trained in scheduling customer orders as they come into the cell, basic machine maintenance, quality assurance, and accumulating and interpreting information. This training increases employee competence in several areas and gives employees the tools and framework to make aligned decisions. In traditional organizations, this structure is undeveloped and is restricted to technical training on a need-to-know basis.

Visualization is the second social coordination structure, again underutilized in traditional organizations where it is restricted to displaying general information on bulletin boards or other easily ignored platforms. Lean processes, however, thrive on visualization! Visual metric boards, kanbans, and other platforms are examples of the extensive use of visual coordination methods. Lean practices use visual cues not only to display information, but also as a trigger and to regulate work activities. In his book on the visual factory, Michel Greif argues that "a visual workplace is a work environment that is self-explaining, self-ordering, self-regulating and self-improving—where what is supposed to happen does happen, on time, every time, day or night."[18]

The third social coordination structure is peer pressure. Some may consider this a subtle form of guidance, but it is a powerful one. Evidence of the effects of peer pressure can be seen in different areas in a lean environment, again built into the operational processes, not the manager's policy book. For example, one-piece flow reduces staging before individual process steps, making the efficiency of the cell team member visible to coworkers. If one cell team member slows down, the result is a similar slowing of the entire cell, which becomes very visible in the following empty staging areas. Another example where peer pressure influences desirable behavior is in visual cell metric boards. Production and quality information is visible for employees external to the cell. Better performance results on the board instill pride in the cell team members. The cell's training matrix can have a similar effect. The use of color dots to signify level of expertise motivates cell team members to ask for additional training.

To summarize, traditional command-and-control thinking has left an almost universally accepted linguistic legacy that undermines lean and is very difficult for most people to relinquish. Guidance systems do not go away in lean environments—they take on a different dimension. It is easy to see why this change occurs. In a traditional environment, managers make all the decisions and direct employees. In the vertical, highly controlled environment, output controls have been designed to dominate decision making. In the transformation to lean, organizational structure flattens and managers should no longer make all the decisions. Organizations need assurances that decisions and process changes are directed toward accomplishing the correct goals. Lean organizations leverage behavioral and social coordination structures based on work processes to operationally regulate activities and motivate appropriate behavior.

5.7 SUPPORTING LEAN PERFORMANCE MEASUREMENT

There are five guidelines that both accountants and nonaccountants must keep in mind when developing information systems that support the lean organization. These five tenets build upon the five principles of lean thinking: value to customers, value stream, flow and pull, empowerment, and perfection. Exhibit 5.3 summarizes the tenets of lean measurement.

First, lean measurement systems capture the *voice of the customer*. Traditional enterprises set goals with respect to historical performance. Internal benchmarking does little to identify and promote innovative value for the customer. Instead it can even perpetuate spending in wrong areas that add to the cost burden but not to value. The lean enterprise continually questions value

Voice of the Customer
Quality—defect rates and product complaints
Delivery—line item fill rates and on-time delivery
Service—overall customer satisfaction

Process Excellence
Pull production—day-by-the-hour and operational equipment effectiveness
Quality—scrap rates and standardized work processes
Employee skills—employee training, 5S, and safety performance
Continuous improvement—inventory turns, average actual cost per unit, and efficient
use of space

Visibility
Understandable information—value stream statements
Capacity use—people and machine utilization analysis
Accessible information—visual metric boards

Shared Commitment
Cooperation—team-based measures
Shared destiny—enterprise-wide measures

World Class Culture
Internal reference point—actual historical performance
External reference point—world-class benchmarks, competitors' prices

EXHIBIT 5.3   The Five Tenets of Lean Measurement

delivery to the customer in all its activities. Tracking measures such as on-time delivery, defect rates, cost of poor quality, and overall customer satisfaction highlight delighting customers as a priority. Using target costing methods during product development and product management can lengthen the useful life of products as well as selectively include features the customer desires. Together, these measures define the extent to which the enterprise is meeting customer expectations.

Second, a lean measurement system tracks measures related to *process excellence*—the guiding principle of lean management. Traditional measures are outcome oriented, focusing only on volume and efficiency. In a lean measurement system, cell team members are responsible for smooth work flow as measured by day-by-the-hour and operational equipment effectiveness (OEE) of the bottleneck resource. Quality is monitored through cross-training, defect rates, and most importantly, SOPs. At the value stream level, team members are concerned with monitoring flow through the entire value stream. Measures such as value stream costs, average cost per unit, cost of poor quality, inventory levels, days' supply of inventory, dock-to-dock days, and customer satisfaction focus attention on the larger flow of goods from supplier to customer.

Third, lean measurement systems provide *visibility*. Traditionally, most reporting is accomplished through paper reports distributed to managers periodically. More immediate operational information is accessed through production computer systems. In other words, key information is hidden and can be accessed only on a need-to-know basis before the lean transformation. In a lean environment, hidden information is considered useless and *muda*. Whenever feasible, information should be compiled and maintained by the people who need to use it. This creates employee buy-in and increases commitment to performance goals. All metrics at the cell and value stream boards should be prominently displayed and easily accessible. This ensures that information is current, available, and relevant.

Fourth, lean measures build *shared commitment*. Traditional systems are all about managing the individual—individual goals, individual performance measures, individual appraisal ratings. With these types of measures in place, it is difficult to build a collaborative system that pulls people together. Lean organizations are flatter in structure because they require collaboration across functions to succeed. Reorganized into cells and value streams, enterprise goals and performance measures established for cell and value stream teams may also factor into recognition programs. In addition, supporting initiatives, such as cross-training and 5S, promote interest and commitment across all cell team members.

Fifth, lean measures motivate a *world-class culture*. In traditional environments, budgets and standard costs are used to gauge progress toward financial goals. Conversely, in a lean environment, a world-class culture is encouraged by creating two points of reference. Lean culture is a shared mind-set that demands excellence in providing customer value. The first point of reference is actual historical performance within the enterprise. Rather than striving to barely meet an internally established budgetary or financial standard, the lean goal is to continuously improve the actual performance of the overall system and its processes at the fastest rate possible. The second point of reference is external indicators such as world-class benchmarks and competitor prices. The logic is simple—if a company's actual historical performance is improving at a rate of 5 percent per year but external indicators suggest that its competitors are improving at a rate of 10 percent, then 5 percent is not good enough. Striving to exceed world-class benchmarks should be the goal.

These five tenets of lean performance measurement guide the development of specific metrics. Chapter 4 discusses more thoroughly the process of strategically linking measures with company goals and offers a useful starter set of measurements as well as implementation advice.

5.8 ACCOUNTING, LEAN PERFORMANCE, AND THE EMPOWERED WORKFORCE

The transformation from a traditional to a lean workplace begins with a keen understanding of the power of the intrinsically motivated workforce and a good idea of what it takes to develop an enterprise culture that supports innovation and empowerment. The five tenets of lean measurement support the transformation by providing guidelines to ensure the development of appropriate lean measures. Now, what is the accountant's role in this emerging lean environment? Lean accountants can help build an organizational culture of intrinsic commitment by promoting five enterprise-wide behaviors (see Exhibit 5.4).

First, lean accountants *enable process ownership*. They do this by providing timely information that is actionable and easily understood by nonfinancial coworkers. The accounting traditional enterprise language that uses terms like absorption costing, variances, overapplied overhead, and month-end close is useless to employees who lack accounting training and who need to make decisions in the moment rather than after the month-end close. Lean accountants also encourage process ownership by developing performance measures

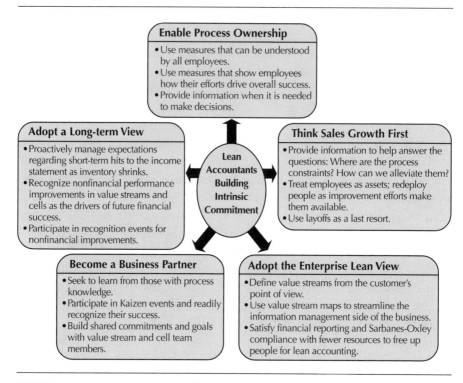

Enable Process Ownership
- Use measures that can be understood by all employees.
- Use measures that show employees how their efforts drive overall success.
- Provide information when it is needed to make decisions.

Adopt a Long-term View
- Proactively manage expectations regarding short-term hits to the income statement as inventory shrinks.
- Recognize nonfinancial performance improvements in value streams and cells as the drivers of future financial success.
- Participate in recognition events for nonfinancial improvements.

Lean Accountants Building Intrinsic Commitment

Think Sales Growth First
- Provide information to help answer the questions: Where are the process constraints? How can we alleviate them?
- Treat employees as assets; redeploy people as improvement efforts make them available.
- Use layoffs as a last resort.

Become a Business Partner
- Seek to learn from those with process knowledge.
- Participate in Kaizen events and readily recognize their success.
- Build shared commitments and goals with value stream and cell team members.

Adopt the Enterprise Lean View
- Define value streams from the customer's point of view.
- Use value stream maps to streamline the information management side of the business.
- Satisfy financial reporting and Sarbanes-Oxley compliance with fewer resources to free up people for lean accounting.

EXHIBIT 5.4   Lean Accountant Behaviors

that link each employee's actions to a unifying set of lean strategic objectives that support overall enterprise success. Accountants should participate fully as value stream teams establish performance metrics and develop the data collection processes. Chapter 4 also emphasizes the need for relevant and timely performance measures that align and support lean principles and provide a framework to assist the enterprise in establishing a performance profile that specifically supports enterprise goals and processes.

Second, lean accountants *build a lean culture by thinking and talking sustainable growth first.* Rather than obsessing with the expense side of the income statement and targeting employee layoffs, lean accountants recognize that net income can also be increased through sustainable sales growth. Using redeployable human resources to alleviate constraints and grow the business increases employee commitment to the organization.

Accountants can help in this change of focus by identifying growth opportunities as people, machines, and space become available. For example, traditional accounting is compelled to allocate 100 percent of occupancy costs to products. Lean accounting allocates only the costs associated with the space utilized by enterprise value streams. This process highlights two key benefits. First, the value stream is motivated to continually reduce their footprint, including any idle inventory storage. Second, the space and the cost of unutilized resources are made visible to decision makers whose task it becomes to grow the business—either increase sales or develop new markets. A customer service representative at a manufacturing plant said that by knowing the additional capacity he can look at the orders and see where he can cut deals in order to optimize capacity. He is now looking ahead and identifying lulls in orders. He actively seeks business during that time. This same plant recognized that it had enough floor space to establish a new work cell that increased the total capacity of the facility.

Third, lean accountants *embrace a long-term perspective when analyzing enterprise performance.* Obviously, pressures from Wall Street to meet the analysts' quarterly earnings forecasts is a non-negotiable fact of life in a world dominated by traditional thinking. Nonetheless, lean accountants can strike a better balance between the short-run and long-run views of the enterprise. For example, inventory levels usually drop substantially during a lean transformation, as discussed in Chapter 2, which in turn causes a drop in absorption net income. The accountants can react to this artifact of the financial accounting process by either seeking to assess blame or proactively managing the expectations of senior managers by giving them an advance warning of the short-term "hit" to earnings. Lean accountants can also champion a longer-term view by emphasizing nonfinancial lean performance measures that drive future financial performance.

A surefire recipe for demoralizing employees who commit time, energy, and resources to an improvement initiative with desirable long-term benefits is to criticize them if the short-term financial implications of their efforts appear unfavorable. Rather than suffering from short-term Wall Street myopia, lean accountants participate in recognition events such as celebratory dinners that acknowledge short-term nonfinancial improvements that are the leading indicators of long-term financial success, sustainability, and enterprise well-being. Using the box score for weekly reporting and financial analysis helps to keep everyone focused on balancing short- and long-term views. This technique is also detailed in Chapter 4.

Fourth, lean accountants *build internal commitment by becoming business partners with their nonfinancial coworkers.* Creating a culture of cooperation is better than maintaining arm's length relationships with those who supposedly need to be monitored and controlled. Lean accountants seek to learn from their operational business partners who possess process knowledge not only because it improves the quality of the cross-functional, team-based decision-making process, but also because it builds the self-esteem of those doing the educating. Similarly, lean accountants seek to build a shared commitment to common enterprise goals by participating in Kaizen events across the organization. At one manufacturing company we visited, there is an accountant assigned to each value stream. As a matter of fact, one accountant is actually the value stream manager as well!

Fifth, lean accountants *adopt an enterprise view of lean.* This means defining value streams from the customer's point of view—even if the value streams span numerous departments, plants, or distribution centers. It also means organizing the finance function around the needs of customers. Opportunities to streamline accounting processes can be identified by creating current and future state value stream maps that encompass all information management processes.

A controller at Germaine Industries[19] decided to employ value stream mapping with the original intention of demonstrating to the owners that there was a need to hire another person. What he found was that by mapping current and future states, his accounting personnel were able to identify enough redundancies and non-value-added tasks that the new person was not necessary to meet normal reporting needs. However, the controller learned so much about the potential of the lean way of thinking that he was able to present a case for a new position that interfaced with and supported the value stream teams. Streamlining the labor time consumed by financial reporting requirements and Sarbanes-Oxley compliance frees up time for accountants to actually do contributive managerial accounting.

5.9 SUPPORTING THE TRANSFORMATION TO LEAN

Historically, enterprises have relied on extrinsically motivating employees to perform to predetermined, policy-based standards, and maybe that was adequate because there was little else of value offered to employees. Decision making and relevant information was and still is reserved for managers in traditional companies. Employees have few opportunities to contribute with such constraints.

With the evolution of lean principles, employees are called upon to contribute in ways they have never before been allowed. They collaborate on teams and are asked to continuously create and innovate—stretch the envelope—to drive the enterprise to excellence. This is the essence of lean performance. Lean employees achieve higher levels of performance because they are intrinsically motivated due to challenging and more interesting responsibilities. In turn, lean managers must learn to respect and empower employees, recognizing that their composite ingenuity and talents propel the enterprise to achieve greater customer value propositions.

Accountants hold critical keys to this transformation—data and information. It is their chief responsibility to support the development of the lean culture with timely and relevant support. The five tenets of lean measurement—voice of the customer, process excellence, visibility, shared commitment, and world-class culture—guide the strategic development of lean performance metrics that daily guide employees as they apply lean-thinking principles to their operational processes. In order for accountants to fully participate in the lean process, they also need to adopt five lean accountant behaviors: (1) enable process ownership, (2) think sustainable growth first, (3) adopt a long-term view, (4) become a business partner to nonfinancial employees, and (5) adopt the enterprise view of lean. These behaviors are essential for accountants to remain relevant contributors to lean enterprises.

What are the very first steps for accountants in an enterprise beginning the transformation from traditional to lean performance practices? Sometimes it is difficult to make the leap from describing necessary information and resources to a logical action plan to fulfill those needs. Begin with an assessment of the relevance of current performance reporting. The following first steps help to launch the lean performance measurement path:

- Establish a cross-functional team that includes operations and users of accounting reports from all areas of the plant.
- Bring regularly distributed reports as well as those provided on a request basis. Identify who uses this information and what decisions are being made with it. Determine whether this is still useful information for that decision. If not, eliminate.
- Establish information gaps. Identify what information is needed and what it should look like when the transformation is complete.
- Identify the actions necessary to provide that information.
- Assign responsibilities and estimate dates of completion.

NOTES

1. Bill Bufe and Leslie Murphy, "How to Keep Them Once You've Got Them," *Journal of Accountancy*, December 1996, pp. 57–61.
2. Karl Sveiby, *The New Organizational Wealth* (San Francisco: Barrett-Koehler, 1997).
3. Brian Becker, Mark Huselid, and Dave Ulrich, *The HR Scorecard: Linking People, Strategy, and Performance* (Boston: Harvard Business School Press, 2001).
4. James P. Womack and Daniel T. Jones, *Lean Thinking: Banish Waste and Create Wealth for Your Corporation* (New York: Simon & Schuster, 1996).
5. Dave Ulrich and Norm Smallwood, "Capitalizing on Capabilities," *Harvard Business Review*, June 2004, pp. 119–127.
6. T. M. Amabile, R. Conti, H. Coon, J. Lazenby, and M. Herron, "Assessing the Work Environment for Creativity," *Academy of Management Journal*, Vol. 39, No. 5, pp. 1154–1184.
7. Deborah Porto and Michael Smith, "Re-making Furniture Making at Hickory Chair Company," *Target*, Vol. 22, No. 1, pp. 16–34.
8. See note 7, p. 23.
9. Robert Simons, *Levers of Control* (Boston: Harvard Business School Press, 1995), p. 5.
10. K. L. Sim and J. A. Carey, "Organizational Control and Work Team Empowerment: An Empirical Analysis," *Advances in Management Accounting*, Vol. 11 (2003), pp. 109–141.
11. Peter B. B. Turney, "Beyond TQM with Workforce Activity Based Management," *Management Accounting*, September 1993, p. 30.
12. Bradley L. Kirkman and Benson Rosen, "A Model of Work Team Empowerment," *Research in Organizational Change and Development* (Stanford, Conn.: JAI Press, 1997), pp. 131–167.
13. Harvey Robbins and Michael Finley, *The New Why Teams Don't Work* (San Francisco: Berrett-Koehler, 2000).
14. Susan A. Mohrman, Susan G. Cohen, and Allan M. Mohrman, Jr., *Designing Team-Based Organizations* (San Francisco: Jossey-Bass, 1995).
15. Jeff Owens, "In Pursuit of Excellence: How Leaders Set the Agenda," *Target*, Vol. 21, No. 2, pp. 8–13.
16. See note 1.
17. See note 1, p. 59.
18. Michel Greif. *The Visual Factory: Building Participation through Shared Information* (Portland, OR.: Productivity Press, 1991), p. 21.
19. Germaine Industries is a fictitious name used at the request of the actual company, which asked that its name be withheld. The situation described is an actual event.

PART III

LEAN ACCOUNTANCY

6

ON TARGET: CUSTOMER-DRIVEN LEAN MANAGEMENT

DR. C. J. MCNAIR, CMA

The more you know about your customers, the better you can serve and sell them.[1]

Lean management is shaped by a core set of assumptions and values, the first of which is that success is defined by profitably meeting customer expectations. As noted by Maskell and Baggaley,[2] *"The first principle of lean thinking is customer value . . . (and) understanding how we create this value." Without the customer, lean management becomes unfocused. Without the customer, value and waste cannot be defined. Without the customer, changes made in the name of lean management and continuous improvement can do more harm than good.*

Building the customer into lean management starts with the initial design of a product or service and continues through post-purchase sales and support. To be effective, customer-driven lean management (CLM) has to reflect the *economics of the market*—the trade-offs customers make to get the most satisfaction from their purchases while consuming the minimal number of their own resources. The goal of effective CLM is not to provide all customers with infinite value, but rather to focus on the key attributes that customers value most.

CLM is about more than making customer requirements visible and actionable—it is about choosing which value attributes to emphasize and which to ignore. Not every customer places the same amount of value on a product or service feature. Maximizing the returns from CLM starts with determining

121

what customer segments will provide the greatest short- and long-term profits for a given set of products and services. It is not about meeting the needs of all customers, but rather about being the best at meeting the needs of the customers you choose to serve.

The discussion that follows first lays out the key concepts of customer economics and how they affect lean practices, including the need to develop value-based customer segmentation strategies. Later sections emphasize building the customer into accounting and control systems as well as the challenges and opportunities resulting from the implementation of CLM.

6.1 THE ECONOMICS OF THE CUSTOMER

When you offer the customer a service, make sure it's what they want.[3]

The definition of *value-add* starts with the customer. If not, it becomes a "feel good" concept used by management to justify its resource decisions. Within the lean management literature, understanding customers and their requirements is the starting point for identifying and prioritizing process improvement efforts.

Value from a customer's perspective is defined by the fit of a product's characteristics, or value attributes, with customer preferences.[4] Customers don't care what it costs to produce a product or provide a service, only what the item will do for them should they decide to purchase it. The challenge faced by a company, then, is to determine what set of product characteristics will create the optimal value for customers and hence the greatest competitive advantage for the firm.

In lean accounting, the customer perspective is developed through target cost management. Target cost management builds customer-defined value into the design phase of a product. Using value engineering and similar tools and techniques, the trade-offs between the cost and features of the proposed product are used to discipline the development process. The basic formula used to make this analysis is:

Target (desired) price	$100.00
Less: Desired Profit	20.00
Allowable cost	80.00
Less: Curent Cost	95.00
Target cost	($15.00)

If the desired features lead to a product cost that exceeds the allowable cost, such as the example above, the design process continues. Why? Because the "target" or excess cost has to be removed before the product can be moved into production. Excess costs, though, cannot be addressed by simply removing features—if the features are critical to the customer's definition of product value, then improved methods have to be identified to deliver the value. Customer preferences drive the process and are non-negotiable.

Customer preferences help a company prioritize its decisions during the design of a product and the improvement of the processes used to provide it. To be effective, though, the customer perspective needs to extend beyond design to shape the entire management process. The customer's preferences have to be built into the daily language of the firm and the measurements it uses to track profits and performance.

6.2 COST: A CUSTOMER'S PERSPECTIVE

Examining the costs incurred by a firm from the customer's perspective leads to a simple separation of costs and activities into two categories: value-adding and non-value-adding. While this fits the customer's view of value, it is not adequate for management's purposes. Why? Because the organization's long-term survival depends on work that today's customers may not value directly, such as the activities that build future capabilities and products and those required to support the organization today.

A more comprehensive view of value-defined cost structures is embedded in Exhibit 6.1. Specifically, the costs incurred by an organization can be broken down into five distinct categories:

1. *Customer value-add:* The costs incurred in direct support of attributes the customer is willing to pay for. These are the only costs that generate revenue.

2. *Business value-add—current:* Costs incurred to support customer transactions, but that do not translate into revenue. They can serve as dissatisfiers, but not value-creating activities.

3. *Business value-add—future:* Costs incurred to create new products and services for future customers. While these are vital to the company's survival, today's customers are unlikely to want to reimburse the firm for these costs.

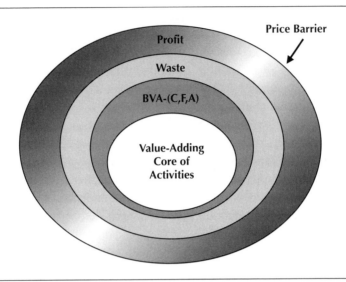

EXHIBIT 6.1   Cost: A Customer's Perspective

4. *Business value-add—administrative:* These costs are caused by internal activities that do not have an impact on today's or tomorrow's customers. Caused by paperwork, meetings, or other "feeding the bureaucracy" activities, these costs are a primary target for minimization in a lean implementation.

5. *Non-value-add or waste:* No one benefits from these costs. The wasted resources never generate value or support organizational growth. They are the primary target for elimination in a lean system.

Most of the lean accounting literature has two to three of these cost categories embedded in the discussion. That being said, when one is looking at individual activities, it is often hard to sort an activity uniquely into one "bucket" or another. Additionally, the behavioral impact of these terms cannot be overlooked. Seldom will employees willingly admit that everything they do is non-value-added. The expansion of the costing language, then, to include the five major categories of activities is an essential first step to implementing CLM.

Moving to customer-driven lean accounting, though, does not stop simply by using activities defined as one form of cost (value-add) versus another (e.g., waste). It is important to ensure that the costing system does not hide the waste and administrative tasks that are embedded in all activities. Instead, each activity has to be analyzed for its contribution to any or all of the five underlying customer-defined cost pools.

To further complicate a customer-based analysis, two other factors need to be recognized. First, lean management is defined within a process structure (e.g., value streams). That means the activities have to be knit together to create a horizontal flow of value creation from supplier to customer. Second, customer value analysis is attribute based, emphasizing costs incurred to provide different product or service attributes. The combination of these factors results in a multidimensional cost analysis that supports the analysis of overall structure, process costing, value-based costing, and finally customer-attribute cost analysis. It also serves to pinpoint interdependencies within the organization—value streams cross functional areas. To accurately capture all of these cost dimensions requires an expansion of traditional activity analysis and data collection methods. An example will illustrate the resulting methodology.

6.3 CUSTOMER-DRIVEN LEAN MANAGEMENT: AN EXAMPLE

Information gathered during a study at the U.S. Coast Guard Academy illustrates the application of customer-driven, multidimensional lean costing. As part of a study to pilot the implementation of activity-based management (ABM) at the Academy, managers of every department were interviewed to identify their activities, costs, and traceability to the Academy's value proposition.

The first step in applying the lean management concept was to identify the core processes that define the Academy and support its mission. Using the APQC Process Classification schematic as a starting point, a total of 17 processes were identified ranging from recruiting candidates for the program on through graduation and deployment of the new ensigns to Coast Guard field units. In addition to these core processes, the Academy also has a number of support and management processes typical of most organizations, such as managing personnel, and others unique to academe, such as managing academic/accreditation records.

Every product or service has its own unique set of value attributes that comprise the value proposition it is offering to its customers. Having summarized the structure of the Academy in process format, attention was turned to identifying the *value proposition* for the Academy—what aspects of its activities

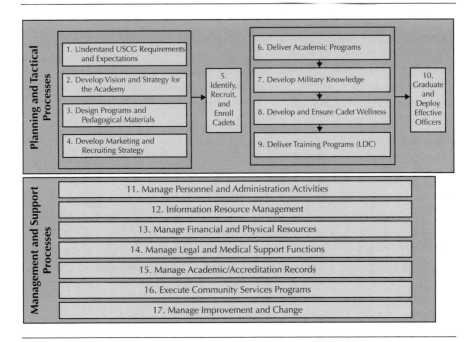

EXHIBIT 6.2   U.S. Coast Guard Academy Process Classification Framework

were seen as adding the most value to its final product: a "fleet-ready" ensign.
Seven distinct attributes were identified:

1. Quality of education
2. Breadth of course/major options (variety)
3. Responsiveness to cadet needs
4. Cadet personal skill building
5. Cadet leadership readiness
6. Shaping cadet integrity and values
7. Develop cadet physical readiness

These attributes are clearly unique to the Academy's mission. For a company
that makes a physical product, they would more likely include attributes such
as ease of use, durability, and quality. The key point is that these attributes do
not exist separate from the activity and cost analysis—they are an integral part
of the costing system.

After identifying the core processes and the attributes comprising the value proposition, attention turned to data collection. Specifically, each activity was analyzed in stages. First, activities were identified through a series of interviews with managers of key units in the organization (see Exhibit 6.3). This information served as the basis for developing activity cost estimates.

For a service firm, such as the Academy, the emphasis is placed on describing the work completed by employees. Other resources are attached to activities using one of two options: (1) they support the work done by people so they are attached in the same proportion as people time to activities; or (2) they are used in only one or a few activities and are directly assigned to these activities in the latter stages of the cost analysis.[5]

The output of the first stage of the activity analysis for one department at the Academy is illustrated in Exhibit 6.3. As can be seen, individuals are assigned to activities to support cost analysis. In addition, the activities are cross-tabulated by department and process, which results in a multidimensional costing array.

Having completed the simple activity analysis, managers were then asked to look at each of the activities in isolation and assign some or all of their cost to one of the five cost categories (value-add, business value-add—current, etc.). As can be seen from Exhibit 6.4, these cost categories were given names that would resonate more clearly within the Academy culture—cadets were not seen as customers. The prior information on the department, process codes, and activity names automatically mapped into the second part of the spreadsheet, allowing the manager to focus on the new question—what types of costs were contained within each activity.

To complete the cycle for its customer-driven lean analysis of the Academy and its activity/cost structure, the value-add costs then had to be mapped to the seven attributes that defined the value of the education process at the Academy. Managers faced a grid that contained only those activities that had been previously suggested to be value-adding and a columnar list of the defined value attributes. Results for the analysis are shown in Exhibit 6.5.

Having gathered the desired information on all the key dimensions needed to support customer-driven lean analysis of the department, the data was combined with the payroll and other costs incurred by the department to create a summary of the costs by activity and value attribute (see Exhibit 6.6).

Combining this data from across the entire Academy resulted in the following comprehensive analysis of the costs and their relative capability to create

EXHIBIT 6.3 Activity/Process Analysis

Please identify key activities performed by this department, the number of employees engaged in this effort, and the percentage of their time (on average) dedicated to completing the activity.

# of FTEs: 3

CC	Process Code	Activity Description	Number of Employees Doing Activity	% of Their Time Spent on Activity	"People" Equivalent Time	Cumulative People Time
gp	14	Generate transcripts	1	30%	0.3	0.3
gp	3	Build master schedule	1	44%	0.44	0.74
gp	12	Decision support—CGA	1	75%	0.75	1.49
gp	11	Manage/evaluate personnel	1	5%	0.05	1.54
gp	12	Register students	1	5%	0.05	1.59
gp	12	Produce cadet schedules	2	5%	0.1	1.69
gp	12	Add/drop activities/adjustments	2	5%	0.1	1.79
gp	6	Academic reviews	1	2%	0.02	1.81
gp	12	Degree audits	1	5%	0.05	1.86
gp	12	Registration audits	1	1%	0.01	1.87
gp	15	Field inquiries from depts, students, etc.	2	5%	0.1	1.97
gp	14	Filing and record-keeping	1	20%	0.2	2.17
gp	2	Manage information system development	1	30%	0.3	2.47
gp	11	Professional development	2	5%	0.1	2.57
gp	3	Product course catalog—maintain	2	15%	0.3	2.87
gp	14	Meetings/projects—administrative	2	5%	0.1	2.97
gp	3	Meetings/projects—curricular	1	1%	0.01	2.98
gp	2	Planning meetings/committees/projects	2	1%	0.02	3
gp					0	3
gp					0	3
gp					0	3
		Totals	N/A	N/A	3	

128

EXHIBIT 6.4 Value-Based Cost Analysis

For each activity from step (1), please estimate the percentage of this effort that would be considered customer value-add (a customer would pay for it), business value-add (C, F, or A), or non-value-add.

CC	Process Code	Activity Description	% Direct Student Benefit	% Indirect Support of Student Activities	% Future Academy Value-Add	% Acad Admin	% Non-Value-Add	Total (Must equal 100%)
gp	14	Generate transcripts		80%		10%	10%	100%
gp	3	Build master schedule	60%	20%		10%	10%	100%
gp	12	Decision support—CGA		30%	30%	20%	20%	100%
gp	11	Manage/evaluate personnel				80%	20%	100%
gp	12	Register students	60%	20%		10%	10%	100%
gp	12	Produce cadet schedules	60%	20%		10%	10%	100%
gp	12	Add/drop activities/adjustments	60%	20%		10%	10%	100%
gp	6	Academic reviews		40%	0%	30%	30%	100%
gp	12	Degree audits			60%	20%	20%	100%
gp	12	Registration audits			60%	20%	20%	100%
gp	15	Field inquiries from depts, students, etc.		30%	30%	20%	20%	100%
gp	14	Filing and record-keeping				80%	20%	100%
gp	2	Manage information system development			80%	20%		100%
gp	11	Professional development			80%		20%	100%
gp	3	Product course catalog—maintain	60%	20%		10%	10%	100%
gp	14	Meetings/projects—administrative				80%	20%	100%
gp	3	Meetings/projects—curricular		30%	30%	20%	20%	100%
gp	2	Planning meetings/committees/projects		30%	60%	20%	20%	100%
gp	0	0						0%
gp	0	0						0%

EXHIBIT 6.5 Activity to Value Attribute Weighting

For each activity you noted to be value-adding, please assign the percentage of that value that corresponds to one or more of the value attributes.

CC	Process Code	Value-Adding Activity	Quality of Education	Breadth of Course/Major Options	Responsiveness to Cadet Needs	Cadet Personal Skill Building	Cadet Leadership Readiness	Shaping Cadet Integrity and Values	Develop Cadet Physical Readiness	Total (must be 100%)
gp	14	N/A								0%
gp	3	Build master schedule		50%	50%					100%
gp	12	N/A								0%
gp	11	N/A								0%
gp	12	Register students		50%	50%					100%
gp	12	Produce cadet schedules		50%	50%					100%
gp	12	Add/drop activities/adjustments		50%	50%					100%
gp	6	N/A								0%
gp	12	N/A								0%
gp	12	N/A								0%
gp	15	N/A								0%
gp	14	N/A								0%
gp	2	N/A								0%
gp	11	N/A								0%
gp	3	Product course catalog—maintain		50%	50%					100%
gp	14	N/A								0%
gp	3	N/A								0%
gp	2	N/A								0%
gp	0	N/A								0%
gp	0	N/A								0%

130

EXHIBIT 6.6 Activity Cost Analysis

NAME: Registrar
PHONE:

Cost Center: gp
# of FTEs: 3

CC	Process Code	Activity Description	Budget / Activity Costs	% Direct Student Benefit	% Indirect Support of Student Activities	% Future Academy Value-Add (Personnel)	% Acad Admin	% Non-Value-Add (Operating)
		Calculation Section	$ 306,900		$ 284,900	0	$ 22,000	
gp	14	Generate transcripts	$ 30,690	$ —	$ 24,552	$ —	$ 3,069	$ 3,069
gp	3	Build master schedule	$ 45,012	$ 27,007	$ 9,002	$ —	$ 4,501	$ 4,501
gp	12	Decision support—CGA	$ 76,725	$ —	$ 23,018	$ 23,018	$ 15,345	$ 15,345
gp	11	Manage/evaluate personnel	$ 5,115	$ —	$ —	$ —	$ 4,092	$ 1,023
gp	12	Register students	$ 5,115	$ 3,069	$ 1,023	$ —	$ 512	$ 512
gp	12	Produce cadet schedules	$ 10,230	$ 6,138	$ 2,046	$ —	$ 1,023	$ 1,023
gp	12	Add/drop activities/adjustments	$ 10,230	$ 6,138	$ 2,046	$ —	$ 1,023	$ 1,023
gp	6	Academic reviews	$ 2,046	$ —	$ 818	$ —	$ 614	$ 614
gp	12	Degree audits	$ 5,115	$ —	$ —	$ 3,069	$ 1,023	$ 1,023
gp	12	Registration audits	$ 1,023	$ —	$ —	$ 614	$ 205	$ 205
gp	15	Field inquiries from depts, students, etc.	$ 10,230	$ —	$ 3,069	$ 3,069	$ 2,046	$ 2,046
gp	14	Filing and record-keeping	$ 20,460	$ —	$ —	$ —	$ 16,368	$ 4,092
gp	2	Manage information system development	$ 30,690	$ —	$ —	$ 24,552	$ 6,138	$ —
gp	11	Professional development	$ 10,230	$ —	$ —	$ 8,184	$ 6,138	$ 2,046
gp	3	Product course catalog—maintain	$ 30,690	$ 18,414	$ 6,138	$ —	$ 3,069	$ 3,069
gp	14	Meetings/projects—administrative	$ 10,230	$ —	$ —	$ —	$ 8,184	$ 2,046
gp	3	Meetings/projects—curricular	$ 1,023	$ —	$ 307	$ 307	$ 205	$ 205
gp	2	Planning meetings/committees/projects	$ 2,046	$ —	$ —	$ 1,228	$ 409	$ 409
gp	0	0	$ —	$ —	$ —	$ —	$ —	$ —
gp	0	0	$ —	$ —	$ —	$ —	$ —	$ —
		TOTALS	$ 306,900	$ 60,766	$ 72,019	$ 64,040	$ 67,825	$ 42,250

continues

131

EXHIBIT 6.6 Continued

CC	Process Code	Activity Description	% Direct Student Benefit	Quality of Education	Breadth of Course/Major Options	Responsiveness to Cadet Needs	Cadet Personal Skill Building	Cadet Leadership Readiness	Shaping Cadet Integrity & Values	Develop Cadet Physical Readiness
gp	14	Generate transcripts	$ —	$ —	$ —	$ —	$ —	$ —	$ —	$ —
gp	3	Build master schedule	$ 27,007	$ —	$ 13,504	$ 13,504	$ —	$ —	$ —	$ —
gp	12	Decision support—CGA	$ —	$ —	$ —	$ —	$ —	$ —	$ —	$ —
gp	11	Manage/evaluate personnel	$ —	$ —	$ —	$ —	$ —	$ —	$ —	$ —
gp	12	Register students	$ 3,069	$ —	$ 1,535	$ 1,535	$ —	$ —	$ —	$ —
gp	12	Produce cadet schedules	$ 6,138	$ —	$ 3,069	$ 3,069	$ —	$ —	$ —	$ —
gp	12	Add/drop activities/adjustments	$ 6,138	$ —	$ 3,069	$ 3,069	$ —	$ —	$ —	$ —
gp	6	Academic reviews	$ —	$ —	$ —	$ —	$ —	$ —	$ —	$ —
gp	12	Degree audits	$ —	$ —	$ —	$ —	$ —	$ —	$ —	$ —
gp	12	Registration audits	$ —	$ —	$ —	$ —	$ —	$ —	$ —	$ —
gp	15	Field inquiries from depts, students, etc.	$ —	$ —	$ —	$ —	$ —	$ —	$ —	$ —
gp	14	Filing and record-keeping	$ —	$ —	$ —	$ —	$ —	$ —	$ —	$ —
gp	2	Manage information system development	$ —	$ —	$ —	$ —	$ —	$ —	$ —	$ —
gp	11	Professional development	$ —	$ —	$ —	$ —	$ —	$ —	$ —	$ —
gp	3	Product course catalog—maintain	$ 18,414	$ —	$ 9,207	$ 9,207	$ —	$ —	$ —	$ —
gp	14	Meetings/projects—administrative	$ —	$ —	$ —	$ —	$ —	$ —	$ —	$ —
gp	3	Meetings/projects—curricular	$ —	$ —	$ —	$ —	$ —	$ —	$ —	$ —
gp	2	Planning meetings/committees/projects	$ —	$ —	$ —	$ —	$ —	$ —	$ —	$ —
gp	0	0	$ —	$ —	$ —	$ —	$ —	$ —	$ —	$ —
gp	0	0	$ —	$ —	$ —	$ —	$ —	$ —	$ —	$ —
			$60,766	$ —	$ 30,383	$ 30,383	$ —	$ —	$ —	$ —

EXHIBIT 6.7 A Process Perspective on Costs

Process Code	Process Description	Budget — Total Process Cost	$ 52,657,653 % Direct Cadet Benefit	Salaries % Indirect Cadet of Student Activities	$ 44,691,653 % Future Academy Value-Add	Operating Budget % Acad Admin	$ 7,966,000 % Non-Value-Add
1	Understand USCG requirements and expectations	$ 389,474 0.74%	$ 5,962	$ 45,686	$ 214,115	$ 96,651	$ 27,059
2	Develop vision and strategy for the Academy	$ 813,652 1.55%	$ 22,185	$ 28,515	$ 451,463	$ 194,834	$ 116,655
3	Design programs and training materials	$ 2,014,872 3.83%	$ 552,422	$ 214,176	$ 727,977	$ 431,289	$ 89,008
4	Develop marketing/recruiting strategy	$ 488,642 0.93%	$ 18,269	$ 22,026	$ 266,451	$ 114,625	$ 67,271
5	Identify, recruit, and enroll cadets	$ 2,151,132 4.09%	$ 600,453	$ 108,261	$ 922,490	$ 418,757	$ 101,169
6	Deliver academic programs	$ 10,866,769 20.64%	$ 7,041,154	$ 1,377,721	$ 1,686,168	$ 548,099	$ 213,626
7	Develop military knowledge and preparedness	$ 1,948,208 3.70%	$ 1,383,351	$ 188,788	$ 289,193	$ 74,063	$ 12,813
8	Develop and ensure cadet wellness	$ 6,279,520 11.93%	$ 5,180,351	$ 646,221	$ 176,381	$ 268,348	$ 8,218
9	Deliver training programs (LDC)	$ 511,201 0.97%	$ 278,938	$ 45,634	$ 118,061	$ 61,788	$ 6,780
10	Graduate and deploy effective officers	$ 792,767 1.51%	$ 323,427	$ 71,508	$ 89,877	$ 245,183	$ 62,772
11	Develop and manage human resources	$ 2,939,062 5.58%	$ 131,324	$ 834,703	$ 393,367	$ 1,268,007	$ 311,661
12	Manage information	$ 1,398,218 2.66%	$ 180,739	$ 303,269	$ 252,578	$ 523,673	$ 137,960
13	Manage financial and physical resources	$ 11,944,076 22.68%	$ 4,609,590	$ 3,707,617	$ 1,095,870	$ 2,042,805	$ 488,194

continues

133

EXHIBIT 6.7   Continued

		Budget	$ 52,657,653	Salaries	$ 44,691,653	Operating Budget	
Process Code	Process Description	Total Process Cost	% Direct Cadet Benefit	% Indirect Cadet of Student Activities	% Future Academy Value-Add	% Acad Admin	% Non-Value-Add
14	Manage legal, military, and academic records and relationships	$ 6,033,439 11.46%	$ 220,532	$ 1,608,384	$ 1,850,427	$ 1,900,493	$ 453,602
15	Execute outreach/public relations programs	$ 3,311,819 6.29%	$ 590,984	$ 501,197	$ 1,506,113	$ 551,215	$ 162,310
16	Manage improvement and change	$ 774,804 1.47%	$ 180,745	$ 127,813	$ 373,986	$ 28,590	$ 63,669
	TOTALS	$ 52,657,653 100.00%	$ 21,320,427 40.5%	$ 9,831,519 18.7%	$ 10,414,517 19.8%	$ 8,768,421 16.7%	$ 2,322,768 4.4%

value for the Academy's stakeholders: the U.S. Coast Guard and the American public. In a for-profit firm, these results could be compared to the relative amount of revenue generated by each of the value attributes (e.g., revenue equivalents) to derive a measurement of the alignment of firm efforts and expenditures with customer preferences. Absent revenues, as is the case in nonprofit and governmental organizations, the information can instead be used to redistribute resources and discipline spending.

Of the total budget (modified for presentation) for the year, over 43 percent was determined to be directly of value to cadets (see Exhibit 6.7). This is a very high level of direct value-add, but fairly typical of a small university setting where almost everything that is done touches the students directly or indirectly. The low level of waste, or non-value-add, actually reflects the culture of the organization. Coast Guard employees pride themselves on doing much with little, and hence had significant problems with classifying anything that they did as unimportant or wasteful.

The responses received at the Academy to the "waste" questions underscores how important it is to add depth to the cost management language. People respond to the language being used and how those terms resonate within their culture. Accounting is not a behaviorally neutral science. It is, instead, one of the strongest forms of management control in use today. Activity accounting makes events visible that were hidden in prior accounting approaches. Not only are new things more visible, they are amplified in importance because they have an economic value attached to them.

Summarizing the example and points so far, customer-driven lean cost management has the following unique features:

- It is multidimensional, building the process, department, activity, value attribute, and value-creating dimensions of cost into its structure.
- It enhances lean modeling by including multidimensional cost structures.
- It prioritizes areas for performance and cost improvement by identifying those activities and processes that have the lowest percentage of customer-value-add.
- It reduces the potential of cutting resources from apparently "non-value-add" areas by ensuring that interdependencies are built into the model.
- It supports process analysis by creating a structure where process shortfalls, redundant activities, and related process problems become apparent during the natural process of analyzing costs by process.

- It identifies major interdependencies and allows a more comprehensive understanding of the vast array of departments that contribute in some way to the work embedded in a process. In other words, it moves beyond departmental assignment to processes to reflect the impact of individuals across the organization on the performance of these key processes.
- It shifts attention away from people to processes, emphasizing the need to improve the workflow. This reduces the negative behavioral consequences of activity-based costing techniques.

Customer-driven lean cost management, then, provides depth as well as the ability to link activities across the organization. It supports the lean process because it recognizes that waste is embedded in everyone's activities and work flows, not just in specific activities or departments. It makes the identification and elimination of waste everyone's job. Having explored the basic methods used in the development of customer-driven lean cost management systems, the discussion now focuses on using this information in strategic planning.

6.4 VALUE SEGMENTATION

I don't know the key to success, but the key to failure is trying to please everybody.

Bill Cosby[6]

One of the most common challenges faced by an organization is identifying and securing customers who will value what the firm does best. Customer segmentation is done in many ways in traditional organizations—by geographic area, by customer demographics, by division, or by product lines. In other words, some characteristic of the company or its potential customers is used to generate a market segmentation strategy that is then used to shape the marketing strategy of the firm.

Customer-driven lean cost management takes a different slant on developing segmentation strategies for the market. Specifically, customers are analyzed and grouped based on a common set of preferences for specific product value propositions. Not every customer wants the same type of product nor expects the same level of durability or quality. In fact, we know that customers differ significantly in their expectations. An effective market segmentation strategy starts with customer preferences to build products and services that meet or exceed the needs of specific *value segments*—customers who have similar expectations.

The reason why value segmentation is important in any lean initiative is that what is of value to one customer may well be waste to another. In lean management, the focus is on eliminating waste. This cannot be done unless customer preferences are understood and used to guide product and marketing development efforts.

A simple example illustrates this point. One of the seven deadly forms of waste targeted for elimination by lean management techniques is excess inventory, which is often caused by poor methods and systems. At Western Electric in the early 1980s, management was faced with a significant challenge. Inventories of their various phones were on the rise in the face of increasing pressure by customers to offer phones in a wider variety of shapes and colors. Waste was being created in the effort to meet changing customer requirements.

After careful analysis using lean logic and process analysis, management came to the recognition that the only real variety in its phones was their shape. The color differences were the result of adding an inexpensive plastic cover, nothing more. A decision was then made to stock phones without their plastic covers, snapping the customer's desired color cover on at the last minute. Variety was pushed to the end of the process, allowing the company to take waste out while maximizing customer satisfaction with its offerings. Lean concepts were used to reduce the cost of meeting customer demands.

At Western Electric, meeting diverse customer requirements resulted in a win-win situation where all customers were given what they wanted with what was actually one standard product. In many cases, the decision to modify a product or service to meet the preferences of one customer will significantly reduce its value to other customers. In this situation a company has to deploy lean techniques to minimize the impact of product variety on the performance of its processes. These initiatives usually emphasize removing unnecessary variation from the product, pushing variety as close to the customer as possible, or using standard handling procedures (e.g., quick changeover dies) to reduce the impact of variety. If the effects of variation cannot be minimized using the traditional lean techniques, then value-based segmentation becomes necessary.

Moving to value-based segmentation strategies moves a company away from a "vanilla" product offering, or the one-size-fits-all approach to securing sales. Instead of searching for ways to convince customers to accept a product's value proposition as given, products are tailored to the preferences of targeted groups of customers. Customers with similar preferences may correlate to traditional segmentation strategies, but it is just as likely that they will not. Securing a competitive advantage in a value-driven world requires focused strategies that maximize the value created for specific customers.

Value-based segmentation creates a challenge for market research. When customers are asked what features they want in a product or service, they usually want everything. Until customers are required to describe their trade-offs, to identify which attributes matter the most to them, their input cannot be effectively put to use in the design of a product or service. Customers may want everything if it is free, but become much more specific when asked to spend their own money on a specific feature or product attribute.

Returning to the Coast Guard example, two senior cadets at the Academy[7] completed a survey of over 300 individuals, asking them to rate the missions performed by the U.S. Coast Guard (USCG) in terms of importance. As shown in Exhibit 6.8, all of the 15 core missions supported by the USCG were deemed to be very important by respondents. Looking at this information, it would be very hard for Coast Guard command to choose where to put its resources.

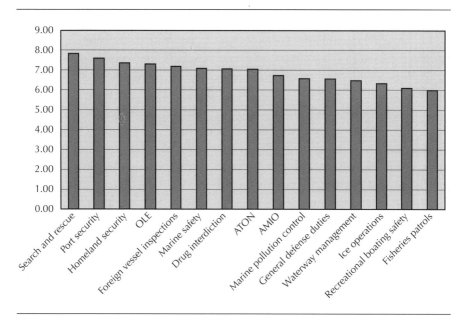

EXHIBIT 6.8   Importance of Coast Guard Missions

The problem identified here is the one often faced by companies. When asked what they want, customers want it all. Everything is important. Making choices about features and attributes then comes down to internal decisions about what the firm can afford to do—making attribute trade-offs based on internal preferences, history, or "gutfact."

When respondents were instead asked to assign a percentage of the total budget of the USCG to specific missions, with a total not to exceed 100 percent, a very different pattern of responses emerged, as shown in Exhibit 6.9. There were clear differences in the rankings of the different missions under the revised scenario—economic realities that require trade-offs were used by the respondents. Specifically, the search-and-rescue (SAR) mission was assigned 16 percent of the total USCG budget by the respondents, while fisheries patrols were only allotted 0.2 percent of the total budget. When faced with realistic economic trade-offs, customers provide very different views of the relative importance of different products or services and their features.

These preferences can now be compared to the actual spending of the USCG against the defined missions (see Exhibit 6.10 for 2005 actual expenditures,

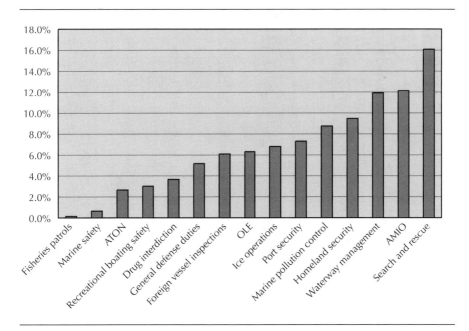

EXHIBIT 6.9   Value-Based Performance

Allocations	Search and Rescue (SAR)	Marine Safety (MS)	Aids to Navigation (ATON)	Ice Operations (ICE OPS)	Marine Environmental Protection (MEP)	Living Marine Resources (LMR)	Other Law Enforcement (OLE)	Illegal Drug Interdiction (DRUGS)	Undocumented Migrant Interdiction (MIGRANTS)	Ports, Water-ways, & Coastal Security (PWCS)	Defense Readiness (DR)
	Percent of USCG budget attributed to each of its eleven mission-programs										
2005 Actual	11.8%	7.9%	14.9%	2.4%	3.3%	9.3%	1.2%	13.2%	7.1%	21.0%	7.9%
2006 Enacted	11.5%	8.9%	13.1%	1.8%	4.7%	9.8%	1.7%	14.6%	5.6%	20.9%	7.4%
2007 Request	10.4%	8.0%	12.6%	1.7%	3.9%	9.6%	1.8%	14.7%	5.8%	24.2%	7.2%
USCG Mission-Programs (per HSA §888)	Search and Rescue (SAR)	Marine Safety (MS)	Aids to Navigation (ATON)	Ice Operations (ICE OPS)	Marine Environmental Protection (MEP)	Living Marine Resources (LMR)	Other Law Enforcement (OLE)	Illegal Drug Interdiction (DRUGS)	Undocumented Migrant Interdiction (MIGRANTS)	Ports, Water-ways, & Coastal Security (PWCS)	Defense Readiness (DR)
Budget	Total Appropriations (Dollars in thousands)										
2005 Enacted	910,887	613,843	1,152,794	185,926	255,124	720,113	94,642	1,017,478	548,675	1,625,391	612,554
2006 Enacted	956,039	741,574	1,086,817	151,406	387,232	809,441	143,924	1,211,218	462,011	1,734,717	615,814
2007 Request	$879,796	$677,699	$1,060,816	$146,938	$331,710	$808,968	$152,569	$1,239,474	$486,625	$2,034,848	$602,632
Performance	Where: ■ = Performance target for that fiscal year was met; ● = performance target for that fiscal year was not met; ◆ = to be determined										
2003 Results	■	■	■	■	■	■	■	◆	Not reported		●
2004 Results	■	■	■	●	■	●	●	■	Not reported		●
2005 Results	■	■	■	■	■	●	■	■	■	■	●
2005 Actual	86.1%	1,304[1]	1,825	0 days	18.5	96.4%	171	137.5[2] metric tons	85.5%	14% reduction[3]	67% of assets maintained C2 rating[1]
2005 Goal	Save mariners in imminent danger on our Nation's oceans and waterways	Eliminate maritime fatalities and injuries on our Nation's oceans and waterways	Eliminate collisions, allisions, and groundings by vessels on our Nation's oceans and waterways	Maintain operational channels for navigation, limiting channel closures to 2 days (during average winters) and 8 days (during severe winters)	Eliminate oil spills and chemical discharge incidents	Achieve sustained fisheries regulation compliance on our Nation's oceans	Reduce the number of vessel incursions into the United States' Exclusive Economic Zone (EEZ)	Reduce the flow of illegal drugs entering the U.S. via non-commercial maritime shipping sources	Eliminate the flow of undocumented via maritime routes to the U.S.	Reduce homeland security risk in the maritime domain	Support our national security and military strategies by ensuring assets are at the level of readiness required by the combatant commander
2005 Target	86%	1,317 or less	1,831 or less	2 (avg); 8 (severe)	20 or lower	97% or above	200 or less	19% or more	at least 88%	n/a	100%
2006 Target	86%	1,280	1,748 or fewer	2 (avg); 8 (severe)	19 or less	97%	199	22%	89%	14%	100%
2007 Target	86%	1,273	1,664 or fewer	2 (avg); 8 (severe)	19 or less	97%	199	26%	91%	15%	100%
CG Strategic Goal	Maritime Safety		Maritime Mobility		Protection of Natural Resources		Maritime Security				National Defense
HSA mission	Non-Homeland Security						Homeland Security				

140

EXHIBIT 6.10   USCG Budget

2006 projected expenditures, and 2007 requests). As can be seen, SAR receives a significant amount of the overall budget at 11.8 percent in 2005. This is roughly 4 percent less than the respondents felt it should receive. Over the course of the three years of data, though, the SAR percentage of the budget actually drops to 10.4 percent, further increasing the gap between "stakeholder" value preferences and actual spending.

On the other end of the spectrum, Marine Safety is allotted 7.9 percent of the USCG budget in 2005, growing to 8.9 percent in 2006 and then back to 8 percent in 2007 (projected). In contrast, the respondents to the survey only placed 0.7 percent of the total value-based budget against this mission. Once again, a significant gap between stakeholder preferences and USCG spending is identified, this time as a significant overspend on marine safety and an underspend on SAR missions.

Clearly, the missions and structure of the USCG is not based solely on the preferences of the public for its services—it supports a vital set of missions that have both short- and long-term implications for maritime and port safety and security. In addition, stakeholder preferences are swayed by more immediate events. The responses received in the wake of Hurricane Katrina efforts are clearly different than those that would have been given immediately after 9/11. That being said, there is still directional information in the stakeholder preferences—Coast Guard missions that directly impact the public are seen as more valuable than those serving a smaller, less public constituency.

6.5 USING CUSTOMER PREFERENCES IN SEGMENTATION

The USCG cannot segment its market providing mission support to one group and not another. Its missions and efforts are driven by natural disasters, geographical and commercial characteristics, and national priorities. In sharp contrast, for-profit organizations need to build the information about customer preferences into their segmentation strategies to ensure that they provide the right services with the right mix of features to the right customers. Product/service attributes generate revenue only when a customer values them. If features are added that are not valued by a customer segment, they become waste—a waste that lean management should target for elimination. Using diverse customer preferences to guide the development of product/service variety that increases value, not waste, is the challenge. A second example helps illustrate these points.

General Telecom, Inc. (GTI)[8] was a large telecommunications firm that entered the late 1990s struggling to remain competitive. It provided traditional
voice communication services for residential and commercial customers in
both the local and long distance markets. It was also entering the digital market,
reflecting the growing competition from cable providers for their customers.
Faced with an unregulated digital market, a recently deregulated long distance
market, and the threat of deregulation of its local service markets, GTI was
facing significant competitive challenges that lay outside of its traditional business models.

To get a better understanding of what its customers preferred, GTI embarked
on a study of customer value preferences. Starting from a recap of key customer
complaints over the last two years, GTI's marketing group worked with a focus
group of customers across its three primary product lines (long distance service, Internet service, and local service) to identify key product attributes for
its various customers. The results of the focus group were then used to generate a telemarketing survey study to understand differences in customer preferences for these attributes.

To put this problem into lean terms, the extra services required to secure Internet customers' business was waste to local customers, while friendly operators so essential to the satisfaction of local customers was a form of waste
for Internet customers. The definition of waste, which drives lean process improvements, shifts radically between these customer segments. If GTI tries to
serve everyone's needs with one business model, one product/service bundle,
it builds waste into its processes. Each customer segment places value on
unique types and quantities of attributes, transforming the definition of waste
and by extension the focus of the lean management initiative. One size would
not fit all.

As Exhibit 6.11 summarizes, the customers evaluated the services provided by GTI on six primary attributes: price of service, speed/ease of access
to network, responsiveness/friendliness of operators, convenient bill paying
locations, easy to understand statements/billings, and variety of packages or
services available. As the exhibit also suggests, there were significant differences across the three primary customer-product segments in terms of the importance of the attributes. Where long distance customers were price sensitive,
local customers wanted friendly operators. Internet customers placed most of
their value in the speed and ease of access to the network.

Having identified the different preferences for these three primary types of
services, GTI then compared its actual spending on attributes versus those desired by customers in the different segments, as shown in Exhibit 6.12. Clearly,

EXHIBIT 6.11   GTI Customer Segments

Value Attribute	Long Distance Customers	Internet Customers	Local Service Customers
Price of Service	40%	30%	10%
Speed/ease of access	0%	50%	0%
Responsiveness	20%	0%	40%
Convenient locations	10%	0%	20%
Easy to understand bills	15%	0%	10%
Variety of services available	15%	20%	20%
TOTAL	**100%**	**100%**	**100%**

the firm was not aligning its spending with the desires of any part of its market. It was approaching the market with a "vanilla" strategy that did not differentiate service offerings or intensities by customer segment, but rather offered the same range of options to the entire market. Costs were assigned to match the vanilla strategy, with cost per account of $119.57 serving as the primary metric for assessing profitability of segments.

At the time of the study, GTI was facing $10 million in cost with revenues just over $8 million—it was losing $2 million per year. Its lack of alignment with customer requirements, a slowly responding structure ill designed to deal with a nonregulated business environment, as well as the increasingly competitive marketplace was driving GTI into bankruptcy. The misalignment of spending and the actual revenues and costs per segment are noted in Exhibit 6.12.

Under the generic costing model, it appeared that the local customers were the "dogs" of the business, with revenue of $94.42 on average costs of $119.57, or a loss of $24.15 per year per customer. On the other hand, Internet customers looked quite profitable, with revenues of $152 per year, suggesting a profit of $32.43 per customer. When costs were traced more accurately to the segments, it became clear that all customers were unprofitable, with Internet customers causing $121.60 more in cost than they were generating in revenue, or an annual loss rate of 80 percent.

Average cost estimates reduce the accuracy and reliability of activity-based costing methodologies. What separates customer-driven lean cost management is its ability to pinpoint the areas where overspending and underspending are taking place, allowing management to focus its actions on areas that will yield the greatest positive impact on customer value creation. For instance, GTI needs to eliminate any spending on friendly operators, convenient bill paying, and easy-to-understand statements for the Internet users. They place no value on these attributes, so every dollar spent on these attributes is waste. On the other

EXHIBIT 6.12 GTI Customer Profitability and Value-Added Spending Alignment

	Long Distance	Internet	Local
Total costs traced to segment	$ 337,405	$ 68,400	$ 670,359
Average cost per customer	122.69	273.60	111.73
Total revenues traced to segment	$ 217,750	$ 38,000	$ 566,500
Average revenue per customer	79.18	152.00	94.42

	Desired Spending Pattern		Actual Spending Pattern		Over (Under) Spending	
Long Distance	%	$'s	%	$'s	$'s	%
Price of service	40.0%	$ 20,244.28	30.0%	$ 15,183.21	$ (5,061.07)	−25%
Speed/ease of access to network	0.0%	$ —	10.0%	$ 5,061.07	$ 5,061.07	
Responsiveness/friendly operators	20.0%	$ 10,122.14	15.0%	$ 7,591.60	$ (2,530.53)	−25%
Convenient locations to pay bill	10.0%	$ 5,061.07	5.0%	$ 2,530.53	$ (2,530.53)	−50%
Easy to understand statements	15.0%	$ 7,591.60	10.0%	$ 5,061.07	$ (2,530.53)	−33%
Variety of packages or services available	15.0%	$ 7,591.60	30.0%	$ 15,183.21	$ 7,591.60	100%
Local Service						
Price of service	10.0%	$ 10,055.38	30.0%	$ 30,166.14	$ 20,110.76	200%
Speed/ease of access to network	0.0%	$ —	10.0%	$ 10,055.38	$ 10,055.38	
Responsiveness/friendly operators	40.0%	$ 40,221.52	15.0%	$ 15,083.07	$ (25,138.45)	−63%
Convenient locations to pay bill	20.0%	$ 20,110.76	5.0%	$ 5,027.69	$ (15,083.07)	−75%
Easy to understand statements	10.0%	$ 10,055.38	10.0%	$ 10,055.38	$ —	0%
Variety of packages or services available	20.0%	$ 20,110.76	30.0%	$ 30,166.14	$ 10,055.38	50%
Internet Users						
Price of service	30.0%	$ 3,078.00	25.0%	$ 2,565.00	$ (513.00)	−16.7%
Speed/ease of access to network	50.0%	$ 5,130.00	15.0%	$ 1,539.00	$ (3,591.00)	−70.0%
Responsiveness/friendly operators	0.0%	$ —	5.0%	$ 513.00	$ 513.00	
Convenient locations to pay bill	0.0%	$ —	5.0%	$ 513.00	$ 513.00	
Easy to understand statements	0.0%	$ —	5.0%	$ 513.00	$ 513.00	
Variety of packages or services available	20.0%	$ 2,052.00	45.0%	$ 4,617.00	$ 2,565.00	125.0%

hand, for local customers GTI is underspending on delivering service to these attributes, reducing customer value and satisfaction with the company's service.

As company spending begins to align with customer preferences, it gains a strategic advantage that translates into improved profitability. It also gains an ability to choose one customer over another based on the optimal match between what the company does best and what the customer wants. Improved alignment reduces the waste from overspending on attributes that do not add value in the customer's eyes and increases the probability that the firm can invest more effectively in the attributes its customers value most. At the least, a company that uses customer-driven lean cost management gains the ability to craft unique market strategies that optimize the value delivered to customers based on customer-defined, not management-defined, needs.

A second factor affecting the way a company spends its scarce resources to meet customer needs is the realities of its competitive landscape. At GTI this issue was ultimately split into two dimensions: table stakes and revenue enhancers. *Table stakes* were defined as features that every product in the marketplace had to have to even be considered for purchase. For a window, the table stake features would be a window that allows light in and keeps rain out. There are a range of product attributes that must be present. After dealing with these generic, or commodity, features, attention turns toward the right set of *revenue enhancers*, or product/service attributes that can give the firm a competitive advantage.

If a firm fails on table stake issues, it won't be in the market for long. Conversely, if it fails to create a unique value proposition for its customers (e.g., few or no effective revenue enhancers), it becomes caught in an unrelenting cost-profit squeeze that makes it more and more difficult to survive. Both of these are "lose-lose" strategies. Only if a firm understands what comprises the table stakes for the product or service, provides them as efficiently and effectively as possible, and carefully develops revenue-enhancing attributes that customers value highly will it create a sustainable competitive advantage. The key to profitability lies in carefully managing the firm's value proposition to continuously provide the greatest value for dollar of price—as defined by the customer, not the company. Using the customer perspective to shape strategies and action is the ultimate goal.

Lean management is driven by the desire to eliminate waste from the processes and procedures that are used to provide products to customers. Unfortunately, a well-designed process that has no "waste" in its flow may itself be waste to some customers if the attribute it supports is not valued by the customer. To summarize the discussion of value-based segmentation and how it influences lean management initiatives:

- Lean management emphasizes removing waste from products and processes.
- The definition of waste is based on customer preferences.
- Not all customers value the same set, or quantity, of product/service attributes.
- What is waste for one customer is value creating for another.
- Effective lean management has to begin from a detailed understanding of the diverse expectations of its primary customer segments. If this step is skipped during a lean implementation, attributes that are critical to one segment may be accidentally lost or impaired in value, transforming the entire product into waste.
- If every customer's wants are built into every product, waste will be created for everyone.
- Only when customers have to make economic decisions about attributes will this information become available to companies. Changing to a lean mentality in managing a business has to start with changes to the heart of its market research and product segmentation strategies.
- Once identified, customer/product segment performance has to be tracked against metrics *unique to that segment*. The management control system has to be modified to ensure that value, not waste, is created in the customer's eyes.
- Only when the correct set of product/service attributes are identified by customer segment should lean initiatives be put in place to improve the processes that deliver this value. Being on time with the wrong mix of product attributes is not a winning strategy, no matter how lean the underlying process is. *Waste cannot be defined from the inside—it is defined by the customer.*

6.6 PUTTING THE CUSTOMER PERSPECTIVE INTO ACTION

You can have big plans, but it's the small choices that have the greatest power. They draw us toward the future we want to create.

Robert Cooper[9]

The basic structure of customer-driven lean cost management is presented in Exhibit 6.13. As can be seen, CLM starts with the mapping of resource costs to activities and their related value streams or processes. Having completed this basic cost analysis, attention turns toward analyzing the percentage of value-add, business value-add, and non-value-add cost and effort embedded in each activity. Activities are seldom all value creating or waste, but somewhere in between. In addition, these definitions of value-add cannot be made by management. Value is defined solely in the eyes of the customer. What is value creating to one customer may be waste to another.

Mapping costs against customer preferences, then, is a multidimensional activity that has to *begin* with the customer's preferences, including preferences by segments. Unfortunately, far too many lean costing initiatives take a "hands-off" view of the value proposition. Whatever features marketing or management note as critical become value-adding, but studies completed over the last few years suggest that managers are not very good judges of customer value preferences.[10] Over and over again, significant misalignment of company spending on various product and service attributes has been documented, suggesting that companies may need to increase the use of active dialogues with their current, past, or potential customers. Part of this discussion

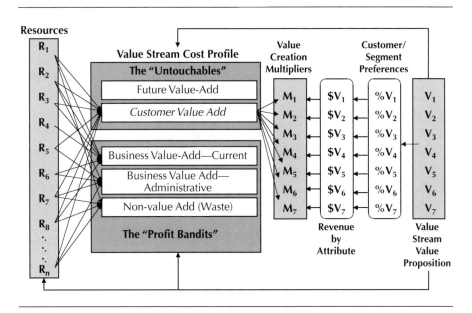

EXHIBIT 6.13   Customer-Driven Lean Cost Management

has to emphasize the underlying economic trade-offs for any given product or service from the customer's perspective—not all attributes are created equal nor equally valued by all.

A simple example of how a failure to match customer value to product attributes can create opportunities for competitors is the Tupperware story. As any owner of Tupperware knows, it is a superior product that lasts for years. It is also relatively expensive—its price reflects its planned useful life from the company's perspective. Unfortunately, the original owner of a Tupperware container seldom retains "custody" for the entire life of the product—it is instead left at parties, "borrowed" by college-age children, or meets some other fate that shortens its useful life for the original customer. The excess value in Tupperware left it open to competition from products that more closely match the customer's experienced value. Gladware and related multiuse, inexpensive storage container providers have moved into the space created by Tupperware's failure to match its products to customer economics.

Having identified customer preferences and used this information to analyze the current spending within the firm, attention should turn to develop metrics that will become a permanent part of the performance management system. Several potential metrics would be:

- *Value multiplier.* The ratio of revenue generated by attribute using the customer's preferences compared to the value-added dollars being spent to deliver on those attributes. Low or negative multipliers are an indication of excessive spending, while high multipliers suggest either a competitive advantage (customers respond they are satisfied with company performance) or a value shortfall, which will harm the firm's competitiveness and profits.

- *Cost-value gap.* Assessment of the total dollars spent to deliver an attribute versus the spending preferred by the customer. This metric may be done with either total costs, leading to a target-costing methodology, or with value-added costs only. Overspending is waste, whether or not value of some sort is being created.

- *Value-add ratio.* Analysis of percentage value-added cost to total cost by activity, value stream, or in total. It has been determined that a company with a value-add ratio of less than 20 percent will normally be experiencing losses.

- *Customer-to-administrative cost ratio.* Direct customer value-add costs can be compared to the costs of running the business (business value-add: administrative). If the company is spending as much or more money on administration as it is on serving the customer, it is on a dangerous path.

- *Cost-to-value ratio.* A measure of a product's comparative quality against its comparative life cycle costs, both taken from the customer's perspective. The goal is deliver the highest quality for the lowest cost.

The key in all of these metrics is that emphasis is placed on capturing the economics of a product or service from the customer's perspective—they make customer preferences *visible* and hence actionable.

6.7 BUILDING THE CUSTOMER IN: A SERVICE PERSPECTIVE

The examples used in this chapter have emphasized the need to build the customer perspective into products and services. There have been numerous articles and books written about target cost management, which is used to focus attention on key product characteristics in manufacturing firms. To date, most of the lean cost management discussions of customer value have taken a manufacturing-centered approach, integrating lean concepts with the target costing model.

It is no secret that today the U.S. economy is comprised of more service organizations than manufacturing companies. Lean concepts, though, apply to all forms of value streams. The USCG can use the concepts to focus its spending on more highly valued missions, or at least in making the public more aware the ways that some of the USCG's less valued missions impact them. Telecommunications firms can use the customer perspective to differentiate their service and support structures to provide only what is valued, at a competitive price, effectively stepping away from the tendency to keep adding more and more features in the hope of gaining share or keeping customers. More may be less for many service customers.

In the GTI discussion, the concept of a "vanilla" strategy was developed. This is perhaps the greatest danger faced by service-based organizations—the potential that they may present the same "face" to all customers. One final example may help to underscore the importance of building the customer into a company.

Impact Communications is a small, boutique public relations firm in Boston. Several years ago it began to experience profitability problems. Value-based analysis uncovered the fact that while the firm and its entrepreneurial owner were defining its value proposition around "cause-related" marketing strategies, the majority of its customers were coming to them for basic "smile and dial" public relations work. The latter customers, who made up 80 percent of the firm's annual revenues, seldom stayed with the firm for more than one or two PR campaigns because the firm simply did not meet their service expectations. Impact's view of its customers' requirements and what customers really wanted for their service dollars were totally out of alignment.

After completing a value-based analysis, management decided to take a very different approach to managing its engagements. Instead of negotiating for a project at a set fee, managers began to build the engagement budget from customer preferences. In initial negotiations, the customer was asked what their expectations were—how would they define a successful engagement? These preferences were used to develop the budget for the engagement and to tailor the initial quote to ensure that only the services expected by the client would be included. This customer-driven proposal could then be reviewed by the customer to clear up discrepancies and ensure that the project was properly focused and scoped.

Once the engagement was secured, management used the original value-based budget to control project costs. Monthly reports were made to clients that detailed spending against customer expectations and preferences. By building the customer perspective into the basic management control system of the firm, Impact was able to improve performance and profits. In addition, it helped clarify the communication between customers, management, and employees.

6.8 CLM: THE PATH FORWARD

The field of customer-driven lean cost management is in its infancy. There remains open debate on how to define customer value, how to segregate costs to best support the creation of superior levels of customer value, and how to build the lean concepts into the everyday reporting cycles of the organization. What is not in question is the critical need to build the customer perspective into both lean and nonlean costing management initiatives.

Lean costing techniques have to be embedded in the management control system of the firm, from initial setting of strategies through the development of performance measurements and management incentive and reward systems. This embedding endeavor has to be driven from the customer perspective to ensure that activities and processes that create customer value are protected from cost reduction initiatives. While all activities have some form of business-value-add or waste embedded in them, cutting the activities closest to the customer requires a precision that is not yet mastered in costing circles. Simply knowing where these boundaries are, though, is a positive start.

There is no simple way for a firm to transition from traditional costing methods to customer-driven lean cost management. That being said, the path forward can be taken in incremental steps that will maximize the payoff a firm receives for its efforts in building the customer into its daily operations, including:

1. *Collect value preferences from current, potential, and past customers.* Understanding where your customers are really coming from is the critical first step. Often, the customers that leave are a better source of information than those who stay. Put in place a regular system for gaining customer input.

2. *Force customers to make trade-offs.* Unless customers are required to prioritize their choices, they happily accept higher and higher levels of value from companies for the same, or perhaps even a lower, price. Excess value, as seen in the Tupperware example, can actually become waste. Customers will accept the excess, but that doesn't mean they will pay for it.

3. *Abandon "cost plus" thinking in all areas of the business.* Regardless of how a company is managed or costed, it is never guaranteed the right to "cover its costs" in the price charged to customers. Companies have the right to earn a profit for their value-creating efforts, not cover excessive costs.

4. *Undertake activity cost analysis at a high level.* Part of building toward a customer-driven lean cost management system is creating the demand for this type of information. By using simple pilot studies such as that completed at the USCG Academy, managers can gain an understanding of what the technique will do for them. CLM changes the definition of "success" within the organization away from controlling the greatest amount of resources to delivering the most value with the least amount of resources. In addition, a pilot study can help management understand how close, or not, the firm comes to profitably meeting customer expectations.

5. *Build the platform for cooperation between marketing and finance.* More than any technique developed to date, CLM requires the active

collaboration of marketing and finance professionals. As noted in one company, the primary value they received from implementing CLM was that everyone in the organization was able to speak the same language—the language of customer value, not costs.

6. *Accept that cost and value are not linear functions.* One of the key ideas often lost in a discussion of waste and lean management is the fact that all dollars are not created equal. A dollar invested in customer value will generate more than one dollar of revenue growth. If the threshold for profitability is 20 percent or more of a firm's costs be value-added, then this simple rule of thumb suggests that value-added dollars generate at least five dollars of revenue for a firm at breakeven. Conversely, a dollar that is wasted can never be leveraged in the future—it is a dead weight loss to the firm's value-creating ability that multiplies over time as the impact of these lost resources ripple through the firm.

7. *Dollars freed up from non-value-added work need to be reinvested.* A natural tendency when cost savings are gained during a lean initiative is to use them to bolster sagging performance in other parts of the firm, to pay them out as dividends or profit sharing, and so forth. In reality, these funds should be immediately reinvested in increasing the amount of customer value created and delivered by a firm. Each dollar that is reinvested generates a cycle of growth.

8. *Build customer value into the management control system.* CLM makes customer value creation visible to all in the firm. That being said, unless the management control system is modified to include metrics that capture performance on key dimensions affecting customer satisfaction and value creation, CLM will become just another fad given nodding acceptance by employees. Placing the emphasis on customers in budgeting, in product planning, in all forms of management evaluation, drives home the message that management intends to keep the "customer in" in all of its efforts.

Whether the goal is to create a customer-driven organization, or to find ways to align costing systems with a customer-centric culture that already exists, the focus must remain on ensuring that the economics of the market drive the CLM initiative. Leveraging customer preferences requires making choices, choices that can only be assessed against economic trade-offs made by customers in choosing among products. This fact, combined with the care-

ful development of market segmentation strategies that ensure the optimal leveraging of a firm's competencies with those attributes valued by the market, provide the basis for sustained, profitable growth—to keep a firm *on target*.
Make your organization chart customer-oriented.

Joe Griffith[11]

NOTES

1. Joe Griffith, *Speaker's Library of Business Stories, Anecdotes, and Humor* (New York: Prentice-Hall, 1990, reprinted in 2000 by Barnes & Noble Books), p. 80.
2. Brian Maskell and Bruce Baggaley, *Practical Lean Accounting* (New York: Productivity Press, 2004), p. 11.
3. See note 1, p. 79.
4. There is a fairly extensive literature in economics on product/service character-istics and customer utility functions. Based on early work by Lancaster (K. Lan-caster, "Competition and Product Variety," *The Journal of Business, Vol. 53*, No. 3, Part 2 (July, 1980), pp. S79–S103.), this literature emphasizes the trade-offs made by consumers when choosing among products with similar but slightly dif-ferent attributes. Maximizing profitability is tied to effective matching of the op-timal mix and weighting of attributes or characteristics with those demanded by the largest segment of the consuming public. The key to competitiveness is the superior matching of products with preferences.
5. Due to the exploratory nature of this study, salaries within departments were charged to activities based on an average cost. Further analysis could improve the accuracy of this assignment but would create other issues that were deemed out-side the scope of this project.
6. Allen Klein, *The Wise and Witty Quote Book* (New York: Gramercy Books, 2005), p. 136.
7. The data presented here was obtained by Ens. Greg Batchelder and Ens. Kevin Laubenheimer as part of their senior independent study. All rights to this infor-mation are retained by these two individuals for use in future publications.
8. GTI is an acronym for an actual telecom firm that requested it remain anonymous in all publications. The data presented is from actual company information, with translations that maintain key relationships but hide actual financial details of the firm.
9. See note 5, p. 130.
10. See, for example, C. J. McNair, L. Polutnik, and R. Silvi, "Cost Management and Value Creation: The Missing Link," *European Accounting Review*, Vol. 10, No. 1 (2001), pp. 33–50.
11. See note 1, p. 79.

7

VALUE STREAM COSTING: THE LEAN SOLUTION TO STANDARD COSTING COMPLEXITY AND WASTE

BRIAN MASKELL AND NICHOLAS KATKO

7.1 THE PROBLEM WITH STANDARD COSTING

Companies transforming to a lean business strategy quickly confront the issue of their standard costing system. Standard costing was initially developed to value inventory, but its use has expanded over the years into a system that measures operating performance and is used to make many business decisions. One of the best ways to understand the impact of using a standard costing system in a lean environment is to review how a standard costing system works in a traditional manufacturing company.

For a traditional mass production manufacturer, a standard costing system (or another full absorption accounting system) works based on the assumptions of mass production. As discussed in Chapter 2, traditional manufacturers assume that profit is a function of high resource utilization. The busier its machines and people are working the more money will be made. A standard cost system reinforces this assumption in the ways that labor and overhead costs are absorbed for inventory valuation purposes. High resource utilization ensures high overhead absorption, which transfers manufacturing costs from the income statement to the balance sheet, improving profits.

Another assumption of traditional manufacturing is that performance can be measured primarily by focusing on resource efficiency and utilization. The detailed tracking and reporting of material and labor in a standard costing system

155

creates actual-to-standard variances, which supports this assumption. Traditional manufacturing also assumes that direct labor is the most important conversion cost. Most standard costing systems use labor as the driver for allocating all other manufacturing costs to products, even though labor usually is the smallest component of total product cost.

As a result of these assumptions, traditional manufacturers believe that excess capacity is bad for the business and traditional top-down management must be used to control the business. The wealth of data that a standard costing system produces comparing actual to standard production, material, labor, overhead, absorption is used by management to evaluate the performance of manufacturing operations and operators. In a traditional manufacturer, operations receives little to no real-time operational performance information, and therefore people must react and make decisions based on management's analysis of standard costing information.

Most routine business decisions in a traditional manufacturer are made using standard costing under the assumption that the standard costs of its products are correct. For example, sales and marketing departments demand standard product cost information to determine prices, usually to achieve desired margins. Inevitably, one of two scenarios occurs when sales and marketing receives standard product cost information. If the standard cost is perceived to be high, sales and marketing disputes the standard cost. This dispute leads to a review and checking of the standard setting process. If the standard cost is perceived to be low, then sales and marketing assumes that the margin on such products is greater than planned, and all effort are made to sell more of these "high-margin" products.

Decisions to make a product or source it from a supplier, determining the profitability of special orders, customers and products, and capital purchases are made by comparing standard cost to a corporate standard cost target. Because traditional manufacturers focus on cost reduction, if the standard cost of what is being evaluated is less than corporate standard cost target, the decision is made to stop incurring the higher than desired standard cost. This leads to products produced in-house being outsourced because of the perceived savings. Product lines and customers with low margins are dropped owing to "low margins" and capital purchasing decisions are made primarily on their impact on standard cost.

Using standard costing for inventory valuation purposes requires the maintenance of a complex system of generating and monitoring all the necessary standard rates. A standard costing system values inventory from the individual product level. This means that any inventory valuation requires the ability to drill down from a top-level inventory valuation to detail information on how the standard cost of each individual product in inventory was valued. Information such as bills of material, routings, work centers, overhead rates, direct labor rates, and direct/indirect allocations must be maintained, updated, and available to address any inventory valuation issues.

7.2 STANDARD COSTING IS ACTIVELY HARMFUL TO LEAN

Standard costing is actively harmful to companies pursuing a lean business strategy for two reasons. First, the principles in which a lean company operates are fundamentally different than those of a traditional mass production manufacturer. Second, the foundation of standard costing system contains an inherent flaw—comparing standard rates, based on estimates, to actual information to evaluate performance.

Lean companies make money by maximizing flow on the pull from the customer, not by maximizing resource utilization. Lean companies realize that maximizing resource utilization leads to overproduction, inventory, and large batches. Thus, using standard cost utilization and efficiency information as performance measures creates a mixed message—that operational improvements to provide customer value, such as creating flow, are not working.

Lean companies relentlessly eliminate waste to create available capacity to meet increasing customer demand—and generate more profits. Again, standard cost information will send the wrong message—that resources are being underutilized even though customer-focused operational performance such as improved on-time shipments, are improving. Operational performance in a lean company is measured by improvements in cycle time, productivity, quality, flow, and cost. Standard cost information does not provide any relevant performance measures in any of these areas. Indeed, standard costing systems provide information that motivates people to take actions that sabotage lean operational improvement.

The foundation of a standard cost system is based on a static set of estimates. Rate setting for work center production and absorption based on product mix sales forecasts are based on estimates. A great deal of effort is made by companies to compare estimates to actual, but the fact remains that the future cannot be predicted. Many companies continue to make the assumption that actual information should be compared to standards because standards are reality. A lean company must rely on real-time accurate information, both operational and financial, to manage the business. Standard costing uses estimates, which precludes it from being helpful in conjunction with lean.

Additionally, the process of setting standards assumes a fixed assignment of resources. During the standard-setting process, assumptions are made regarding how certain products will be made according to a predetermined production routing and how production resources will be permanently assigned to specific work centers. In a lean environment, where continuous improvement is a way of life, changes in operation processes and the resources used to produce product is the norm. Attempting to update standards in a continuous improvement environment is virtually impossible.

The solution is for lean companies to replace their standard costing system with a value stream–based system of costing and to use value stream costing to make business decisions and value inventory. Additionally, a lean performance measurement system should replace traditional utilization and efficiency measures. The standard costing approach is not inherently wrong, but it is wrong for lean. Standard costing (and other methods like activity-based costing or full absorption actual costing) was designed to support the mass production of the mid-twentieth century. It is unsuitable for organizations making the transformation to a lean enterprise.

7.3 VALUE STREAM COSTING

One of the essential principles of lean thinking is the value stream. Lean companies identify their value streams so they can organize and manage the enterprise around them to enhance the value they provide to their customers. As value streams become the primary organizational requirement for a lean enterprise, it only follows that a company's income statement be organized in the same manner. Value stream costing is the process of assigning the actual expenses of an enterprise to value streams, rather than to products, services, or departments. This chapter focuses on an analysis of value stream costing in manufacturing, but the principles apply to service enterprises as well.

The value stream costing process begins with a value stream map. The value stream mapping process generates the necessary information on material flow and resource allocation that can then be applied value stream costing. The material flow defines which products flow through any particular value stream. The mapping process determines how people, equipment, and space are used by each value stream. From this information, actual value stream costs can be calculated. All costs within the value stream are considered direct costs to the value stream. No effort is made to allocate costs excluded from the value stream into the value stream. Exhibit 7.1 illustrates typical value stream costs.

Value stream *labor costs* come from a company's payroll, based on the actual people who work in the value stream as defined in the value stream map. There is no distinction between "direct" and "indirect" labor in value stream costing, nor is there a distinction between the work activities of specific employees. Whenever possible, people are assigned directly within a single value stream irrespective of whether they are traditionally "direct" employees or people who support the processes. The distinction focuses on whether or not an employee is assigned to work in the value stream and includes employees who make product, move material, maintain the facility, make sales, or perform purchasing.

Value stream *material costs* are calculated based on the actual material used by the value stream. The actual material used by the value stream can be based on actual material purchased or actual material issued to the value stream from raw material inventory. The decision to use actual purchases or actual issues is a function of a company's raw material inventory. If raw material inventories are low (30 days or less, for example) and under control, then actual material purchased can be charged to the value stream. This amount can be calculated

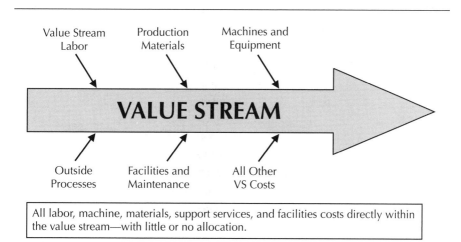

EXHIBIT 7.1   Costs Included in Value Stream Costing

from cash disbursements made through accounts payable. If raw material inventory is high, then value stream material cost is calculated based on raw material issued to the value stream. This figure can be calculated from bills of material of product issued to production or from calculating the month-end inventory plus purchases less the previous month-end inventory. Exhibit 7.2 shows a typical value stream map. This is not a "perfect" value stream, but it shows how Caspian Corporation has been organized into value stream teams.

Outside processing costs can be calculated from cash disbursements in accounts payable. In some cases, the outside processing vendor bills paid in a period may be for work performed in the prior period. If outside processing costs are significant and vary period to period, this could have an impact on value stream costs. If this situation exists, a possible solution is to accrue a monthly outside processing charge to the value stream, rather than the actual cash disbursement.

Machine costs for value stream costing is the depreciation expense of the machines, in addition to costs such as spare parts, repairs, and supplies. Depreciation expense can be calculated from a company's detailed fixed asset and depreciation system. One question that often arises during a lean transformation is what to do about fully depreciated assets. Generally, no depreciation

Caspian Corporation - OEM Products Value Stream

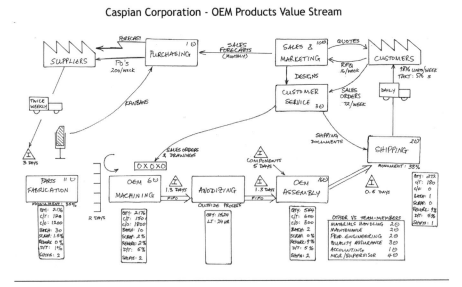

EXHIBIT 7.2   Example of a Value Stream

is charged to a value stream for fully depreciated assets. However, some companies determine that they would like to impose a "replacement value" charge on value streams for fully depreciated machines. This is acceptable, provided that replacement value is simple calculation.

Other costs of running machines, such as spare parts, repairs, and supplies can be charged to the value stream as part of machine costs if these costs are readily identifiable by value stream in the general ledger. In some cases, these machine costs cannot be easily identified by specific machine or by value stream in the general ledger. An example of such an expense would be fuel or spare parts that are used on many machines. In such cases, these costs can be considered a monument and assigned to the value stream using a simple allocation process.

Monuments are machines or departments shared by more than one value stream. The lean goal is to minimize monuments, but when monuments exist it is necessary to allocate their costs across the affected value streams. The best allocation method is a simple one based on the activities of the monument. It is important to avoid tracking usage of the monument to create the allocation basis. Use a simple analysis at the beginning of the year to establish the allocation rates and adjust the rates annually. Exhibit 7.3 shows the value stream income statement for the Caspian Corporations OEM Motors value stream.

Value stream *facility costs* consist of the actual costs such as rent or lease (interest expense if owned), repairs and maintenance, and utilities. Facility costs are allocated to value streams on the basis of square footage of the value stream. The total facilities costs are divided by the total square footage of the building to get the cost per square foot. The square footage of the value stream

EXHIBIT 7.3   Value Stream Income Statement

Revenues	$326,240	
Material costs	$111,431	34.2%
Employee costs	$49,515	3.4%
Machine costs	$8,113	2.5%
Outside processes	$32,433	9.9%
Facilities costs	$12,750	4.1%
Tooling costs	$4,843	1.5%
Other costs	$3,290	1.0%
TOTAL COSTS	$222,375	68.2%
Value stream profit	$104,865	
Return on sales	31.8%	

is multiplied by the cost per square foot. This is the only allocation used regularly within value stream costing, specifically for the purpose of motivating the value stream to reduce the amount of floor space used by the value stream. In fact, some companies charge the unused space to sales and marketing!

Questions often arise about *utility costs*, which can be for both general facilities and/or specific machines. Typically utility costs can be assigned to specific machines and general facilities if the machines are metered and utility bills are broken down by meters. In other cases, certain machines are obviously the primary consumers of utilities and facility utilities are a small portion of the entire bill, in which case the entire utility bill could be charged to the specific value stream. What is important to remember when dealing with such issues is to keep any methodology both simple and apply it in a consistent manner.

Support costs for a value stream typically consist of traditional "indirect" costs such as maintenance, quality, engineering, supervisors, materials management, scheduling, and purchasing. When companies first adopt value stream design and costing, they often encounter the problem of sharing these functions across value streams, which makes them monuments. Three methods can be used to charge support costs to value streams—direct charge, monument allocation, or no charge to the value stream.

The preferred approach is to assign the actual support costs to a value stream based on a future state value stream map. If the future state of the value stream includes employees in the value stream who will be performing support functions, then these support costs should be assigned, even if the actual assignment of the employees has not yet occurred. If assigning support employees to value streams is not being considered due to complexity or other reasons, then these support functions should be considered monuments. As described earlier, a simple allocation rate should be established to allocate the costs and support function usage should not be tracked.

Allocating these costs is acceptable when first starting to use value stream costing, but it is important to directly assign people to the value streams. The primary reason for directly assigning people to the value stream is that lean organizations work as teams. It is important to include *all* the relevant people within the team: people making product, people moving materials, people providing engineering support, purchasing, customer service, lean improvement, accounting, changeover, and maintenance. It is difficult to develop the kind of teamwork required when these support people are organized by traditional departments and work across multiple value streams.

The second reason to avoid allocating support costs to the value streams is that it makes the cost assignments complicated and opaque to operational people. The financial information is not clear-cut, and people do not understand it. This inevitably leads to meetings where the value stream managers argue about their level of cost allocation. None of this creates more value for the customer, and none of this moves lean improvement forward.

7.4 THE ADVANTAGES OF VALUE STREAM COSTING

Value stream costing has several advantages over traditional cost accounting. Traditional cost accounting gathers and collects costs at the product and work-order level and rolls up these costs to income statements. This requires a complex system to be maintained and managed because of the number of products and services companies offer. The high-mix, low-volume trend in manufacturing (e.g., mass customization) proliferates the number of products that need to be maintained in a traditional costing system. In some instances, companies must create standards for products that may be produced and shipped only once. Value stream costing collects costs at a higher level in the organization, eliminating the need for maintaining a complex product costing system.

Eliminating the need to maintain a traditional cost accounting system opens up the opportunity to eliminate many of the transactions associated with traditional cost accounting. In value stream costing, labor costs are derived from payroll records. This eliminates the need to report labor transactions to work orders and "earn" labor to specific jobs.

Similarly, most material tracking transactions can be eliminated under value stream costing. Material does not have to be assigned to specific work orders because it is charged directly to the value stream based on cash disbursements or total material issued. Material-related job tracking transactions such as back-flushing can be eliminated.

Eliminating the need to track labor and material to specific jobs brings into question the reason why work orders are even necessary, especially if a lean company has implemented a pull system. When a pull system is in place and effective, visual management methods like kanbans, supermarkets, first in–first out (FIFO) lanes, and visual work instructions completely eliminate the need for production tracking documents.

Because the reason for having work orders has been eliminated with lean value stream costing, work orders and the maintenance of work orders can also be eliminated. It is no longer necessary to maintain routings, work centers, and labor and overhead rates. Elimination of these transactions and the maintenance of the system frees up the time of the shop floor employees, who enter transactions, and the finance people, who analyze, review, and manage transactions. This freed-up shop floor capacity can now be redeployed to produce more product, and the freed-up finance capacity can be used to drive further lean improvements.

Another aspect of the simplicity of value stream costing is the reduction in cost centers in the general ledger. It is no longer necessary to track costs by a multitude of department cost centers broken into detailed cost elements. Costs are collected at the value stream level and can be summarized into a few cost elements such a labor, materials, facilities, and support. Cost reduction is accomplished through the elimination of waste through continuous improvement. Continuous improvement is accomplished by focusing on operational performance measurements, which in turn focus on the wasteful activities that are creating the costs. This process gets to the root causes of costs and, over time, eliminates these causes and the need for detailed cost information.

The elimination of overhead cost allocations in value stream costing is another reason it is simpler than traditional standard costing. Most people work in the value streams of a company. However, there are employees whose work is unrelated to value streams (such as financial accounting) or their work crosses all value streams (such as ISO 9000 support). In value stream costing, instead of allocation of these costs, they are treated as business-sustaining costs. These costs are budgeted and controlled, and cost reduction is accomplished through the application of continuous improvement practices, office Kaizens, for example. There is no need to maintain any system to allocate these costs, and there is no need for the complexity and fruitless meetings associated with these kinds of allocation.

The reason these business-sustaining costs are not allocated to value streams is that the value stream has no control over managing these costs. Lean companies want their value streams to focus on reducing direct costs through continuous improvement. If sustaining costs are allocated to value streams, the only method to reduce these costs is to reduce the allocation percent, which means questioning an imperfect allocation system rather than focusing on value-added activities that enhance customer value.

People in a lean transformation often argue for allocation of sustaining costs, reasoning that there is a value stream cost for the support these activities provide to the value stream. In value stream costing, this is accomplished through targeting a higher return on sales that the value streams must achieve to "pay for" sustaining costs and generate the required company profitability.

7.5 CLOSING THE BOOKS

Value stream managers use value stream income statements to control costs and improve their value streams. These statements are usually created weekly so that the value stream manager has up-to-date, fresh information leading to better decisions. When it comes to closing the books at the month-end, value stream income statements are prepared for each value stream each month. These income statements are summed—together with the business-sustaining or support costs—to create month-end reporting for the whole location or division of the company.

Exhibit 7.4 shows a month-end consolidation for Caspian Corporation. The company has three revenue-earning value streams: OEM Motors, Systems, and Spare Parts. There is a fourth value stream called New Product Design. This is a different kind of value stream that has no revenue, but creates value by developing new products that meet the customer value needs. The fifth column shows the business support costs that are outside of the value stream and are not allocated.

The total income statement for the company is calculated by summing the costs for all four value streams and the nonvalue stream support people. To bring the month-end financial reports into line with reporting regulations, it is necessary to make some adjustments, and these are made "below the line" so that the adjustments are not confused with the operational management of the business. The example in Exhibit 7.4 shows two of the most common adjustments required; inventory change and allocation of external overheads.

It is a common mistake to think that generally accepted accounting principles (GAAP) requires full standard costing. In fact the opposite is true. GAAP requires financial reporting to be done using *actual* costs. Value stream costing uses actual costs for all reporting. There is no need for month-end (or quarter-end) adjustments to standards or variance application calculations. In many organizations this greatly simplifies the month-end close process.

EXHIBIT 7.4 **Plant-wide Income Statement**

		VALUE STREAMS				
	Motors	Systems	Spare Parts	New Product Design	Support Costs	TOTAL DIVISION
Sales	$326,250	$748,894	$453,215			$1,528,349
Additional revenue	$0	$0	$12,422		$12,422	
Material costs	$111,431	$232,774	$149,561	$87,909	$12,764	$596,439
Conversion costs	$57,628	$70,406	$81,579	$203,769	$37,645	$451,027
Outside process costs	$32,433	$22,991	$22,661		$7,531	$85,616
Other costs	$16,040	$57,816	$29,459	$72,721		$176,036
Tooling costs	$4,843	$12,544	$6,588			$23,975
Value stream profit	$103,865	$352,363	$175,789	($364,399)	($57,940)	$209,678
ROS	31.8%	47.1%	38.8%	−23.7%	−3.8%	13.7%

Opening inventory	$925,314
Closing inventory	$918,807
Inventory change	($6,507)
Corporate overhead	$51,147
Division profit	$152,024
Division ROS	9.9%

7.6 USING COST INFORMATION TO MANAGE THE VALUE STREAM

Value stream costs are reported by value streams each week, along with operating performance measures and capacity information in a box score format. Exhibit 7.5 shows the box score for the OEM Motors value stream at Caspian Corporation. This illustrates the three dimensions of value stream performance using a box score. The purpose of the box score is to present the relevant value stream performance data simply and on a single sheet of paper.

The three dimensions of box score performance are interdependent, and value stream managers must consider each dimension when managing a value stream. Value streams have the responsibility of improving operations through continuous improvement, which is managed through the value stream performance measures in the upper section of Exhibit 7.5.

The middle section of Exhibit 7.5 shows capacity information. Productive capacity is the percentage of total capacity used for value-adding activities, which are defined by total cycle time × units shipped. Nonproductive capacity is the percentage of total capacity time spent on wasteful activities, such as producing scrap, overproduction, waiting time, and setup time. Available capacity is the difference between total capacity less productive and nonproductive

EXHIBIT 7.5   Value Stream Weekly Box Score

Caspian Company
PA
Motors

Current		5-Feb	12-Feb	19-Feb	26-Feb	5-Mar	12-Mar	19-Mar	26-Mar	GOAL 31-Mar
OPERATIONAL	Units per person	31.77	30.46	32.51	32.19	33.71				35.2
	On-time shipment	96.2%	98.2%	98.5%	97.6%	97.2%				98.0%
	First time thru	42%	44%	43%	47%	54%				62%
	Dock-to-dock days	12.50	11.9	10.94	9.33	8.90				8.0
	Average cost	$115.78	$115.78	$114.62	$112.66	$111.74				$107.01
	AP days-AR days	8.0	8.0	8.0	8.0	8.0				8.0
CAPACITY	Productive	22%	22%	22%	21%	21%				22%
	Nonproductive	58%	58%	58%	41%	41%				37%
	Available capacity	20%	20%	20%	38%	38%				41%
FINANCIAL	Revenue	$366,487	$321,499	$331,546	$325,481	$326,240				$325,000
	Material costs	$112,196	$109,812	$113,243	$111,172	$111,431				$111,007
	Conversion costs	$92,564	$95,743	$95,233	$99,463	$98,194				$94,039
	Inventory	$310,622	$295,712	$271,857	$231,848	$221,163				$198,798
	Value stream profit	$161,727	$115,944	$123,070	$114,846	$116,615				$119,953
	Value stream ROS	44.13%	36.06%	37.12%	35.29$	35.75%				36.91%

46.00%   Hurdle rate

capacity. In a box score, improvement in operational measures means waste is being eliminated and nonproductive capacity is being turned into available capacity.

The value stream profit and loss (P&L), in the lower section of the box score, is the "report card" of how well the value stream is meeting customer demand (revenue), how well it has eliminated waste (cost reduction), and how well the company has utilized the created available capacity by growing revenue.

Box score information is reported weekly and compared to the goals that the value stream team has set for performance improvement, capacity creation, and financial outcomes. These goals are established for the value stream teams by linking continuous improvement plans to strategic plans for revenue growth. The continuous improvement plans establish the operational capacity improvement and cost reduction. These objectives are then communicated to senior management, where the strategic sales and marketing decisions can be made to drive revenue growth.

For many companies, the primary financial benefit of lean transformations is not cost cutting but creating the capacity to allow the company to grow the top line without comparable increases in costs. Lean transformations eliminate waste and create newly available capacity. As this capacity is utilized for increased sales, opening new markets, and creating more customer value, the company's cash flow and sustainable growth are driven to previously impossible heights.

Over the longer term, lean manufacturing is *the* low cost way to manufacture products and provide services, but these financial benefits do not usually accrue in the short term. It often takes several years for the lean initiative to introduce the new enterprise products, open up the new markets, and develop new and highly value-adding services. Lean transformation requires tenacity and patience of the enterprise executive team. Executives who stress short-term cost reduction and emphasize quarterly earnings and stock price inevitably undermine the company's ability to make the transformation to a lean enterprise.

7.7 BUSINESS DECISION MAKING USING VALUE STREAM COSTING

Traditional manufacturers use standard product cost to make many important business decision such as pricing, make/buy, customer and product margin analysis, product and customer rationalization, capital purchases, and performance measurement. In a lean company, value stream costing is used to make these decisions. In evaluating the financial impact of a business decision, a lean business looks at the impact of the decision on value stream profitability and sustainability rather than the "margin" on the individual product.

Lean companies recognize that standard costs and margins are very misleading when making routine business decisions. Margin analysis using standard costs is wrong because it assumes that all the costs included are variable when—with the exception of materials—most of the costs included in the standard are fixed. Some traditional companies attempt to solve this by using some kind of *contribution margin* and excluding the fixed costs. This often assumes that all the costs (except materials) are fixed, when in fact a particular order or make/buy decision may well impact costs other than the traditional "variable costs." When making these kinds of decisions in lean organizations, ask, "Which costs in the value stream will change?" This gives more accurate and valid information for making the decision.

Exhibit 7.6 shows a decision process about accepting a special order from a new customer. This new customer has come to Caspian requesting 100 units per month for three months and is willing to pay a price of $140 per unit. Caspian has determined that it will cost $65 per unit for material costs. Caspian determined that it has available capacity to produce these units without adding people or machines. Should Caspian accept this order?

Yes, if Caspian has the available capacity and can achieve the customer's quality and delivery requirements, it should accept the order. This special order will generate $7,500 of additional value stream profit per month. Lean

EXHIBIT 7.6   Customer Order Decision with Available Capacity

	Current State	Change	Future State
Sales quantity	1,876	100	1,976
Average price	$173.90	$140.00	$172.18
Revenue	$326,236	$14,000	$340,236
Materials	$111,434	$6,500	$117,934
Conversion costs	$110,947		$110,947
Total costs	$222,381		$222,381
Value stream profit	$103,855		$111,355
Value stream return	32%		33%

EXHIBIT 7.7   Customer Order Decision with No Available Capacity

	Current State	Change	Future State
Sales quantity	1,876	100	1,976
Average price	$173.90	$140.00	$172.18
Revenue	$326,236	$14,000	$340,236
Materials	$111,434	$6,500	$117,934
Conversion costs	$110,947	$6,000	$116,947
Total costs	$222,381		$234,881
Value stream profit	$103,855		$105,355
Value stream return	32%	0%	31%

companies earn a profit by maximizing the flow of customer orders through their value streams. There are, of course, many other business issues involved in this decision; but from a financial perspective, this order is good business.

Exhibits 7.7 and 7.8 show the same business decision, except that Caspian does not have any available capacity to produce these 100 units per month for three months. Caspian's management has three alternatives: build the order in house, outsource production, or decline the order. If Caspian builds the order in house (Exhibit 7.7), it must purchase a machine costing $1,000 per month and hire three people at a total cost of $5,000 per month. Producing in house, Caspian will earn $1,500 of profit per month for three months. However, the newly hired people and purchased machine will become available capacity after three months, unless Caspian can find other customers for this product.

In Exhibit 7.8, Caspian has identified a supplier that can produce this product and will charge Caspian $100 per unit. The supplier will meet all quality and delivery requirements for Caspian. The value stream P&L indicates that purchasing this product from this supplier will generate $4,000 per month. Because this customer has committed to only three months of orders, it may makes operational sense for Caspian to use a supplier to produce this order because it doesn't have to invest in expanding capacity as shown in previous example. Additionally, outsourcing production in this case is also the more profitable decision.

Currently, Caspian spends $32,433 per month on outside processing costs. In Exhibit 7.9, Caspian has created available capacity in its workforce through continuous improvement and is considering bringing these outside processing

EXHIBIT 7.8   Customer Order Decision with Outsourcing

	Current State	Change	Future State
Sales quantity	1,876	100	1,976
Average price	$173.90	$140	$172
Revenue	$326,236	$14,000	$340,236
Materials	$111,434	$10,000	$121,434
Conversion costs	$110,947		$110,947
Total costs	$222,381		$232,381
Value stream profit	$103,855		$107,855
Value stream return	32%	0%	32%

activities in-house. To do this, Caspian must purchase a machine, at a cost of $10,000 per month, and hire a supervisor, at a monthly cost of $4,000 to manage this new operation. To evaluate the financial impact of this decision, Caspian would look at the change in costs to bring the outside processing activities in-house. The value stream P&L illustrates there is a net decrease in costs of $18,433, so it makes sense financially to bring these outside processing activities in house.

EXHIBIT 7.9   In-Source Items Currently Outsourced

	Current State	Change	Future State
Sales quantity	1,876	0	1,876
Average price	$173.90		$173.90
Revenue	$326,236	$0	$326,236
Materials	$111,434	$0	$111,434
Outside process	$32,433	($32,433)	$0
Other conversion costs	$78,514		$78,514
Additional labor	$0	$4,000	$4,000
Additional machine	$0	$10,000	$10,000
Total costs	$222,381		$203,948
Value stream profit	$103,855		$122,288
Value stream return	32%	0%	37%

Exhibits 7.10 and 7.11 illustrate a capital investment decision, which improves operations and allows Caspian to sell 25 more units per month but creates available capacity in Caspian's workforce. To evaluate this decision, Caspian must look at the total impact on value stream profitability. The purchase of this machine would increase the value stream contribution (sales less material costs) by $2,863; however, it would also add $5,000 of machine costs per month. At this point, the freed-up operators cannot be moved out of the value stream; their costs remain in this value stream. So the additional cost of the machine and additional sales volume is not enough to offset the cost of the freed-up operators. Purchasing this machine is not profitable to the value stream, unless it can find a way to transfer the freed-up people out of the value stream.

Exhibit 7.11 shows the financial impact of the purchase of the new machine, where Caspian is able to transfer the available operators out of the motor value stream into another value stream. Because the OEM Motors value stream is able to transfer these operators to another value stream, the purchase of the machine is a financially profitable decision. In addition, Caspian is able to meet the needs of another value stream for additional operator capacity by transferring existing employees, rather than hire new employees.

EXHIBIT 7.10   Purchase Machine and Increase Production

	Current State	Change	Future State
Sales quantity	1,876	25	1,901
Average price	$173.90	$173.90	$173.90
Revenue	$326,236	$4,348	$330,584
Materials	$111,434	$1,485	$112,919
Outside process	$32,433	$0	$32,433
Other conversion costs	$78,514	$0	$78,514
Additional labor	$0		$0
Additional machine	$0	$5,000	$5,000
Total costs	$222,381	$6,485	$228,866
Value stream profit	$103,855		$101,718
Value stream return	31.8%		30.8%

EXHIBIT 7.11   Value Stream Implications

	Current State	Change	Future State
Sales quantity	1,876	25	1,901
Average price	$173.90	$173.90	$173.90
Revenue	$326,236	$4,348	$330,584
Materials	$111,434	$1,485	$112,919
Outside process	$32,433	$0	$32,433
Other conversion costs	$78,514	$0	$78,514
Additional labor	$0	($4,000)	($4,000)
Additional machine	$0	$5,000	$5,000
Total costs	$222,381	$2,485	$224,866
Value stream profit	$103,855		$105,718
Value stream return	31.8%		32.0%

Lean business decisions are addressed with reference to the profitability of the value stream as a whole, not the individual product. Using a standard cost to make business decisions in a lean company is very dangerous. The standard cost almost always leads to the wrong decision. The financial analysis of business decisions in areas such as accepting customer orders, make/buy, capital investment, new products, and rationalization of customers and products should always be made by analyzing the impact of the decision on the profitability of the value stream as a whole.

7.8 VALUING INVENTORY

One of the primary reasons for maintaining a standard costing system is for inventory valuation purposes. Traditional mass production companies are characterized by high work in process and finished goods inventory and low inventory turns. Inventory is often the largest current asset on a traditional manufacturer's balance sheet. This means that the valuation of inventory is very material to accurately stating a traditional manufacturer's income. Traditional manufacturers also use their inventory asset as collateral for bank lines of credit, because so much of a traditional manufacturer's cash is tied up in inventory.

A standard costing system is often the easiest method for inventory valuation purposes because companies are required to value inventory at actual cost to comply with GAAP. GAAP also requires that the cost of inventory match the actual costs of the period the inventory was produced. Thus, a company with inventory turns of 2.00 has six months of inventory on hand, which means it must use the actual production costs for the last six months to value inventory. Maintaining an actual cost system in this environment is impractical.

Traditional manufacturers develop standard cost systems that create standard unit costs for each product where the inventory value on the balance sheet is the roll up of the actual quantity on hand for each product multiplied by its standard unit cost. This requires the periodic testing of actual costs to standard to determine if standards need to be adjusted approximate actual. If a manufacturer using traditional standard costing is audited, the auditors test the standard costing system to determine if it represents actual. The result of such audit testing often results in financial statement adjustments to bring inventory value to actual. This very complex system is maintained to get to the actual cost of inventory.

Lean companies have a different view of inventory. Managers in lean companies with pull systems know how much inventory must be in place to create single-piece flow for all work cells in a value stream. All excess inventory is considered waste and must be eliminated. The goals of lean companies are low to nonexistent work in process and finished goods inventory with high inventory turns. The inventory value on a lean company balance sheet shrinks and becomes a smaller percentage of total current assets. Because lean companies with low inventory generate lots of cash, bank lines of credit become less important and inventory is not needed as collateral.

As a result, lean creates opportunities to use a true actual costing system to value inventory and replace the complex, wasteful standard costing system. Companies that are successfully implementing lean often see their inventory turns increase to 20 or higher. As a result, any inventory on hand at the end of a period was produced in that period and it becomes very simple to match the quantity to its actual costs of production.

Exhibits 7.12 and 7.13 illustrate examples of actual cost calculations for inventory valuation. The inventory days method uses a daily material cost and conversion cost rates to value inventory. The daily rate information comes directly from the value stream costing information and is simply multiplied by the days on hand of each inventory component to calculate the value to inventory.

EXHIBIT 7.12   Valuing Inventory Using the Number of Days Method

Days in the Month	Total Material Cost	Material Cost per Day	Total Conversion Cost	Conversion Cost per Day
20	$849,526	$42,476	$876,550	$43,828

	Days	Material Value	Conversion Value	Total Value
Raw material	10	$424,763	$0	$424,763
Work in process	3	$127,429	$65,741	$193,170
Finished goods	4	$169,905	$175,310	$345,215
TOTAL INV VALUE	17	$722,097	$241,051	$963,148

The average cost per unit method (Exhibit 7.13) resembles traditional inventory valuation by multiplying the quantity on hand of each inventory component by the actual material and conversion costs per unit. The difference is that the quantity on hand is the totals number of units across the company's entire product range. The calculation is not done for each individual item but for the inventory as a whole. The underlying assumption of this method—that the inventory represents the mix of products sold and made—is true for companies using a lean pull system and supermarket approach.

EXHIBIT 7.13   Valuing Inventory Using the Unit Quantity Method

Total Units	Total Material Cost	Average Material Cost per Unit	Total Conversion Cost	Average Conversion Cost per Unit
19,433	$849,526	$37,16	$876,550	$38.34

	Quantity	Material Value	Conversion Value	Total Value
Raw material	11,430	$424,709	$0	$424,709
Work in process	3,430	$127,450	$65,752	$193,202
Finished goods	4,573	$169,921	$175,326	$345,247
TOTAL INV VALUE	19,433	$722,079	$241,078	$963,158

Both examples illustrate how inventory valuation can be greatly simplified in a lean company and remain compliant with GAAP. In both examples, it is not necessary to know the cost of any specific product, nor is it necessary to maintain a standard cost system. The simplification of the inventory valuation process eliminates much non-value-added work in finance, creating available capacity to work on strategic lean improvement projects.

7.9 CHAPTER SUMMARY

Standard costing was developed to support mid-twentieth-century mass-production companies. Standard costing (and other full-absorption costing systems) is not a suitable method for lean manufacturers because it drives behaviors that are harmful to lean thinking. In addition, the maintenance and use of a standard costing system requires complex and wasteful processes that are out of place in a lean organization.

Value stream costing provides simple and valid information for cost control, internal decision making, and external financial reporting. Value stream costing requires very little work and provides reports that are immediately understandable to everyone and can be used throughout the company.

Using value stream costing for routine decision making leads to better decisions because the information is up to date, accurate, and understandable. Using standard costing for decision making often leads to wrong decisions from a financial point of view and damages the company's growth and profitability.

Lean organizations can take advantage of value stream costing because lean methods bring processes under control, enable visual management, and significantly reduce inventory.

8

OBSTACLES TO LEAN ACCOUNTANCY

LARRY GRASSO

When H. Thomas Johnson and Robert Kaplan published Relevance Lost
*in 1987, they gave voice to a feeling of dissatisfaction with management
accounting held by many managers. Johnson and Kaplan said that
management accounting practice had stagnated since the 1920s.
Management accounting was irrelevant, even a detriment to managers
facing increased competition and rapid change in the global economy
of the late twentieth century.* Relevance Lost *affirmed the feelings of
many managers who had been grumbling about management
accounting information for years, and it served as a wake-up call for
management accountants.*

Management accounting has changed since 1987 through two major developments, activity-based cost management (ABCM) and the balanced scorecard
(BSC), as well as other techniques such as life-cycle costing, target costing,
Kaizen costing, throughput accounting, back-flush costing, and cost of quality reporting. More recently, resource consumption accounting (RCA), a vari-
ant of the German marginal costing system *grenzplankostenrechnung* (GPK)
incorporating activity-based concepts, has been receiving a great deal of attention in the United States. Despite these developments, management accounting
is still considered a barrier to implementing lean production and lean management. Twenty-two percent of managers in a recent Lean Enterprise Institute
survey said their cost accounting system was an obstacle to their progress in

implementing lean (as reported in an email message from Jim Womack). The movement toward adopting lean management in the United States occurred at about the same time new developments began to emerge in management accounting. Why is management accounting still a barrier to implementing lean management?

Exhibit 8.1 illustrates the importance of the link between management accounting and lean. The exhibit emphasizes that strategy, actions, and measures influence each other, creating a self-reinforcing cycle. Suppose a company adopts a strategy best executed by adopting a lean management system. Appropriate measures inform and lead to successful actions, and successful actions lead to desirable results. Favorable results measures and successful actions reinforce an evolving strategy based on lean management. As a management accounting domain, performance measurement is a positive force enabling lean.

Unfortunately, the reinforcing cycle works both positively and negatively. Lack of information inhibits continuous improvement, and poorly measured results encourage behaviors that subvert lean management. If management accounting cannot enable lean, it should at least get out of the way, but the self-reinforcing cycle makes neutrality difficult. Management accounting works either for or against lean management. Today, management accountants too often find themselves on the wrong side of the lean transformation.

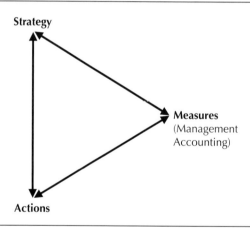

EXHIBIT 8.1   Strategy, Actions, and Measures

Source: Adapted from J. Robb Dixon, Alfred J. Nanni, and Thomas E. Vollmann, The New Performance Challenge (Homewood, Ill.: Dow Jones-Irwin, 1990), p. 6.

For most companies, a lean transformation represents an enormous change, and many companies have found or are finding the transformation difficult to achieve or sustain. Exhibit 8.2 shows the use of management tools related to lean as reported in the Management Tools and Trends surveys conducted by Bain & Company. Trends are difficult to assess from the aggregated data because recent samples of companies are more worldwide compared to earlier samples when responses were more concentrated in Europe and North America. Nonetheless, a large number of companies worldwide use tools and practices associated with lean management. Mark Deluzio is a consultant with extensive experience in lean management, and he estimates that no more than 5 percent of U.S. companies truly use lean management as a comprehensive management system (in a conversation at the 2005 Lean Accounting Summit). While not all companies using tools related to lean management are really interested in comprehensively adopting lean, the vast gap between the isolated use of lean tools reported by Bain & Company and Mark Deluzio's estimate of successful lean management systems suggests that a lot of companies are having difficulty implementing lean.

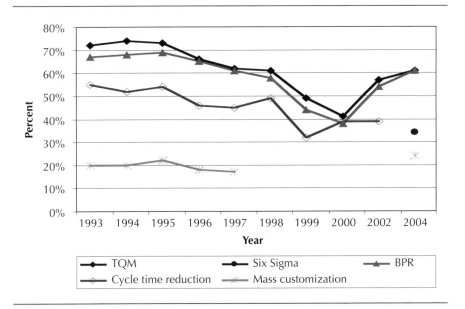

EXHIBIT 8.2 Lean Management Tool Usage Rates

Source: Bain & Company, Management Tools and Trends Survey.

Given the magnitude of the change required, it comes as no surprise that management accountants encounter many difficulties as they attempt to support lean transformations. The same cultural issues that make lean transformation difficult across the organization create problems for accountants. (See Chapter 3 for a discussion of ways that executives can enable the transformation of traditional cultures.) In addition, some of the same professional and educational factors that led to the decline of management accounting present further obstacles for accountants attempting a lean transformation. If these obstacles can be overcome, the self-reinforcing cycle can be turned in a positive direction, and management accountants can increase the likelihood the organization will sustain its lean transformation. This chapter examines the obstacles to lean accounting, and offers suggestions for overcoming these obstacles. The evolution and adoption of the recent management accounting developments are also examined for insights that may apply to developing accounting to support lean management.

8.1 UNDERSTANDING LEAN AS A MANAGEMENT SYSTEM

Anyone who has ever been involved in a significant accounting system change knows that successfully implementing such a change is a challenge. A lean transformation, however, transcends the accounting system. Orry Fiume, former vice president of The Wiremold Company, maintains that a major cause of the low rate of successful lean transformations is managers' failure to see lean as a total management system. When managers hear "Toyota Production System," they typically believe that lean applies only to production or manufacturing. They believe that lean is an isolated set of techniques that they can pass along to their factory managers to implement with little impact on the rest of the organization. Or they see lean as a tool box from which managers can pick only the tools they like best, or the tools they feel most comfortable with, or the tools they believe will be easiest to implement. Reflecting the patterns of the Bain & Company research, these managers leave the rest of the tools in the toolbox, adopt only the tools they have chosen within their existing management system, and believe they have implemented lean.

Many management accountants have difficulty with lean transformations, struggling to implement piecemeal tools from a system meant to be applied as a unified whole. Unfortunately, most organizations use a piecemeal approach to enterprise change initiatives, so this common misconception about lean is understandable. This also makes it easy for accountants to dismiss lean as a "manufacturing thing" that really does not affect accounting. Accountants who actually understand lean as a management system recognize that they are confronted with a management system change that mandates an accounting system change. While the change seems more daunting for management accounting, it is also more critical because the existing accounting measurement system can be a significant barrier to change for all areas of the company struggling with the lean transformation.

8.2 CULTURAL COMPATIBILITY WITH LEAN MANAGEMENT

An environment where people have to think brings with it wisdom, and this wisdom brings with it kaizen [continuous improvement]. The 'T' [in Toyota Production System] actually stands for thinking as well as for Toyota.

Teruyuki Minoura[1]

Lean management derives its power by capturing the creative abilities of all people. Ideas for improving processes, products, and services come from everyone in the organization, even those outside the organization such as customers and suppliers. All participants in the value stream share in the waste elimination and value creation gains for the end-use customer. People usually will not contribute their creative powers to improvement efforts unless they are asked, they believe their suggestions will be taken seriously, and they believe they will share in the benefits derived from their suggestions. A cooperative organizational culture must be in place, or lean management will not work.

Most companies begin their lean transformations without having a cooperative culture in place. "Business as usual" in the United States is the command-and-control culture outlined in Exhibits 8.3A and 8.3B. The command-and-control culture evolved from scientific management and the economic assumptions of self-interested individuals governed by market forces and enforced contracts. Military analogies are often used to describe management's role in formulating and executing strategies. The relationship between management and labor is presumed to be adversarial. Extrinsic rewards are required to get labor to follow management's orders, and monitoring is needed to ensure compliance. In contrast, the cooperative, continuous improvement culture required for lean management emphasizes teamwork, creating win-win solutions benefiting all stakeholders. The distinction between management and labor is blurred. Everyone is working to better serve the customer and create more value to be shared by all stakeholders.[2]

The cultural differences outlined in Part A of Exhibit 8.3 have enormous implications for management accountants. Managers are the owners and users of knowledge in the command-and-control environment. Workers are supposed to act, not think. Periodic reports provided to management by accountants are reports *on workers* to enforce compliance. Management accountants guard the information and prepare the reports used by management to enforce compliance and "control" the business. Everyone has to think in the lean environment. Innovation and improvement is everyone's responsibility, and everyone needs information. Real-time, nonfinancial data are critical to respond to customer needs, and improve processes and value streams. Information is *for workers*, and workers usually gather and control the data they need to perform their roles in satisfying customers and improving processes. Managers are workers that coach and enable other workers. Management accountants become primarily information system consultants.

The different assumptions underlying command-and-control and cooperative cultures encourage and enable different actions. These actions are summa-

EXHIBIT 8.3A   Cultural Comparisons: Assumptions

Business as Usual— Command and Control	Lean—Cooperative, Continuous Improvement
• Shareholder perspective	• Stakeholder perspective

• Competing individuals:
  Market forces and contracts
	• Cooperating teams: Shared
	  goals and values

• Product focus	• Customer focus
• Products cause costs	• Work causes costs

• Managers are source of
  change, workers are costs
	• Workers are source of
	  innovation and learning

• Managers own information	• Workers own information

• Accounting reports **ON**
  workers—compliance
	• Real time operational and
	  customer data **FOR**
	  workers—learning

• Efficient use of committed
  resources
	• Remove constraints,
	  eliminate waste

rized in Part B of Exhibit 8.3. A command-and-control culture is not likely to lead to lean behaviors. In fact, a worker or manager in a command-and-control culture is likely to perceive and use information quite differently than a manager or worker receiving the same information in a cooperative culture. Kaizen costing, for example, appears to be nearly identical to conventional budget-based performance evaluation when viewed from a command-and-control perspective. Aren't the Kaizen cost targets really just budgets? Aren't differences between the targets and actual results just variances? If Kaizen targets are adjusted more frequently than traditional budget targets, isn't that just a more onerous version of conventional budget-based performance evaluation? Is this just a Japanese term chosen for novelty or to encourage a consulting engagement? If more frequent budget target changes are all that there is to Kaizen costing, management accountants can ratchet down budget targets with anyone! The difference is not so much in the data as in how the data are used and in how the culture enables the data to be used.

Bob Emiliani, president of the Center for Lean Business Management, maintains that the two fundamental principles of lean are continuous improvement and respect for people. Many U.S. managers have embraced the continuous improvement concept, but they try to foster or force continuous improvement in a command-and-control environment where respect for people is lacking. Emiliani describes this as "imitation Lean" as opposed to "real Lean."[3]

EXHIBIT 8.3B   Cultural Comparisons: Actions

Business as Usual—Command and Control	Lean—Cooperative, Continuous Improvement
• Persuade and sell	• Customer relationships
• Price-driven purchasing	• Supplier relationships
• Manipulate output to control costs	• Produce output (on time) to actual demand
• Unbalance and decouple	• Balance and integrate
• Elimate workers, cut spending	• Train workers in self-management
• Build for scale and size	• Build for flexibility
• Local optimization	• System-wide improvement
• Bureaucratic control procedures	• Empowered local action

In sum, a cultural change and a management system change are necessary for a successful lean transformation, and a successful lean accounting transformation requires an accounting system change on top of that. Exhibit 8.4 depicts the lean transformation environment. The model in Exhibit 8.1 has been expanded to include structure and culture dimensions. A structure dimension is added as well as the culture dimension because most lean transformations include structural changes that unstack the pyramid organizational structure typical of most command-and-control company cultures. Lean principles enable the reorganization of company structure around value streams because the value stream clarifies the contingent relationship between strategy, structure, culture, actions, and measures for all employees. Each of the five dimensions influences all the others.

Assume a strategy change is the impetus behind the desire for a lean transformation. For people in a company with a strong cooperative culture already in place, the strategic demands and cultural influences will directly (and indirectly through their effect on actions) support the transformation to lean management and lean accounting. Since most companies attempting lean transformations do not have cooperative cultures in place, these companies have to

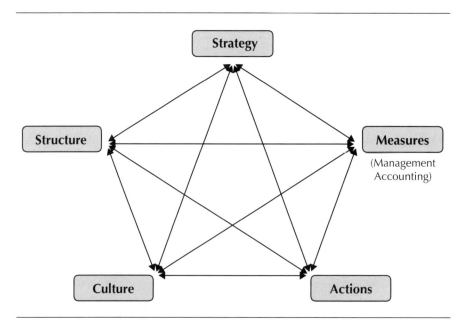

EXHIBIT 8.4   Accounting, Culture, and the Lean Transformation

make a cultural transformation at the same time they are making the lean transformation. Everything hangs in the balance. The culture can help build momentum for positive change, or a failed cultural transformation can generate push-back, impede necessary actions and accounting (measurement) changes, and support reversion to a strategy more compatible with a command and control culture. Lean transformation champions want management accountants to be change agents, helping to build and reinforce the cooperative culture necessary for lean to thrive. The change to a cooperative culture can be subverted, dooming the lean transformation to failure if the accounting system continues to support a command-and-control culture.

8.3 OBSTACLES TO ACCOUNTANTS CHANGING TO LEAN ACCOUNTING

A cause-and-effect diagram (also known as a fishbone or Ishikawa diagram) for the failure to implement lean accounting is presented in Exhibit 8.5. Causes are organized in the four classic categories, Man, Machine, Materials, and Methods, and the two most commonly added categories, Measurement and Environment. Detail of the Man category is presented in Exhibit 8.6.

(a) Machine, Materials, and Methods

Many firms have invested in enterprise resource planning (ERP) systems to expand their data-gathering analysis and reporting capabilities and efficiency. Other firms have less-integrated systems with more or less stand-alone accounting information systems (AISs) and production support systems. Because the vast majority of firms follow traditional management practices, the developers of the ERP, AIS, and production support systems have designed their systems for a traditional management environment. Managers engaged in a lean transformation find to their dismay that their systems, representing a substantial investment in software and training, are not well suited to lean management.

Because lean accounting emphasizes simplicity, most of the changes required involve turning off features of the existing systems rather than an extensive investment in new features and systems. For example, the manufacturing resource planning (MRP) system may be unplugged for production scheduling, but still used for generating bills of materials and for rough capacity

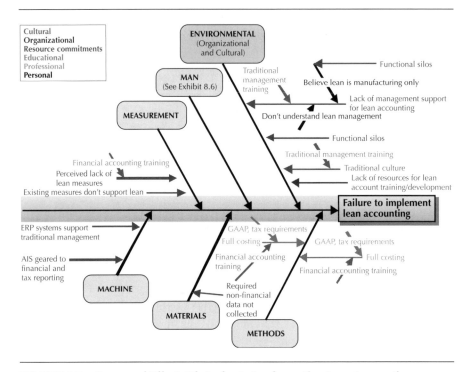

EXHIBIT 8.5   Cause and Effect: Obstacles to Implementing Lean Accounting

planning. Labor reporting is greatly simplified, and variance reporting may be eliminated. The machine (systems incompatibility) obstacle is more a reluctance, given the sunk costs, to limit the use of the existing system than it is a requirement of massive investment in new systems.

Lean management relies primarily on operational measures rather than financial measures for operational control and to support continuous improvement. Because of the financial measurement orientation of traditional accounting systems, some operational measures desired for lean accounting may not currently be collected. In other cases, the data are collected by the production system, but they are not currently made available when and where needed. (This is part of the systems problem discussed above). Converting to lean accounting often requires accountants or more likely, other workers to manually collect operational data or to program systems to collect additional operational data. In most cases, the additional work required is more than offset by the elimination of other unnecessary work, such as detailed labor tracking and inventory tracking.

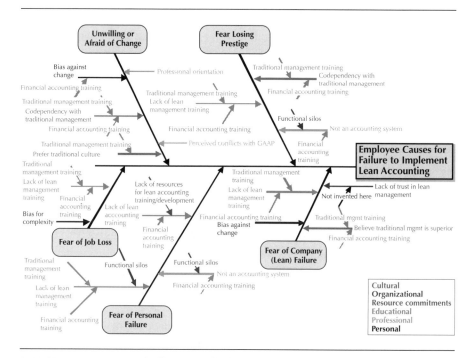

EXHIBIT 8.6   Cause-and-Effect Detail: The Man Category

For years, accountants have taken financial data gathered in systems de-signed to support financial and tax reporting and have used that data to gen-erate management accounting reports. Generally accepted accounting principles (GAAP) for financial reporting and income tax rules require that full-absorption costing be used to value inventory and cost of goods sold. Full-absorption costing measures reward overproduction and penalize just-in-time produc-tion, as discussed in Chapter 2. The problem is especially acute during the crit-ical early stages of a lean transformation. Of course, managerial reporting is not bound by financial and tax reporting rules. It is a relatively simple matter to adjust from an inventory value supporting lean (valuing inventory at direct material cost, or maintaining inventory at the value of standard work in process plus a standard buffer of raw materials and finished goods) to an inventory value satisfying GAAP. For example, the appropriate amount of conversion cost can be added to inventory valued at direct material cost with a single ad-justing entry because only the total value of inventory needs to be adjusted to full-absorption cost.

Implementing lean accounting usually requires changes to machines (systems), materials (data), and accounting methods. Like any changes, these changes require an initial investment in effort, equipment, and training. However, the investments required are relatively small. Were they the only obstacles to implementing lean accounting, machine, materials, and methods obstacles would be easily overcome.

(b) Measurement

If traditional accounting measures supported lean management, there would be no need for an accounting system change. Accounting would not be viewed as an obstacle to lean management, and the discussion of lean accounting would be limited to the elimination of waste from accounting processes. Faced with the reality that traditional measures do not support lean management, the obvious follow-up question is, "What measures do support lean management?" Many accountants are at a loss to provide the answer to that question, but their lack of awareness does not mean the answer is not available. The measurement problem is not a lack of suitable measures but a lack of awareness of those measures. This lack of awareness can be overcome through education in lean management and lean accounting—education that, unfortunately, is missing in the traditional financial accounting–oriented education and training in the accounting profession.

(c) Environment (Organizational and Cultural)

Cultural change is difficult for everyone regardless of discipline or functional area. For accountants, however, cultural change may be particularly difficult. Despite the widespread dissatisfaction with traditional accounting and claims of lack of relevance, traditional accounting reports (based on internally generated financial measures of cost and revenue) continue to be the dominant form of information for management control and decision making in command-and-control cultures. H. Thomas Johnson refers to this as "remote control management." Top managers allocate corporate resources to divisions based on reported financial results, similar to the way mutual fund managers allocate invested cash to different corporate stocks. If division managers cannot manage operations to yield the desired reported earnings, they manage earnings.[4] Many earnings management practices, such as producing unneeded inventory, channel stuffing, and deferring maintenance or research-and-development efforts are changes in action that harm long-term company performance. Even earnings management practices like changing accounting estimates, which only distort the financial reports, may hurt future performance if business decisions are based on the distorted reporting.

As harmful to long-term company performance as remote control management may be, the immediate results may be personally rewarding to managers adept at delivering the desired reported earnings. And who better than the accountants to deliver the desired reported earnings? Accountants assume a leading role in any company whose managers consider reported earnings their most important product. Because delivering reported earnings to satisfy the financial markets has been increasingly believed to be as important or more important than satisfying customers, more and more chief executive officers (CEOs) have been drawn from finance and accounting. The codependent relationship accountants have with like-minded managers who consciously or unconsciously resist cultural change and cling to their command-and-control reports may be the biggest barrier to accounting system change.

Managers must abandon their role as remote commanders and controllers in the lean environment. They have to take on the role of enablers or coaches and serve the workers. Accountants in turn must move from their central role in delivering reported earnings. Reported earnings are no longer viewed as the most important product. Reported earnings are simply one outcome from efficiently and effectively providing value to customers. Providing value to customers becomes the focus of the organization, and accountants play a supporting role, helping the workers build the information systems they need to continually improve the process of providing value to customers. In lean, managers and accountants are required to leave a culture where they had leading roles, and adopt a culture where they will have supporting roles. They must give up roles they were comfortable taking, roles for which they were educated and trained, and take on roles for which they have no comfort, experience, or training. Accountants very likely are having trouble making a lean transformation because they are locked in a codependent relationship with managers that have not embraced or even comprehended the cultural change that must accompany a lean transformation.

(d) Organizational Obstacles

Many companies are organized in functional silos, with sales, marketing, engineering, accounting, and finance personnel isolated in their own areas, physically segregated from other functional areas. The factory floors of many traditional companies display similar segregation, with all machines of a particular type (such as drill presses and milling machines) grouped together where they can be easily operated by a specialized labor force. Accountants located in functional silos are isolated from operations, the area where the lean transformation usually begins. Consequently, accountants operating in a traditional silo structure are less likely to understand lean or have the opportunity to see its power in practice. The physical separation and the functional specialist mind-set it encourages means that accountants may more easily isolate themselves from lean and treat it as an operations issue with no relation to accounting. Whether or not they are attempting a lean transformation, most companies recognize the communication problems and misunderstandings that may be caused by functional silos. Integrating accountants into operations and having accountants participate in lean training and Kaizen is critical to a lean accounting transformation. The accounting silo must be eliminated.

(e) Man—Personal Obstacles

Accountants also face educational, professional, and other personal barriers that reinforce their ties to the traditional command-and-control environment and inhibit their embracing a cooperative culture and the transition to lean accounting.

Accounting education has long been oriented toward preparing people for careers in public accounting. According to Johnson and Kaplan, the public accounting orientation of accounting education and its financial reporting focus within the accounting profession were major causes of the stagnation in management accounting from 1920 to 1985.[5] The public accounting orientation in education and in the profession continues to this day. Roughly three quarters of accountants work outside public accounting, but many accountants working for private companies and government began their careers in public accounting. In addition, while a large number of nonaccounting firms each hire only one or a few accounting majors, a small number of accounting firms hire accounting majors almost exclusively. Just as effective control over a company can be achieved by a minority shareholder group with concentrated ownership when the balance of shares are widely dispersed, the concentration of hiring by public accounting firms gives them "controlling influence" over academic accounting programs.

Remote control management and the financial accounting orientation were also supported by the practice of hiring MBAs rather than having managers rise from the ranks of operations. Most MBA programs emphasized training in accounting and finance and use of economic models based on the cultural assumptions of the command-and-control environment.[6] Thus, MBA programs also encouraged remote control management mostly relying on the same financial accounting data as used for financial reporting. Managers educated and trained in the command-and-control approach are predisposed to request financial accounting reports, and accountants educated and trained with a financial reporting orientation are more than happy to comply. At companies with traditional management systems, the continuing training and education of both accountants and managers through in-house training programs, mentoring relationships, and external seminars is likely to reinforce their academic education. This may also be true of continuing education and training for accountants and managers outside production at companies beginning a lean transformation if management views lean as a manufacturing system. Further reinforcing the financial accounting, financial reporting orientation that began in the educational process, the public accounting certificate (CPA) is the accounting profession's primary professional certification in industry as well as in public accounting in the United States.

The lean transformation of accounting is not likely to have substantial help from academia anytime soon. Lean accounting faces obstacles in academia that are, if anything, more formidable than the obstacles in companies. Like companies, business schools have functional silos, but the business schools have professional smokestacks within the accounting silo! Accounting professors, especially at larger schools, often specialize in financial accounting, auditing, systems, or taxation. Many of these professors have little interaction outside their area of specialization within accounting, much less any interaction with operations where they might be exposed to lean management. Financial reporting and auditing dominate because accounting programs are oriented toward public accounting. In addition, the accounting professors, who were themselves trained in programs with a financial reporting orientation and a command-and-control perspective, are training the next generation of professors in PhD programs.

The IMA is trying to promote the management accountant certification (CMA) as more appropriate for careers in industry. The financial reporting emphasis obstacle would be reduced if the CMA becomes the preferred certification for careers in industry. Making an understanding of lean management and lean accounting essential to achieving the CMA could be a major step toward easing the lean accounting transition in the future. In turn, the value of the CMA might be enhanced in the eyes of industry if companies attempting a lean transformation knew that CMAs were familiar with lean management and lean accounting. Thus, a reinforcing cycle could be created with lean accounting enhancing the value of the CMA certificate and the CMA certificate promoting the understanding of lean accounting.

The economics of the textbook market is also an obstacle to innovation in accounting education. In a conversation, Robin Cooper estimated it takes about 20 years for a new idea to be thoroughly incorporated into mainstream accounting text. It is as if we must be sure the idea has stood the test of time before exposing our students to it. The American Literature curriculum would definitely be filled with books by long-dead white males if accountants were teaching American literature! Book publishers want the widest possible adoption, so the publishers, and consequently the authors, play to the comfort zones and the topics desired by the majority of potential adopters. This is not a recipe for innovation. Robin Cooper suggests teaching cases as the quickest route to get new ideas into the curriculum. For this to happen, lean companies have to be willing to share their experiences with the few accounting professors that possess both an understanding of lean management and lean accounting and the inclination to write cases for use in the classroom. Lean accounting will be incorporated more fully into mainstream texts and the core accounting curriculum as more materials are available and more professors are exposed to lean accounting.

Cross-functional problem-solving teams are emphasized in the lean environment. Functional and professional designations lose their meaning and importance in the cross-functional team environment. The focus is on complete processes and value streams, and the entire team takes ownership of and responsibility for the entire process. Although he was officially vice president of finance at The Wiremold Company, Orry Fiume explained that the formal designation was not important. He was a member of The Wiremold Company management team, and titles or designations beyond that did not matter. Managers at The Wiremold Company often had primary responsibilities that differed from the functional area of their formal professional training. Marketers held positions as production managers, while engineers were responsible for sales or marketing, and so on. Accountants, trained to be unbiased and objective in preparation for careers in public accounting, may be more likely to hold on to their self-image as an accounting professional first and be less likely to see themselves as enablers on company teams.

Most people harbor some fear or anxiety about the unknown, and accountants may resist a lean transformation for this reason alone. However, accountants may be more resistant than other people to change and risk taking by training or self-selection. The stereotype of the risk-averse accountant is almost certainly subject to exceptions, and conservatism in valuing assets, estimating liabilities, and recognizing revenue need not imply resistance to change and a desire to preserve existing conditions. The Meyers-Briggs Type Indicator used in most studies of accountants' personalities does not directly measure conservatism or resistance to change. Accountants, however, are frequently called on to provide the downside analysis of what can go wrong with the ambitious proposals other managers present. Robert Kaplan studied the process of justifying capital investments in new technology and found that companies often fail to consider the potential negative consequences of failing to change, revealing a conscious or unconscious bias against change.[7] Accountants frequently have a leading role in preparing these cost-benefit analyses.

There are good reasons for accountants to be apprehensive about a lean transformation. They may anticipate a loss of influence or prestige in the organization. With a lean transformation, accountants will no longer be the keepers and reporters of data used to manage the company. The accountants in the command-and-control environment often take on the role of high priest or oracle, interpreting and explaining the accounting reports for all the employees who lack financial accounting training. With the lean transformation, employees will have more information and more useful information, but the information will be mostly nonfinancial and it will be gathered and used primarily by nonaccountants.[8] The accountants' role will be to support the employees by enabling their data gathering. The accountant goes from oracle to enabler, from high priest to servant. Properly understood, the accountants' new role has greater value, but perhaps in the eyes of many and certainly from a superficial view it has less stature.

Accountants may worry more about losing their job than losing prestige or stature in the organization. In lean, nonaccountants take on the primary role of gathering and reporting operational data. Financial accounting systems are simplified, transaction processing is reduced, and accountants take a support role helping nonaccountants develop their information systems. Fewer management accountants are needed to support the same level of business activity.[9]

Accountants may also fear they will be unable to adapt to the lean environment. Most likely, their education has not exposed them to lean management principles, and they may fear looking foolish as they learn, or they may doubt their ability to become competent in the new environment.

However, accountants may be convinced that the old way is the better way. Steeped in their conventional management education and experience, accountants may believe that the command-and-control approach is superior to lean management. Following these beliefs, they may continue providing accounting reports that support remote control management, impeding creation of a cooperative, continuous improvement culture, and undermining the needed cultural change. As the lean transformation fails in the face of these obstacles, they may see the failure as confirmation of their belief in the superiority of command-and-control management. Successful lean companies can be explained away as rarities with special conditions that do not exist at their company.

Finally, while lean has a bias for simplicity, accountants may have a bias for complexity and detail. Accountants may feel that helping workers develop simple, easily understood information systems, performance measures, visual displays, and reports do not add much value. If the system is so simple that anyone can operate it or understand it, where is the need for accounting professionalism and training? How can simpler be better in such a complex world? Accountants may feel more valuable supplying complex and detailed data that others are unwilling or unable to supply, and they may feel that complex, detailed data are necessary to compete in a complex, highly competitive, and rapidly changing environment.

8.4 MAJOR DEVELOPMENTS IN MANAGEMENT ACCOUNTING

The management accountant's training, professional orientation, predisposition, and personality clearly maintain and reinforce the traditional position in a command-and-control environment. These same factors serve to inhibit their willingness to embrace a culture of continuous improvement and adopt lean management and lean accounting. Now consider the response of management accountants to three major recent developments: activity-based cost management, the balanced scorecard, and the recently emerging resource consumption accounting. The history of adoption of these management accounting changes may provide lessons for overcoming the obstacles to lean accounting.

(a) Activity-Based Cost Management (ABCM)

The Consortium of Advanced Manufacturing–International (CAM-I) Cost Management System Project brought together a number of companies seeking to get improved cost information in the mid-1980s. The developments at CAM-I and at other innovative U.S. companies were synthesized and integrated by Robin Cooper and Robert Kaplan into the activity-based costing framework. Their early articles and the earliest activity-based systems focused primarily on the accuracy of product cost data. However, activity-based costing quickly evolved into a two-dimensional model. A process or activity-based management (ABM) dimension was added to the "vertical" cost assignment or activity-based cost (ABC) dimension. The model was further advanced when Robin Cooper introduced the activity-based cost hierarchy and the implications of unused capacity were considered.

For accountants, ABCM has a number of attractive features. ABCM systems make the work of management accountants more relevant by providing more reasonable and accurate cost assignments than the traditional systems they replace. Accountants usually play an important role in developing the systems, enhancing their stature, and providing job security. ABCM systems often report dramatically different results than the systems they replace, and accountants may be called upon to explain the differences. The systems are more complex than traditional costing systems so the accountants may be needed on an ongoing basis to interpret the results. ABCM deals with cost data and cannot be dismissed with arguments that it is not an accounting system, it was not invented here, or it is the responsibility of another functional area. Ownership of the system and the data often resides in accounting, although Robin Cooper maintains that ownership should reside with the managers for the ABCM to be used successfully as a cost management tool.[10] Most importantly, ABCM systems do not require a change in culture. ABCM systems can be used in a command-and-control environment.

In 1993, Bain & Company conducted their first Management Tools and Trends Survey, investigating the management tools and techniques used by a broad sample of companies. The survey does not distinguish between ABC and ABM, both are considered uses of a single management tool for survey purposes. As shown in Exhibit 8.7, ABM was being fairly widely used by 1993, the first year of the survey. This indicates broad, but hardly universal adoption of ABCM within ten years of its original synthesis and the articles bringing the concepts to the attention of the business community.

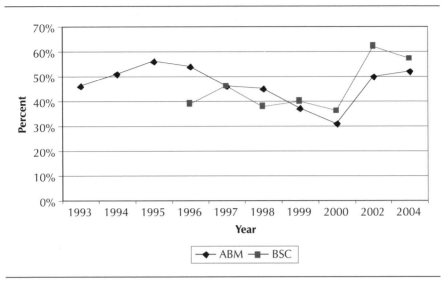

EXHIBIT 8.7   Management Accounting Tool Usage Rates

ABCM was designed to address problems of conventional systems in a command-and-control culture. Will ABCM systems also support lean management? Lean management practices lead to changes in factory layout and work organization by value stream that eliminate much of the product costing distortion that ABC was designed to address. Cooper and Kaplan suggest that ABM can support lean management by making waste more visible and helping managers prioritize improvement efforts.[11] However, most lean management leaders believe that tracking costs does not contribute significantly to reducing waste because costs are an effect of the waste, not its cause. They believe that efforts to identify and eliminate constraints and to understand the root cause of wasteful activities will ultimately be more profitable than efforts spent developing and maintaining an elaborate ABC system.

Often after workflow is reorganized in a lean transformation, "monuments" (machines or equipment usually acquired prior to a lean transformation that are on too large a scale and must be shared by many value streams) remain. Robin Cooper suggests that ABC may be useful for allocating the costs of monuments. This may be a valuable role, but it does mean that ABCM in a lean environment becomes a technique applied on a limited basis. In sum, ABCM has limited value-adding applications in a lean environment, but developing a comprehensive ABCM system with cost pools for all (or even many) activities would be wasteful at a lean company.

(b) Resource Consumption Accounting (RCA)

According to Paul Sharman and Kurt Vikas, Hans Plaut, a German automotive engineer, began developing *grenzplankostenrechnung* (GPK) shortly after World War II because he was dissatisfied with existing cost systems. Plaut wanted to provide more reliable cost information for decision making and correct the product costing "errors" he felt were caused by fixed cost allocations. In 1946, Plaut created a consulting firm to install his cost system at companies. In 1953, he published an article about his cost system. Wolfgang Kilger, an accounting academic, later thoroughly documented the system.[12] GPK is widely used by manufacturing firms in German-speaking countries and since the late 1980s it has begun to be adopted by some service firms in German-speaking countries. As ABC emerged in the United States, activity-based concepts were incorporated into GPK. The resulting system is referred to as resource consumption accounting (RCA) in recent articles in the United States. RCA has been receiving increasing attention in the United States over the past few years. Articles on GPK and RCA have been appearing regularly, and the Institute of Management Accountants (IMA) and CAM-I have special-interest sections exploring RCA.

In RCA, resource elements (costs) are assigned to resource (cost) pools. The pools must have a quantifiable output measure of use by the consumers of the resource. Resources in the pool are classified as fixed or proportional with the measure of output. Proportional resources from the cost pool can then be assigned to consumers of the resource based on the use measure. The cost pool may be an activity cost pool if the consumption measure is an activity. Costs from the resource pool may also be partially or wholly assigned to activity cost pools if activities are the consumers of the resource. RCA is a marginal or incremental costing system. Fixed costs either are not allocated or they are allocated based on a budgeted capacity demanded by the consumer. Neither GPK nor RCA were included in the Bain & Company survey, but the companies using GPK or RCA may have reported using ABM due to the similarity with ABC.

ABC and RCA are conceptually similar in terms of allocation, but they have different orientations. RCA focuses on resources (costs) rather than activities.

RCA systems emphasize the short term for incremental analysis, expenditure, and responsibility. ABCM systems emphasize long-term resource consumption. Many early ABC systems ignored unused capacity in order to fully allocate costs. That distortion would not happen in an RCA system. RCA will almost always result in a system with greater detail and complexity than an ABC system. Assuming resource pools are accurately specified and cost pools are accurately maintained, the more detailed RCA system should yield more precise costs, but the precision comes at a considerable cost.

RCA's apparent cost precision and granular level of detail are the source of its appeal. Detailed costs can then be selected and aggregated to provide precise cost estimates for virtually any decision context. RCA holds out the promise of a having a centralized data repository from which all financial and managerial reports can be generated while not holding management reporting hostage to financial accounting rules. (For example, RCA typically uses replacement costs rather than historical depreciation for equipment costs, and full absorption costing is not used for management reporting.) Many accountants and system developers long for a unified enterprise database the way many physicists long for a unified field theory, so this prospect makes RCA quite appealing.

In the lean environment, however, the additional precision offered by RCA provides little added value for the enormous added cost. Value stream costing can provide incremental analysis for short-term decisions from a system that is much simpler to develop and easier to maintain than an RCA system.

RCA's nonactivity measures may provide more precise short-term allocations from resource pools to cost objects like departments or products. Despite the increased detail, and the more precise or measurable allocations, RCA systems may be less helpful than ABC systems in prioritizing improvement efforts. The process view of ABC almost disappears under RCA's overwhelming emphasis on cost. To the extent that the activities are the root cause of resource consumption, RCA's nonactivity measures may be one step further away from the true cause of resource consumption and of less value for process improvement efforts. That said, remember that ABCM systems are themselves considered of limited value in prioritizing improvement efforts.

GPK/RCA also emphasizes individual responsibility. In principle, in addition to having a quantifiable measure of output, a single responsible manager or employee should be identified for every GPK/RCA cost pool. RCA systems are clearly oriented toward serving a command-and-control culture. Accountants facing an RCA implementation at a firm with a traditional command-and-control culture would certainly not be facing a culture change in addition to the accounting system change. RCA's fit with the traditional command-and-control culture may in fact be an additional source of its appeal among accountants. As with ABCM, RCA adds costing precision that adds little value to a lean company organized in production cells and value streams. As with ABCM, the added precision provided by RCA systems comes at considerable cost. Moreover, the detailed cost data and precise allocations provided by RCA create an added temptation to revert to the traditional command-and-control structure and managing by financial numbers. RCA systems may be the state-of-the-art information system for a command-and-control environment, but they are not compatible with lean business management.

(c) Balanced Scorecard (BSC)

In a 1992 *Harvard Business Review* article summarizing the results of a one-year multicompany performance measurement study sponsored by KPMG's research institute, Robert Kaplan and David Norton presented the BSC, which proposed reporting a few performance measures on each of four perspectives: financial, customer, internal business process, and innovation and learning. The measures would be reported on a single page to make it more difficult to hide perspectives or relegate them to secondary importance. Separate scorecards would be created for business units and for other hierarchical levels with relevant measures on each dimension tied to the overall company strategic measures and performance goals. David Norton became CEO of a new business consulting company in 1993, and he continued to develop the BSC in partnership with Robert Kaplan.[13] The BSC evolved from a strategic measurement system designed to avoid excessive emphasis on short-term financial results into a strategic management system designed to communicate and implement a company's strategy as well as measure the results of tactics used and actions taken to execute the strategy.

Kaplan and Norton have retained their four original scorecard perspectives, but as the BSC has evolved, the character of the perspectives has changed. The financial perspective has changed very little, while the conceptualization of the innovation and learning perspective has changed considerably. The focus of the learning and innovation perspective is on developing human, organization, and information capital. Measures such as developing new products that would have originally been included under "learning and innovation" would now be characterized as measures of "innovation processes" in the internal business process perspective. Kaplan and Norton have also extended the BSC approach by introducing strategy maps. A strategy map is a visual representation of the strategy, linking presumed cause-and-effect relationships and temporal relationships across the four scorecard perspectives.[14] Many companies adopting the BSC use Kaplan and Norton's four perspectives, but others add perspectives, such as a community perspective.

The BSC has been rapidly adopted by businesses. Almost 40 percent of the Bain & Company respondents in 1996 reported using the BSC (see Exhibit 8.7). This was the first year the BSC was included in the Bain & Company survey, and it was only four years after the initial *Harvard Business Review* article. In the last two Bain & Company surveys, over 50 percent of have respondents report using the BSC.

Companies with traditional performance measures that adopt the BSC must add a number of nonfinancial measures, but they may keep their existing traditional financial measures. The BSC does not affect the core transaction processing systems and cost systems. Accountants may find the BSC attractive because they see it as adding to rather than replacing the existing accounting and measurement system and consequently enhancing their role in the company. It also provides more systems development and maintenance work for accountants. That the BSC grew out of a study conducted by a division of a major accounting firm and a well-known accounting academic may also increase its appeal for accountants at U.S. companies. In addition, companies operating in a traditional command-and-control environment can use the BSC.

Although a change to a cooperative, continuous improvement culture is not required to adopt the BSC, it does appear to be compatible with lean management and a cooperative culture. The BSC supports a stakeholder perspective. The customer perspective can support lean's focus on end-use customers, the internal business perspective can support the continuous improvement culture, and the organization capital and human capital facets of the innovation and learning perspective can be used to foster cultural change and respect for people. Companies can add additional perspectives to the BSC framework to suit their unique circumstances. Lean companies, however, do not appear to be using the BSC despite the apparent conceptual fit with lean and growing general popularity of BSC. Lean companies are more likely to use *hoshin* planning. Lean companies may view *hoshin* planning and BSC as competing alternatives for communicating strategy and policy deployment, and they prefer *hoshin* planning. However, the BSC could complement *hoshin* planning if the measurement aspect of BSC is emphasized. Companies already using the BSC prior to embarking on a lean transformation should find the BSC a useful tool for promoting lean.

(d) Lessons for the Development of Lean Accounting

ABCM, GPK/RCA, and BSC have all emerged from management accounting practice. Academics identified common principles and themes in the practices of innovative companies, organized those principles and themes into frameworks, and presented the frameworks to the public. A lean accounting framework might help spread the adoption of lean accounting. The need for a lean accounting framework was discussed during a meeting preceding the main sessions at the Lean Accounting Summit held in September 2005. Brian Maskell, Bruce Baggaley, and Orry Fiume agreed to take a lead role in drafting a framework. An initial draft of the framework appeared in a 2006 *Target* article.[15] The *Target* article framework is not intended to be the last word on lean accounting. It is designed to promote the growth and understanding of lean accounting. In the spirit of continuous improvement, the framework should evolve as lean accounting develops.

The recent major management accounting developments have interest groups (CAM-I for ABCM and RCA, and the Balanced Scorecard Collaborative for BSC), where companies can share their experiences with other users and try to identify best practices. These interest groups have been useful in developing management accounting practices. Lean accounting would benefit from having a similar user group. Management accountants at lean companies could also try to create their own grassroots user groups by connecting with accountants at other companies in their supply chain or perhaps in their industry association.

ABCM and BSC were adopted quite rapidly. A large percentage of companies reported using each of these tools within a few years of their presentation to the public. Perhaps because it appealed to top executives as a strategic management system, the adoption of BSC was especially rapid. BSC may also have been more acceptable to accountants because it is perceived as adding onto the existing accounting and reporting system, while ABCM and RCA generally change the existing accounting system. ABCM could also be viewed as adding to rather than replacing the existing system if it is operated as a stand-alone system. RCA, however, implies a more fundamental change, with a goal of developing the kind of Stage IV system Cooper and Kaplan described in *Cost and Effect.*[16] Cooper and Kaplan's Stage IV system is a unified information system supporting management from which data could be extracted and modified to comply with financial reporting rules. Despite all the attention recently given to RCA, the rate at which RCA systems will be adopted outside the German-speaking world remains to be seen. The cost and complexity of the system development and maintenance is a major obstacle to RCA adoption.

Accountants are confronted with additions to the accounting system with BSC and ABCM, and a complete overhaul of the accounting system with RCA (and possibly also with ABCM). That BSC and ABCM have been relatively widely adopted illustrates that the machine, materials, methods, and measurement obstacles, while significant, can be readily overcome. All three management accounting changes, ABCM, RCA, and BSC can be implemented in a traditional management system and culture. They do not require accountants to simultaneously confront a management system change and a cultural change while making the accounting system change. The principal barrier to lean accounting is the cultural change, not the accounting system change.

8.5 OVERCOMING THE OBSTACLES

The resistance to lean accounting has little to do with the accounting and a lot to do with resistance to lean management and a cooperative, continuous improvement culture. Lean accounting techniques are now fairly well developed and publicly available. The question is not, "What measures should we use?" The question is, "Will we use the measures we should?" At one of the September 2005 Lean Accounting Summit sessions, an attendee remarked that a supervisor at her company was resisting the elimination of direct labor reports. She likened his use of the reports to "a security blanket." Does the supervisor understand that direct labor reports are likely to encourage overproduction and waste, not efficiency? Does he believe that, given the opportunity, workers would like to do a better job and produce quality products? Does he believe that with operational performance measures collected and reported in real time, workers may quickly identify errors and discover process improvements, reducing costs? Does he understand that nonfinancial measures should enable more effective cost management than do the direct labor reports? Does he realize the financial results can be more easily and reliably checked by looking at the trend in total costs in a production cell or value stream than by looking at a detailed cost variance report? A supervisor clinging to a labor report security blanket either does not understand lean management or he does not trust lean management. He is resisting the transformation to a cooperative, continuous improvement culture. He is trying to stay in his comfort zone, the command-and-control culture, and the authoritative role and the illusion of control it provides. Many management accountants are in the same position as this supervisor. With limited or no exposure to lean management and no experience with lean accounting measures and practices, they cling to their comfort zone. They continue to provide traditional standard cost variance reports. These reports allow managers like the supervisor described above to continue the command-and-control culture, managing by financial numbers and blocking a lean transformation.

How can accounting overcome the obstacles and become part of the solution rather than remaining part of the problem? Accountants need to locate the sources of resistance to cultural change, especially if the source is within their own hearts and minds. Discovering this root cause is the first step toward overcoming it and removing the barrier to the lean accounting transformation. Specific actions to be taken will depend on the current state of the lean transformation in the organization.

As the cause-and-effect diagrams illustrate (Exhibits 8.5 and 8.6), many of the obstacles to lean accounting are at least in part caused by a lack of understanding of lean management. To support a lean accounting transformation, accountants must understand the lean management system. Understanding lean overcomes the barriers of fear, lack of education, and the resistance to cultural change. Currently, accounting degree programs offer very little exposure to lean management, so enrolling in degree programs will not overcome the educational barrier, and even recent accounting graduates are likely to have little exposure to lean management. Whatever the state of the lean transformation, management accountants should try to get all the lean training they can. The further along a company is in its lean transformation, the easier it will be to obtain this training within the company. Management accountants at companies just beginning a lean transformation have to rely more on outside workshops.

(a) Supporting a Lean Transformation Begun in Production

Most lean transformations begin in production. Production workers and managers are more likely to have had exposure to lean management concepts in their training, and many companies try to implement some lean tools or concepts in production to keep up with (or gain an edge on) competitors. Often, lean is mistakenly seen as a set of tools for production efficiency rather than as a management system requiring a cultural change. The chances for a successful transformation are much greater if top management understands lean as a management system and supports the transformation to lean (see Chapter 3). Accounting, however, can support the spread of lean management even if it is currently viewed as a production system.

First, management accountants must view the production workers and managers implementing lean as their internal customers. They must break out of the accounting silo, get to know their customers, and understand their needs. They must understand the company's processes, so they can provide the information necessary to support lean management or, more likely, design systems to allow workers and managers to gather and report the information they need. The management accountants must discover what "information" that they are regularly producing and reporting is actually wasted effort on irrelevant data.

Management accountants should take every opportunity to participate in Kaizen throughout the company. This will allow accountants to appreciate firsthand the power of lean. They will also better understand the information needs of the workers and managers performing the processes. Management accountants can then help build systems that better serve the information needs of the users. These systems are usually simple, reporting data collected by the users themselves. Management accountants should place a special priority on attending to the information needs of those who have demonstrated a commitment to lean management and to a cooperative, continuous improvement culture. If workers and managers committed to lean are successful, their success helps convert others and helps reinforce the culture.

Second, accountants should apply lean concepts to accounting processes. Learning about lean, participating in Kaizen, and helping build new information systems take time. If accountants wait for a spare moment, that time may never come. Applying lean to accounting transaction processes should free time to devote to lean education and training and system development. Transforming accounting processes also develops lean management expertise in accounting and it shows by example that lean is a management system rather than just a set of tools for producing goods and services more efficiently.

Finally, management accountants must eliminate reports containing measures that conflict with lean management and that discourage the development of a cooperative, continuous improvement culture. The resistance to lean management and lean accounting lies as much or more in what is taken away than in what is added. A parallel conversion path, leaving the old measures and reports in place while adding the new might appear to be the path of least resistance. A parallel conversion path provides the new information needed, but it leaves the "security blankets" in place. Managers resisting the cultural change and lean management are likely to ignore the new lean measures and keep managing with the old measures, undermining the lean transformation. Eliminating old reports and measures as soon as workers are getting the information they need to manage processes in the lean environment increases the likelihood of successful lean transformation despite the initial resistance and discomfort. Continuing unnecessary reports is also wasteful and contrary to lean management.

Of course, traditional reporting may still be required by corporate management if the lean transformation is taking place in only part of the company. Management accountants can help support lean by explaining (or helping the line managers explain) the reasons for the conflicting signals sent by traditional accounting measures. They can also provide supplementary measures that may not have been included in the corporate reports such as cash flow, inventory turns, throughput rates, defect rates, and on-time-delivery rates that reflect the improvements made through implementing lean.

Production managers can promote the lean accounting transformation by initiating and sustaining the communication with accountants. They should ask for help in gathering the information they need. They should ask why unused and unneeded reports are being prepared. If required by upper management, production managers should ask for help in showing the gains made through lean and in explaining any contradictory signals that may appear in the traditional measures included in the required reports. Production managers should invite management accountants to participate in Kaizen, so they can better understand the processes and information needs, and so they can experience firsthand the power of lean management.

(b) Sparking a Lean Transformation from Accounting

What about companies not currently undergoing a lean transformation? Can accounting drive a lean transformation? Accounting need not trail in the lean transformation, but it would be very difficult to lead a lean transformation from accounting without strong support from top management and support in production. Still, accounting can plant the seeds for a lean transformation by gathering and reporting on operational metrics that support lean management. For example, a report showing favorable efficiency variances could be supplemented with data showing deteriorating on-time deliveries, reduced inventory turns, and poor cash flow. Exposing waste and the dysfunctional consequences of local optimization and financial accounting metrics may spark an interest in lean in operations and in management. Management accountants can also be proactive in establishing communications with production. Accountants can understand existing processes and introduce or suggest measures that support continuous improvement. Through these communications, management accountants are likely to discover production managers and workers familiar with lean management and interested in attempting a lean transformation at least as a pilot project in a small area of the company.

If someone in accounting has significant experience with lean management, accounting can transform the accounting processes and conduct Kaizens, providing an example of lean management for the rest of the organization. By getting employees from other areas to participate in Kaizen and selecting accounting processes with significant interactions with other functional areas, the desire and ability to convert to lean management may spread throughout the company.

A lean transformation requires a cultural change, and cultural change is difficult and often uncomfortable. Cultural change may be particularly difficult for management accountants, who often have a lot invested in the traditional command-and-control culture. Regardless of the state of the lean transformation, accounting can be converted from an obstacle to change into an agent for positive change. Management accountants can even become leaders in the lean transformation!

NOTES

1. Teruyuki Minoura, "The "Thinking" Production System: TPS as a winning strategy for developing people in the global manufacturing environment," *Toyota Special Reports*, October 8, 2003. Toyota Motor Corporation Public Affairs Division.
2. Exhibits 8.3 and 8.4 draw heavily on the work of H. Thomas Johnson, *Relevance Regained: From Top-Down Control to Bottom-Up Empowerment* (New York: Free Press, 1992), especially Chapter 4, pp. 57–72.
3. Bob Emiliani, with David Stec, Lawrence Grasso, and Jim Stodder, *Better Thinking, Better Results: Using the Power of Lean as a Total Business Solution* (Kens-

ington, Conn.: Center for Lean Business Management, LLC, 2003), Chapter 8, pp. 240–267.
4. See Note 2, pp. 16–53.
5. H. Thomas Johnson and Robert S. Kaplan, *Relevance Lost: The Rise and Fall of Management Accounting* (Boston: Harvard Business School Press, 1987), pp. 125–151.
6. See Note 2, pp. 16–32, 175–196.
7. Robert S. Kaplan, "Must CIM Be Justified by Faith Alone?" *Harvard Business Review*, March–April 1986, pp. 87–95.
8. Robin Cooper, "Squeeze Play," *Journal of Accountancy*, January 1997, pp. 46–50.
9. Robin Cooper, "Look Out Management Accountants," *Management Accounting*, May 1996, pp. 20–26.
10. Robin Cooper, "Look out Management Accountants," *Management Accounting* May 1996, p. 21.
11. Robert S. Kaplan, "Management Accounting (1984–1994): Development of New Practice and Theory," *Management Accounting Research*, Vol. 5, 1994, pp. 247–260; Robin Cooper, "Look Out Management Accountants," *Management Accounting*, May 1996, pp. 20–26; and Robert S. Kaplan and Robin Cooper, *Cost and Effect* (Boston: Harvard Business School Press, 1998).
12. Paul A. Sharman and Kurt Vikas, "Lessons from German Cost Accounting," *Strategic Finance*, December, 2004, pp. 28–35.
13. Robert S. Kaplan and David P. Norton, *The Balanced Scorecard: Translating Strategy into Action* (Boston: Harvard Business School Press, 1996).
14. Robert S. Kaplan and David P. Norton, *Strategy Maps: Converting Intangible Assets into Tangible Outcomes* (Boston: Harvard Business School Press, 2004).
15. Brian H. Maskell and Bruce L. Baggaley, "Lean Accounting: What's It All About?" *Target*, Vol. 22, No. 1, 2006, pp. 35–43.
16. Robert S. Kaplan and Robin Cooper, *Cost and Effect* (Boston: Harvard Business School Press, 1998).

9

LEAN APPLICATION IN
ACCOUNTING ENVIRONMENTS

JEAN CUNNINGHAM*

Lean is an ever-morphing support structure attached to all parts of the organization. When a change occurs in one part of the organization, it causes adjustments in many other areas. Everything is connected. Lean is not implemented from the top down. All managers and supervisors must actively engage their area in the lean focus areas. A lean organization can readily identify unengaged departments because of the evident lack of ongoing productivity improvements.

An often unexpected outcome of lean activities is the improved attitude of those involved. There will be a status quo sourpuss here and there, but, in general, people like to be involved in change and improvement when the results are concrete and obvious. Job interest often improves as they engage members of other parts of the organization with whom they have not traditionally worked (see more on this subject in Chapter 5).

Once an enterprise has established lean as a "way of life," the activity is never ending, and when looking back years from now, people will be shocked, amazed, and proud of the productivity and quality improvements it enables them to continually implement. Accounting can directly improve the bottom line. Believe it! Now, enough with the proselytizing and let's figure out how we can effectively adopt lean into the accounting area.

*To Alan Riggs, my husband and partner—Thanks, Jean

9.1 GOAL AND FOCUS AREAS

Accounting organizations may or may not be well integrated into the overall enterprise. Everyone has heard of and probably seen ivory tower chief financial officers (CFOs) and accounting groups who churn out numbers that are rarely seen and never understood by other members of the company. Even groups that are not this extreme may still be very separated from the firm's operations. Lean changes that scenario. To effectively adopt lean, first and foremost the accounting function must adopt a new primary goal: *Add value to the company bottom line for all activities.* Accountants in lean transformations are continually surprised by what actually adds value and what does not.

There are three broad, overarching *areas* for accounting functions to focus on in an organization that has adopted lean as a business strategy (see Exhibit 9.1).

1. Follow the change progression in the organization's operational areas. Then adapt and alter accounting processes and deliverables to support those changes.
2. Investigate and establish how all information currently provided by accounting is or is not being used. Add, modify, or eliminate information as appropriate to support the primary goal.
3. Find and eliminate waste (activities and information that do not add value) in the accounting processes.

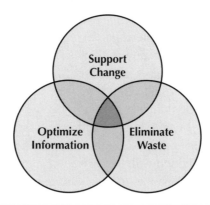

EXHIBIT 9.1   Accounting Focus Areas

Each of the focus areas is essential and highly interrelated with the other two. Accounting should apply them to all activities ongoing with the intensity and impact dependent on the breadth and speed of change in the overall organization.

9.2 KAIZEN EVENTS IN BRIEF

Kaizen literally means "continuous improvement" in Japanese, and that is what Kaizen events do. Well-orchestrated events are essential to successful lean adoption. No Kaizens, no lean! They are a proven, fabulously successful structure for continuous improvement. Participants need this structure to avoid improvement meetings where attendees sit around playing guessing games about what is supposed to happen and result in little or no improvement but a lot of wasted time and upset employees. A thorough definition of Kaizen is beyond this chapter, but this section includes a brief description for the uninitiated.

A Kaizen event lasts 3 to 5 consecutive days. There are 10 to 18 dedicated, full-time participants. This group works together to make significant or breakthrough improvements to a specific, previously identified process. Given the high-impact results, a Kaizen event is *not* an event for "Mr. I'm-too-busy-with-my-other-real-work-to-stick-around" who comes and goes as he pleases while constantly disrupting, demeaning, and lowering the effectiveness of the event. Include this person at your peril.

There are three phases to the event.

1. The event starts by observing and documenting the current process.
2. Improvements based on lean philosophies are brainstormed and accepted or rejected. A plan to revise the process is agreed on.
3. The changes to the process are implemented.

Real, high-impact change is fully implemented in three to five days. Now, that's progress.

The Kaizen team by definition must be from a wide variety of backgrounds. This optimizes the ability to "think outside the box" and allows for a wide variety of knowledge and skill sets to be present.

- About half of the team members should be from inside the targeted process.

- Some members should be employees from upstream or downstream processes.
- There should be employees not associated with or impacted by the process.
- Many of the most successful events also have individuals not employed or otherwise associated with the company that bring a specific expertise to the event that would not otherwise be present.
- Employees of companies who have already adopted Kaizen events as a way of life are more than willing to attend Kaizens of those who are just getting started.

The team facilitator begins the event with lean training, and then helps the team stay focused and step through the Kaizen phases. Goal setting is an essential start-up action for every Kaizen event. A Kaizen event itself needs to be lean, and without stated and understood goals the event will meander into a lot of dead ends and wasted time.

It is often better to define a Kaizen improvement event broadly. Instead of "accounts payable" and looking at only the work of the accounting clerks, look at the *process*, starting when the material or service is received until the supplier receives its payment. This drastically reduces the number of Kaizens over time, and each one tends to accomplish more. Now, that's lean!

The number of people involved in the process will expand beyond accounting. As each part of the process is described in a flowchart, each person in the process sees how their work fits in with the whole, how the data they create is used, and how long the overall process takes. Invariably, with just that much added clarity, the team members immediately see improvements and waste that they want to fix. The relationships of the team members also grows as they gain respect for the overall process, and continue to work on the process long after the Kaizen event is complete.

(a) Personal Kaizen Experiences

Team members make a huge difference in the success of Kaizen events, so work to keep perspectives as broad as possible when planning a Kaizen. When planning a Kaizen for the collections process at Lantech, a packaging equipment company and early lean adopter, we wanted our perspective to be as broad as possible. In addition to the usual invitees from accounting, we also invited a person from the shipping team (upstream from invoicing), the sales

team (downstream from accounting for problem customers), and manufac-
turing (someone outside the process.)

For this event in particular, we also invited someone from a collection firm.
He joined us for two days during the event, and we were able to learn tips and
gain perspective from his professional expertise. As it turned out, he also gained
knowledge on waste elimination that he was able to put to work at his com-
pany. It was a great partnership. In most events where we invite people from
outside the company, it is pretty difficult to tell who is an employee and who
isn't within a few hours. It seems that everyone really enjoys the opportunity
to contribute when empowered for change.

In another recent event, one team member, "John," discovered that the per-
son after him in the process, "Jane"—from a different department—routinely
reorganized the information and "fixed" errors in the data before proceed-
ing. John had no idea that errors were being passed along and was somewhat
embarrassed that it occurred in the first place. Thereafter, he sent the data for-
ward with no errors and even reformatted it to meet the next person's needs.
John hadn't known there was a problem, and Jane simply thought that "was
how it was." The fix was easy and fast and made both people happy.

9.3 HOW TO GET STARTED AND NEVER END

Ten interdependent activities enable enterprises to adopt and support the lean accounting focus areas described in the previous section. While they all overlap,
they are listed in the order that most enterprises are usually capable of following as people become engulfed in the full benefits of adopting lean concepts.

1. Plunge into operation's lean activities.
2. Lead a culture of continuous improvement.
3. Reduce the closing calendar.
4. Optimize financial data usage.
5. Convert to English.
6. Support lean measures.
7. Attack accounting waste.
8. Evaluate and/or eliminate standard cost accounting.
9. Engage kanban.
10. Become a consultative business partner.

These are not "one time and done" activities. They change most or all business processes, everyone's job becomes more productive, and, frankly, everyone's job makes a lot more sense. With ongoing management support, many employees start looking for possible improvements as a matter of course, resulting in continuous gains as the transformation process moves forward.

While using these activities in my accounting group over a five-year period, our company revenue doubled while the accounting group stayed the same size, with two people redeployed to provide entirely new services. In general, our value-add and reputation company-wide rose immeasurably. Each activity is described in the following sections.

(a) Plunge into Operation's Lean Activities

Deploy the accounting members into the various Kaizen and improvement events in the rest of the company. They might well perform the traditional role and "bring finance information" to the event, but they also should function as active participants and full members of the teams by finding and improving the process in other parts of the company. The sooner each accounting team member—and most critically the CFO and accounting managers—get involved with the nonfinancial lean events, the sooner they gain a personal understanding of what is changing in the company and the potential impact in competitiveness, cash flow, and profitability (see Chapter 3 for more on the role of the CFO).

Many of the benefits will not be directly recognizable as financial benefits unless it is observed firsthand. Most traditional financial evaluation tools are focused on the value-adding portions of the process. Traditionally, accountants know how to "value" reducing the cycle time for manufacturing equipment or how to measure the benefit of reducing wasted materials. Tools like discounted cash flow, payback, or return on investment (ROI) are understood and normal for these activities.

Waste elimination steps in non-value-adding activities are not traditionally measured by accounting. For instance:

- Moving equipment closer together to eliminate travel time
- Creating standard procedures for cleaning and maintaining the equipment
- Processing one part at a time

These productivity gains, while apparent to those doing or observing the work, do not often have obvious or immediate benefits found in the results of traditional financial measurement tools.

By directly observing the waste elimination, the financial manager and the accounting team realizes that the traditional tools cannot be effective in understanding the benefit of many lean activities. Further, by working with accounting during Kaizens, other parts of the company grow to better understand accounting's point of view and grow to better present requests with accounting needs in mind. A miracle!

(i) A Personal Plunge Experience *As CFO at Lantech, the manufacturing area presented me with an investment opportunity to purchase reusable containers that would travel from the parts supplier to our manufacturing plant. The reusable container would replace the current use-once corrugated box. The traditional financial assessment would evaluate how costs are eliminated compared to the initial outlay with some type of discounted cash flow or payback measure. Would the new container reduce the product cost because we would no longer buy a corrugated box for each product? If not, there would not be any obvious benefit, and I would have nixed the deal since the new container costs more.*

However, since our accounting team was actively involved in shop-floor Kaizens, we knew that the container was not just a way to protect our parts during shipment. It turns out, the container would also be a compartmentalized visual counting device, as well as a physical signal to the vendor that manufacturing had used up those parts and needed more sent. We understood that the value of getting exact-count parts with built-in reorder signals via the container was going to reduce inventory and stock shortages, which in turn would reduce line stoppage and late deliveries. Finally, the elimination of a purchase order for each order would lower transactional purchasing time. All of these gains are measurable items, and I approved the purchase of the containers with full confidence of the value being added.

(b) Lead a Culture of Continuous Improvement

There are three main types of improvement activities:

1. Everyday improvement
2. Breakthrough Kaizen
3. Planned approach

The first two are the ones that have the most impact. Everyday improvement is an individualized empowerment to improve one's work every day: looking for improvements in cost, quality, safety, and customer satisfaction. Even small improvements—repeated daily—add up over time. Leadership encouragement and support to make changes is critical to ensure that all team members understand this is expected and recognized (see Chapter 5 for more on employee empowerment and leadership's role).

Breakthrough Kaizen events create the opportunity for significant improvement that may result in work changes for a larger group of people. This is rarely achieved by one person's efforts. The beauty of the breakthrough Kaizen event is the empowerment of the team to make big changes very quickly without the bureaucracy of pedantic approvals. By implementing rapidly, the team can quickly see the impact and make further improvements to the process!

Planned approach is the more traditional method, where a team meets every week or so for an hour with updates on progress since the last meeting. The meetings are usually not as effective at moving forward quickly, and often the "outside the meeting" time is not as well utilized because the "normal" work gets in the way.

Introducing these improvement methods is a necessary first step, but to continually apply them and realize their potential, leaders must truly establish a new culture within the accounting team. Management must lead *all* team members into thinking and learning about improvement.

Monthly meetings in the accounting department should be focused on improvement in both the metrics and the process. If the leader asks about improvement ideas in every meeting and then recognizes the gains and individuals from earlier ideas—whether large or small—then the team gets a clear message that this is expected behavior. If the manager does not discuss and check this on a *very* regular basis, the new culture will not develop. Even more effective is when the team can see that the manager has changed some personal behaviors and acknowledges personal activities that needed improvement.

Create a non-negotiable stance that all employees will be part of improving and changing the work. If the company is having cross-functional improvement events, then require that each employee participate in one to three events per year in their performance reviews. Ensure that time is provided in the employee's schedule. Often, to enable the participation, cross-training activities need to be in place. During the first six months of the lean journey, focus on cross-training and thereafter on improvement events, though the need for cross-training recurs from time to time. The key is to make it part of the written performance review, so there is no mistake that this is expected behavior.

No employment is eliminated by lean, but all jobs change. If management has a history of terminating employment because of productivity improvement, it must take measures to build employee trust that this will not happen as a fundamental part of the new lean culture. However, be clear that *every* job is expected to change and the activities that employees perform may change. This could be as small as some additions or deletions to work content, or as drastic as job shifting or even assignment to a pool of people for redeployment. Also, it is *essential* to clarify that as is always the case—with or without lean—if overall *business volume* drops, a reduction in workforce might be an unfortunate, but necessary, outcome.

A less obvious but very important aspect of lean accounting is to pull in the banking and audit partners to observe, understand, and appreciate the changes the company wants to make and solicit their support. Since the bankers and auditors make decisions that impact the process, they're on the team whether you recognize it or not. Many improvement efforts are stifled from the expectation that the auditors will not accept the changes.

All things being equal, the improvement activities that are focused on eliminating waste and adding value increase competitiveness almost immediately and have a compounding effect in the future if the enterprise is continuously improving. The compounding effect is dramatic indeed five or ten years later.

(i) A Personal Experience Leading Continuous Improvement *While championing our lean initiatives, I met with the auditor and our banking relationship manager quarterly to discuss the direction of the company and the reasons the lean strategy had been selected. We discussed the areas of changes that had been completed and areas for focus in the coming months. Particularly with changes to inventory and accounting, I explained why we were simplifying and listened to any input they might have for the company. This led to a very high level of trust, and coincidentally, no major surprises for either party. Using this approach, I did not experience resistance from the auditors or the bankers in either company where I was CFO.*

I used another technique during improvement events when the inevitable "our auditors won't let us do that" resistance occurred. I suggested a call to the auditor to describe the change and its benefits, and to get their "approval," or at least understand what they believed to be the barriers. In nearly every case, the auditor and the team would come up with a good, creative solution or direction. Everyone involved seemed pleasantly surprised by the interaction and cooperation.

(c) Reduce the Closing Calendar

This reduction is actually a series of straightforward steps that result in incredible gains.

- Develop a simple visual map (Exhibit 9.2) of the accounting systems, including points where there is manual intervention. The resulting data can be used in many heretofore unnoticed or underanalyzed areas by pointing to potential waste elimination areas.

- Look at the manual entries made using a Pareto chart based on the dollar value of the entries.

- Create another Pareto chart of how many manual entries are made on each day of closing (Exhibit 9.3).

- Determine what percentage of the total manual entries is specifically for correction.

- Establish a monthly meeting to look at the postclosing entries made each month. Use the team to find ways to reduce the entries and resequence the work to eliminate days from the closing.

- Create a visual map of how information is passed among team members during closing, and try to eliminate handoffs, eliminate need for entries, or reduce queue time between handoffs.

- Look at where information is required from other departments and have a joint improvement event to create a process flowchart of information sources and uses. Discuss quality and timeliness concerns. If all members across departments of the process flow see the entire sequence, they will find opportunities for task improvement, flush out waste, and resynchronize the schedule of events to shorten the closing.

An important aspect in reducing the number of days to close is to first consider what entries can be eliminated. An example would be to decide to *not* make correcting entries unless they were at least $200 (or some other significant figure) or to eliminate the root cause of the correcting entry. Often, correcting errors in other people's work is seen as the work, as opposed to waste. To emphasize this, keep track each month of any input information that is incorrect, and meet with the originator to discuss how to avoid the error including elimination of the duplication of effort. It seems so simple, but frequently correction just becomes "the job." Put the work into the *root cause*, not cor-

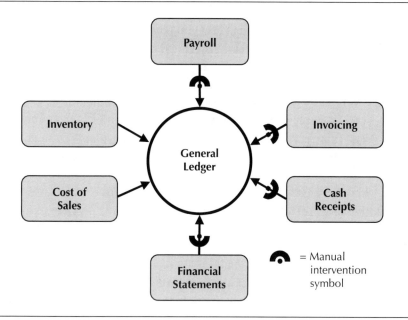

EXHIBIT 9.2   Accounting Systems

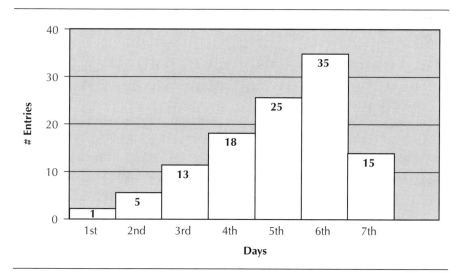

EXHIBIT 9.3   Closing Entries Pareto

recting the error. To quote a Chinese proverb, "Give a man a fish and you feed him for a day. Teach a man to fish and you feed him for a lifetime."

In addition to optimizing closing activities, look for ways to stop batching activities until after the end of the month. If one of the closing tasks is to review the cost of sales for items shipped, perform this task as each item ships or at least on a daily basis. For example, in a machinery manufacturing company, there are typically both shipments of machinery and an after-market spare parts business. The spare parts business typically has a large volume of small-dollar invoices each month. The machinery invoices are fewer in number but much greater in value. Accounting might decide to look at each machine the day after it ships—or completes manufacture, if made to stock—to see if the cost of sales information looks correct, while looking at the spare parts invoices as a group. This not only reduces the time during the closing window, it also identifies problems early in the month before it is duplicated over and over. Also, as accounting later begins producing financial reports on a more frequent basis (weekly or daily), they have accurate input information.

After having reduced or eliminated batching, look for ways to perform more closing tasks prior to the end of the month, so they are not in the closing window. An example would be making the warranty reserve calculation using 29 days of shipments and estimating the thirtieth day. Another is booking all the payroll entries prior to the end of the month.

After accounting has thoroughly leaned down the closing process, make sure technology is being used every way possible and for all it is worth. Adopt the technology to meet the company's specific closing needs with as few touch points as possible. "Once and be done." Focus on getting the information in the system correct the first time and then letting the technology create the entries and adjustments automatically.

The biggest obstacle to technology change is finding the way around the favorite "toys" of the information technology (IT) department and the rumors and false assumptions of many decision makers. Eliminating this obstacle enables system users to thoroughly research systems available and arrive at a consensus with the IT department of which one really adds the most value to the company. The initial cost is typically staggering, but the right system optimized for specific needs still pays for itself many times over.

(i) A Personal Calendar Closing Experience *During the monthly metrics meeting at Lantech, one of the standard agenda items was a trend chart show-*

ing the number of manual entries prepared after the month close. One person was appointed to update this chart each month and bring a list that included what entries were made, by whom, and subject matter. The list was given to all the members to encourage ideas of which entries we might be able to eliminate or move. Those suggestions were shared with the person who created the journal entry, and the author of the entry led the effort to get the changes implemented.

(d) Optimize Financial Data Usage

After getting as many entries out of the closing window as possible, turn to your data output and reporting. All accounting departments deliver data to other parts of the company either electronically or as hard copy. There's a significant amount of time and effort expended on a job that is rarely optimized, and almost without fail includes reports that were requested long ago and far away and haven't been used for years. Make sure you understand the voice of the customer. In this case, the customers are the people inside the company who use the financial data that are a result of the closing process. Discuss with each customer—not just supervisors and up—what reports they use and even what data on the reports is useful.

Really ask the five "Whys," only in this case it is the five "Hows"—the five iterations of diving deeper into the question of "How do you use the financial data output to make decisions for the future?" Ask how they use the data and if the data could be improved. Dig hard on this to understand *exactly* how the information is applied. For instance, a customer response "To see if our costs are in line" would be probed to understand which costs, how much of a variation is relevant, and what they do with their findings. Use this feedback to improve, add, or delete the information provided. This effort leads to significant improvements in what is provided to the customer, including gains in tailoring it to their specific needs. The results may or may not save time in accounting, but the data provided raises efficiencies in the overall company going forward. Just as all business understands the value of focusing on the end customer, so it is valuable to focus on the internal customers.

(i) A Personal Experience Optimizing Financial Data *Recently, one of the accounting teams I'm working with held a Kaizen to reduce the amount of time they spend during the monthly close. The focus was the cost accounting area*

where two accounting team members did all the work. The event was a three-day event with ten team members focused on this opportunity. The Kaizen team members included:

- *Two cost accountants*
- *The division controller*
- *An accounting team leader from a sister division*
- *An inventory control analyst*
- *An engineer*
- *A member of the purchasing team*
- *Three other accountants*

A team comprised of people inside and outside the process creates greater likelihood of breakthrough ideas. After discussing the purpose of the cost accounting information, the team decided they needed more information about how the company used the reports that accounting created each month. The team paired off and visited the offices of eight key managers in the company, including the president, the engineering manager, and several others. Each pair showed the manager six different reports that they received, asked how they used the report, and learned what decisions they actually made because of the information. The accountants also asked how the report could be improved. Each of the pairs then reported back to the Kaizen team.

The team then created a matrix of each report and manager interviewed. As a result, three of the reports were eliminated and one had significant modifications. Several managers were also taken off the distribution list. Did this process discourage the cost accountants to see that the information on which they worked so hard every month needed serious modification? No, because they now understood which information was valuable and used to make decisions. They could focus their efforts going forward on what really was creating value. By the way, along with other improvements from the Kaizen, this team met its goal of reducing the closing time by half. Really good!

(e) Convert to English

When manufacturing begins a transformation to cellular manufacturing, accounting should:

- Convert standard cost reporting to plain English financials.
- Eliminate absorption accounting at the transaction level.

- Create product line financial statements that align with cellular manufacturing.

This is a significant task, and most of the current discussions of lean accounting focus on this topic. Other thorough treatments of this broad topic supply the necessary detail.[1] Conversion to plain English is simultaneously the most difficult challenge for the accounting team, and the most enlightening result for the statement customers.

Despite the training that many people in management have had on financial statements, the accountant must make the language simple to understand. A lean statement of "Shipments Minus Expenses Equals Profit" is a great step toward nonfinancial management and leadership taking ownership for the financial performance of the company. Words like variance, accrual, absorption, direct, indirect, revenue, and other terms truly understood only by financial professionals are all red flags that the statements are not in plain English.

The lean initiatives are as guilty as most other management methodologies of inventing technical jargon that is then used in discussions as if it has existed forever and everyone who has ever crossed a corporate threshold uses daily over coffee. The word *lean* itself connotes a reduction or minimizing rather than improving, and words like *Kaizen*, *poka yoke*, *takt*, and *5S*—all lean staples— are a mystery to most. So accountants have to make a significant and important effort to either talk in plain English or slow down and explain the background and meaning of these terms. It is fun when you are "in the know" of the special language, but it is no fun at all when you do not know and are not helped to understand. And beyond fun, it thwarts accounting's efforts to lean down the company and may relegate good work to the vast dustbin of unrealized quality improvements.

(f) Support Lean Measures

Support all the new measurements needed by the organization either with information systems reports or directly with charts and diagrams at the shop-floor level. Traditionally, almost all the "important information" in a company is felt to belong in the financial statements or in management offices. The lean organization tries to provide key information as quickly as possible—in many cases immediately—and locate the information where it can directly support decisions and lead to ongoing improvement.

As the lean effort expands throughout the organization, new measures will be needed, and many of those measures will be used at point of use. For example, when cellular manufacturing is in place, the immediate feedback to the operators and team leaders on the line points to whether or not they are able to produce to takt time, the customer demand rate, and if not, what were the key reasons. This information is needed in the cell where it can be seen by the team members and discussed at the daily meeting each morning.

Many of the measures will address topics that have traditionally been considered "nonfinancial." For instance, there will be a greater focus on units of customer demand rather than just dollars. Other measures may include:

- On-time delivery
- Lead time
- Batch size
- Percentage of material part numbers procured using visual process (kanban)
- 5S audit scores
- Percentage of team members who have participated in Kaizen events
- Percentage of team members with performance feedback
- Shipments per employee
- Number of overtime hours
- Hours worked safely (or lost hour safety incidents)
- Percentage uptime of any constraint equipment (Percentage update on nonconstraint equipment is unnecessary and can produce counterproductive behavior.)[2]

These measures will usually be tracked in line with either the product families or value streams. The closer to where the activity occurs that the results can be measured and presented, the better. (See Chapter 4 for a more complete treatment of performance measurement and management in the lean environment.)

For instance, let's say production is at a slower rate than planned. With traditional measures, it would show up in the end-of-month statements as a production variance. However, the lean factory would put a flip chart at the end of the line showing the rate at least daily and perhaps more often. The chart would compare the actual to the plan and information to support how the team met the plan or why they might not have been able to make the rate.

(i) Personal Experiences Supporting Lean Measures *At Lantech, the log-in screen for our computers had a banner screen that traditionally was used for* *system notices. We revised this screen to post the daily and monthly statistics for new orders being received by product line compared to plan. All employees using a computer could see the customer demand rate as they began their work each day. This set the tone of the day for everyone—there were no surprises, and no one could justifiably claim to be surprised.*

For similar reasons, the schedule for each manufacturing cell was located in the cell, so all cell team members could see the quantity and type of orders to be produced. Likewise, the engineering cells, organized by product families, also had their schedules on visual boards in the engineering area. Not only could the engineers see what was in their queue, but sales and management also had visual access. This put everyone on the same wavelength concerning capacities and order sequencing.

(g) Attack Accounting Waste

Waste is a normal part of growing and changing firms. Something that was optimized yesterday is top heavy today. Something that was used by all in the 1990s is long forgotten but still being created in the 2000s. Accounting is no different, and in many firms it is an area that has been completely ignored by earlier improvement efforts. Of course, everything can't be improved at once, but, over time, Kaizen events should be launched in the key accounting processes:

- Accounts payable
- Payroll
- Sales tax
- Invoicing
- Accounts receivable
- Audit

Each area of the accounting department is an excellent target for reducing waste.

A good point of view to take when approaching an analysis of accounting waste is to think of the work of the accounting department as represented by the Traditional triangle on the left in Exhibit 9.4. The triangle represents the amount of *time* traditionally spent in transactions, analysis, and consulting. Most of the accounting team labor is consumed by making transactions as represented by the wide bottom layer of the triangle. These are the activities to

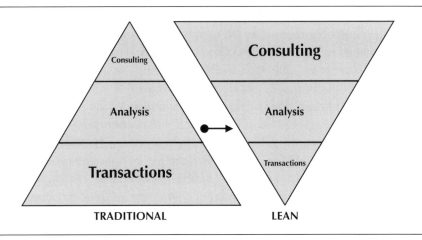

EXHIBIT 9.4   Accounting Work Triangle

record transactions so that accounting can either take action, such as paying vendors, or provide information, such as the monthly financial statements.

The middle layer is the activities that are analyzing the transactions to look for information to provide to the company. For example, by looking at the accounts payable transactions, accounting might be able to identify that metal purchased from Vendor A is less expensive than Vendor B, or that Customer A pays within terms and Customer B takes debit memos and an extra 14 days to pay each month. The amount of analysis could be limitless.

The small top layer of the triangle represents consulting activities. These are the activities that look at the analysis and make recommendations on how to improve performance in the future. For example, the consultative role might include participating in a Kaizen event in the fabrication department and making recommendations on the purchase of different sizes of raw materials to minimize cost while maintaining quality. Or there might be a visit to a difficult customer to work out an improved method of communication so invoices are submitted and paid effectively.

Also, the triangle represents the chronological focus of accounting activities. The transaction layer includes historical activities, which include recording or transacting what has been decided in the past. The analysis layer is about the present and looks at the historical information to see what it means currently. The consulting layer has a future focus asking the question, "What can be taken from the analysis of the current situation to make decisions and actions that will improve the company's future strategic performance?"

The long-term goal of lean accounting is to turn the triangle upside down so accounting activities reflect the lean triangle on the right (Exhibit 9.4). Accounting can add tremendous value to the company by spending most of the time in consultative activities and the least time on transactions. As one might guess, the initial purpose of accounting-related Kaizen events is to eliminate wasted time in transactions so that more time can be spent on analysis and consulting. Start first with accounts payable and payroll. They usually have dramatic opportunity. The key tenet for success is to define the event not as a department or function but as a process. Instead of defining the Kaizen scope as "accounts payable," define the scope from the point a product or service is received until the vendor is paid.

Even a small company that might have only one person involved with accounts payable will see that many people are involved with the process. These usually include:

- The receiving department
- The person who opens the mail
- The person who approves an invoice
- The person who approves the check run
- The person who signs the checks
- The accounts payable clerk

A similar approach would be taken with each accounting area. Not only will improvement and change happen in the accounting department, but also in all the other related process areas. These accounting events might include waste-reduction goals such as:

- Reduce the number of people involved in the process by 50 percent.
- Improve first-pass yield (the completeness and accuracy of the information) by 30 percent.
- Eliminate the need for invoices with two vendors.
- Eliminate 15 non-value-adding tasks.
- Have fun.

The purpose of the goals is to help people understand that big, concrete improvements and major changes to the processes are expected.

(i) A Personal Experience Attacking Accounting Waste *It's much more pro-ductive to not change information systems during the first event in each area. Change the process first. Then after the process is redefined with as little waste as possible, system changes are implemented to support the process changes rather than the other way around.*

When we started business process Kaizens at Lantech, our first event was in customer service. Having learned from our earlier manufacturing experi-ence that people wanted to perform multiple Kaizens in an area before we had the key elements in place, we felt the same would be true in the business processes. At first, team members could see many improvements they wanted in the information system, but if they focused on those changes they would be improving only the current process. But when we said, "No system changes," the team really looked at creating flow and one-piece flow, ended up disman-tling the current process, and put in a completely new process. We had two large events in this area before we really felt we had the key elements. Addi-tional changes were made to the customer service process as we got down-stream into purchasing and engineering. So it was almost a year later before we began to make information system changes in customer service.

(h) Evaluate and/or Eliminate Standard Cost Accounting

Evaluate all the accounting procedures that are done to support standard cost accounting, and change or eliminate them. It is surprising how much transac-tional work is done to support a standard cost accounting system. If the deci-sion is made to eliminate standard cost accounting—yes, this has been done very successfully in lean accounting environments—transactions that made so much sense before may no longer fit. Some examples include vacation ac-counting, allocations, and direct versus indirect labor classification.

If all the manufacturing costs are treated as period cost, vacation account-ing is simplified. A vacation accrual is still needed to represent the liability for future vacation on the balance sheet. But accounting no longer needs the ac-crual to reduce period cost in the current month for days of vacation to avoid showing a labor variance. Significant simplification and time savings result by separating the recording and reporting of the hours of vacation taken from the recording of the vacation dollars paid on the income statement.

Another payroll-related simplification is to ignore direct and indirect labor classification for income statement reporting. As manufacturing moves toward cellular manufacturing, the traditional definitions of *direct* and *indirect* may begin to blur. For instance, if the function of scheduling a manufacturing line is now located on the line and a person who previously worked on the line performs the scheduling function, is it direct or indirect? Or if the person who is identifying what needs to be ordered is the same person who delivers the parts to the work cell, how are they classified? The real answer to these types of questions lies in how the information is used to make decisions that affect profitability in the future.

(i) Engage Kanban

Taken as a whole, the "materials process" is huge and usually full of waste before going lean. Nearly all lean companies eventually adopt kanban as a way to simplify the management of materials process. Kanban is a visual signal process based on the pull of materials through a just-in-time (JIT) manufacturing process.

Some firms only implement kanban internally to move materials between different areas of the factory or factories, and additional accounting involvement is negligible. However full-implementation includes external kanban, which means using kanban with material suppliers and eliminating the use of purchase orders for each purchase. As the company implements external kanban, accounting must become active team members and aggressively change to recognize and support kanban benefits. Processes that are highly affected include:

- Accounts payable
- Inventory management
- Cost evaluation

Every element of the materials process is simplified through kanban. The accounting team must actively participate in the design and implementation of kanban because of the productive impact it has on accounting processes when fully and appropriately implemented. For instance, traditional use of purchase orders is eliminated and replaced with blanket orders with a smaller number of vendors. The potential to eliminate vendor invoices altogether exists and has occurred in some companies. It's simply astonishing how many transactional activities can be changed and simplified by kanban.

After people costs, material purchases for inventory may be the most significant expense to the company. Material purchase expense is one of the most underestimated costs in standard accounting processes. Material purchases consume not only the obvious cost of the material itself, but also (1) the costs of the purchasing, accounting, receiving, and planning departments to keep the flow of materials into the company in place. Then add in the costs of (2) storehousing, (3) counting, (4) weighing, (5) quality assurance, (6) reserving for inventory, and, ultimately (7) disposing, to fully recognize the costs of material inventory.

Inventory reduction is the largest change that results from implementing kanban, and it positively impacts all material purchase expenses. As the inventory levels reduce, the financial significance on the balance gets lower, paving the way for simplified methods of inventory valuation and reserves, as well as a simplified inventory control mechanism. Many companies decide they can eliminate their cycle-count programs altogether, and obsolescence risk is reduced dramatically.

For lending purposes, your banking partners must be informed and understand the kanban concept with the effect of reduced inventory levels to your income statement and balance sheet. You will want your bankers to understand the improved cash flow and company strength that result from these improvements.

There are many ways to implement kanban, so the best way for the accounting team to stay abreast of the changes and requirements related to materials and inventory is to become a team member on these change initiatives from the start. Kanban is an ideal place to apply the time freed up from reducing the transactional accounting activities on earlier lean efforts. Channel the time into consulting opportunities and you're really starting to turn that triangle upside down. A nice aspect for those individuals who might champion kanban is that the results and gains are so visible to most in the company and to external business partners that justifying the cost and time takes care of itself.

(j) Become a Consultative Business Partner

Emphasize this step once lean has been adopted and dramatic improvements have been made in all areas of the company. If a company has a traditional mind-set for accounting functions of "Accounting lives in an ivory tower," "It's us versus them," "Accounting reports are unintelligible," or other negative outlook, then evolving to a consultative business partner takes a lot more work. Usually, employees both inside and outside accounting have the same perception in these negative environments, albeit from a different perspective. The realized gains from waste elimination help to build the relationship, but many may still resist accounting's expanded consulting role. If accounting has fully participated in kaizen activities, most negative attitudes should have been changed. Regardless, to make the most of consulting opportunities, place a priority on growth and waste elimination initiatives.

Ideally, the executive team has also launched some growth initiatives so that the time and energy of the human resources that have been made available through the lean effort have been redeployed so they can contribute going forward. The seed work of those growth initiatives should start to have a positive effect, and this is the time for accounting to focus on evolving the growth into profitability. Growth might include adding new products, adding new sales channels, or acquisition of new companies or technology. These are tangible new sales growth opportunities, which lead to the need for continued improvement focus.

When the income statement is in plain English and the old absorption accounting gobbledygook is gone, forecasting short-term financial performance is much easier. The same inputs to the forecast are used: manufacturing and sales input into what units will be shipped. Since accounting will not be dealing with the major fluctuations that standard cost accounting creates, it can take the true variable margin for each of the product lines against the shipments, less the total spending of the company, to get profit.

Major spending changes (perhaps a trade show or a royalty income) can be added or subtracted to more closely predict the profit number. More importantly, an effective forecasting tool is so simple to create and update that the forecast can easily be prepared on a frequent, weekly basis or with multiple scenarios. The breakeven shipment level becomes obvious as well as trade-off between different product lines. Look at Exhibit 9.5 to see a simple example— easily prepared in Excel—that even a large company or business unit could use. For further reference on this subject, you may want to read Thomas Corbett's *Throughput Accounting*.[3] While it does not deal with Generally Accepted Accounting Principles (GAAP), it is an excellent resource to understand the facile nature of the simplified accounting statement.

Lean tools have the most dramatic result when used together. For instance, the simple forecasting method just described becomes most accurate when the lead time of the products is very short, meaning they are manufactured in one-

EXHIBIT 9.5 Three-Month Forecast Tool for Lean Accounting

Order Entry	Avg Price	Month 1 Units	Month 2 Units	Month 3 Units	Month 1	Month 2	Month 3
Product A	1000	20	30	25	20	30	25
Product B	2000	300	350	400	600	700	800
Product C	3000	55	60	40	165	180	120
Product D	4000	100	300	200	400	1200	800
Product E					300	350	400
Total Order Entry					1485	2460	2145

Shipments	Avg Price	Disc %	Month 1 Units	Month 2 Units	Month 3 Units	Month 1	Month 2	Month 3
Product A	1000	20%	20	30	25	20	30	25
Product B	2000	30%	300	350	400	600	700	800
Product C	3000	40%	55	60	40	165	180	120
Product D	4000	20%	100	300	200	400	1200	800
Product E		25%				300	350	400
Total Revenue						1485	2460	2145
Discounts			27%	25%	26%	405	616	553

	VM %			
Variable Margin	VM %	0	0	0
Product A	45%	9	14	11
Product B	38%	228	266	304
Product C	40%	66	72	48
Product D	56%	224	672	448
Product E	76%	228	266	304
Total Variable Margin		755	1290	1115
Operating Expenses		1000	1000	1000
Interest Expense		50	50	50
Other			40	
Profit before Bonus/Taxes		-295	200	65
Bonus	20%			
Profit after Bonus		-236	160	52

piece flow to customer order with kanban purchasing in small lots. Why? Because in the lean organization:

- Inventory fluctuation is minimal.
- Finished goods are nearly zero.
- Production flow is in concert with customer demand.

In fact, the lean organization may so closely align with cash fluctuations over time that accountants may yet get back to the old cash box accounting!

In competition for those growth initiatives will be additional and never-ending opportunities to continue eliminating waste and creating flow in the organization. And as much as accountants hope that the new processes will work perfectly, change happens, and processes continue to need improving and reinforcing. Old habits can be hard to break. This can be especially true in processes in which it is hard to see the flow physically, like many office processes.

9.4 WHAT TO EXPECT

Every area in the accounting and finance department is enhanced by adopting lean methods. The operational areas of accounts payable and accounts receivable have fewer steps and clearer indicators of the pace of work, and become more integrated into the processes of material procurement and order processing. The fixed asset and capital investment evaluations recognize that small, specific-purpose equipment that supports one-piece flow manufacturing and inventory reduction is of greater value than huge multifunctional batch-based production.

The cost accounting activities focus on teaming with the engineering, purchasing, and manufacturing processes to identify improvements in cost and quality instead of searching down elusive historical variance debits and credits. The budget process recognizes the quickly shifting nature of a lean organization and allows for movement of resources through the processes. There will be people unassigned to a specific department when they are freed up from their current job through lean.

The financial statements are easy to understand and available on the first day of the month, and easy-to-use forecast tools are more valuable than the historical statement. But perhaps the biggest change comes in watching the number of miles accounting feet cover instead of watching people sit in their cubicle day in and day out with no "visitors." Frequently, team members will be out in the organization working on team projects, visiting customers and suppliers, or huddled with other team members on the vital strategic projects for the company. Or the accounting team may be spread throughout the facility with their process partners. Bean counters no more—at least not in the hearts and minds of those outside accounting. And best of all is the personal satisfaction you and many others feel and the recognition you receive as leaders of the lean transformation.

Congratulations! Thanks to your participation in lean, the future of the company is bright. The tools of improvement are adopted in all areas of the company, existing and new customers see and value the products and services of the company, and the workforce is respected and valued for their collective genius, which drives the company forward. Every job in the company has changed for the better, employees are proud of what they and their company are doing, and loyalty even made a comeback!

Now is a great time to get started, and good luck.

NOTES

1. Brian Maskell and Bruce Baggaley, *Practical Lean Accounting* (New York: Productivity Press, 2006).
2. Jean E. Cunningham and Orest J. Fiume, *Real Numbers: Management Accounting in a Lean Organization* (Durham, N.C.: Managing Times Press, 2003).
3. Thomas Corbett, *Throughput Accounting* (Great Barrington, Mass.: North River Press, 1998).

10

SARBANES AND LEAN—ODD COMPANIONS

FRED GARBINSKI

The Sarbanes-Oxley Act (Sarbanes) is one of the most influential-and controversial-pieces of corporate legislation. Its original aim was modest: to improve the integrity of financial reporting. The methods, however, were anything but. We are now nearing the end of the third year of compliance with Sarbanes, and not much has changed in the approaches. Auditors still hold the legislative trump cards and set the direction for managers to follow. Management continues to claim that compliance costs too much and the benefits are too little. On the whole, management is still obediently following the auditor's lead with little voice in setting the direction of its design, implementation, and ongoing development.

There seems to be little momentum to change management's current role. The government (through the Public Company Accounting Oversight Board [PCAOB] and the Securities and Exchange Commission [SEC]) keeps asking auditors to reduce the cost of compliance, but auditors, who know no other model to turn to, continue to unwittingly interpret the rules as they always have: not knowing—or caring—to reinvent their approaches. The government is still imploring auditors to use a more risk-based, top-down approach instead of a bottom-up transaction-based approach. They know the current model is costing too much, yielding too little. However, no one seems to know how to describe the specific direction needed to make compliance with the legislation more meaningful and less costly. In summary, the leadership role seems to be reserved exclusively for the government and the auditors with little to no input from representatives of management. Yet, neither seems to be able to adequately articulate just how management should be reviewing its systems.

This chapter was first drafted in the fall of 2005 with a few modest purposes. The first was to describe how and why the auditors were handed the role they now enjoy in a post-Sarbanes world. The second was to illustrate how a management-led process, such as a lean initiative, with its associated tools like standard work, continuous improvement, and team-based organizations can and does meet the Sarbanes requirements. The final purpose was to get the responsibilities realigned. The premise of the chapter is, and continues to be, that it is management's responsibility, not the auditors, to design and implement effective control processes.

Lean manufacturers demonstrate time and again how lean processes are much more effective and efficient than processes used by traditional, transaction-based mass producers. Yes, lean processes are different, but with their underlying purposes of simplicity, availability, understandability, and capability, their design easily meets the Sarbanes requirements of ensuring the reliability and integrity of financial reporting. In fact, since they are designed with a far greater purpose, it is not much of a stretch to say that they would meet all the other COSO[1] objectives, not just the financial reporting objectives necessary to comply with Sarbanes.

The original purposes of this chapter remain relevant. To accomplish those purposes, this chapter starts with an overview of Sarbanes and then addresses three questions:

1. How we got to where we are. How did we get to the current definition of internal control that is used for Sarbanes compliance, and why is that definition so limited?

2. Where can we go from here? Is there any hope that the Sarbanes control and review requirements can be incorporated into an organization's DNA?

3. Are there common denominators between Sarbanes and lean that can be used as a springboard for the future?

10.1 OVERVIEW OF SARBANES

Did anyone think Sarbanes would be as far reaching or as controversial as it has been? I doubt it. When first enacted, it essentially appeared to be a reemphasis of the Foreign Corrupt Practices Act (FCPA), a typical and, quite frankly, not unexpected response to instances of corporate misconduct. After all, the government has been claiming that self-regulation has not worked and has been threatening for years to regulate auditing. Accountants have been looking over their shoulders for that same period recognizing that as soon as another McKesson Robbins, Equity Funding, or savings and loan crisis occurs, the government will make good on its threats and regulate auditing. Enron, WorldCom, Adelphia, Tyco, and others were just the last straw.

Unfortunately, it's more than just a mere reemphasis of the FCPA. The differences are ominous. With the introduction of a management opinion and the two additional auditor opinions, the work by management and auditors necessary to reach such opinions are enormous. This was hardly just a dusting off of the FCPA.

When it was originally passed, the FCPA made it illegal to fail to maintain an adequate system of internal accounting control. However, due to absence of standards to support the definition of internal accounting control, the FCPA ended up essentially adding some personnel to the internal audit staffs, conducting some additional financial process reviews, and adding a few words to the annual report.

However, Sarbanes requires management to document, test, assess, and express an opinion on whether their controls are effective. Auditors, in turn, need to express an opinion on the effectiveness of management's assessment and an opinion on the controls themselves. The Sarbanes requirements are a far cry from the FCPA requirements and are costing enormous amounts of internal and external time to complete. Why such a radical change? The reasons were set forth in the introductory paragraphs of Auditing Standard No. 2 (AS2).

> The series of business failures that began with Enron in late 2001 exposed serious weaknesses in the system of checks and balances that were intended to protect the interests of shareholders, pension beneficiaries and employees of public companies—and to protect the confidence of the American public in the stability and fairness of U.S. capital markets.
>
> From the boardroom to the executive suite, to the offices of accountants and lawyers, the historic gatekeepers of this confidence were found missing or, worse, complicit in the breaches of the public trust. Congress responded to the corporate failures with the Sarbanes-Oxley Act of 2002, creating a broad, new oversight regime for auditors of public companies while prescribing specific steps to address specific failures and codifying the responsibilities of corporate executives, corporate directors, lawyers, and accountants.[2]

10.2 Q1: HOW WE GOT TO WHERE WE ARE[3]

How did we get to the current definition of internal control used for Sarbanes compliance, and why is that definition so limited? Internal control is hardly a new concept. While no one is certain where it first emerged, the concept of internal control first appeared in the early 1900s with the need for accurate financial information and attestation to secure loans. Borrowers had to convince lenders of their capacity to repay. Financial information became the foundation on which those lending decisions were made. However, lenders needed some assurances that those statements were prepared correctly, and for that assurance, lenders turned to groups of independent accountants. These accountants realized early on that some reliance had to be placed on the underlying processes followed to prepare the statements, and from that need came the first definitions of internal control. While the definition evolved over the years, it began with internal control as a broad concept. In 1949, that definition was subdivided into the internal administrative control and internal accounting control definitions. The latter definition was more acceptable to accountants because it provided a narrower focus for a financial audit. It reduced the risks and the costs. As one author describes the need for this separation:

> . . . it was one of the several initiatives taken by an apologetic accounting profession in the aftermath of the scandal involving McKesson & Robbins. These steps were necessary to prevent the Securities & Exchange Commission from exercising its authority to set accounting and auditing rules for the private sector.[4]

In 1977 the definition of internal accounting control took a giant leap as a result of the enactment of the FCPA. To define internal accounting control, legislators turned to and literally lifted the definitions from the auditing literature. Soon after enactment, however, it became clear that the definitions alone were not suitable, and there were no other standards available to help direct any evaluation of the effectiveness of internal accounting control. It was a veritable free-for-all of explanations covering how to recognize an adequate system of control. The aftermath was that management was simply left to use their judgment to develop and conduct an evaluation of internal accounting control and to render a report thereon. Commentators persuaded the SEC to deal with the situation on a voluntary basis, thereby rendering the act nearly harmless but forevermore embedding the term and definition of *internal accounting control* in law.

Still more financial reporting fiascos in the late 1980s that culminated with the savings and loan scandals, led to further discontent with the understanding of what constitutes adequate systems of internal accounting control. This discontent led to the formation of the National Commission of Fraudulent Financial Reporting (commonly known as the Treadway Commission after its chairman, James C. Treadway, a lawyer and former SEC commissioner) in 1985 to recommend how the various concepts and definitions of internal control could be integrated. The result was the publication by Committee of Sponsoring Organizations (COSO) of its internal control framework document in 1987 and a later amendment in 1992. This two-volume, several hundred-page framework, entitled *Internal Control-Integrated Framework*, contains guidance on not only the reliability of financial reporting (internal accounting control) but on two other categories of internal control—the effectiveness and efficiency of operations and compliance with applicable laws and regulations.

(a) Important Points from a Historical Perspective

The important points to keep in mind from this historical perspective are:

- The accounting profession has managed the thinking on internal control for most of the twentieth century, and those definitions were influenced by the questions raised concerning the extent to which auditing work was necessary.
- The work of COSO was strongly influenced by the perspectives of the independent accountant, even though other interested parties participated in developing this framework.
- Recognition was growing that the internal control over financial reporting—while remaining very prominent—is but one aspect of internal control. COSO, for example, concluded on three categories that need to be effective: effectiveness of operations, reliability of financial reporting, and compliance with applicable laws and regulations.

(b) Sarbanes's Major Provisions

Enacting Sarbanes, some argue, will become known as the perfect financial storm,[5] citing all three elements of the impending disaster: the heat from the rising stock market that swept the nation throughout the 1990s; the cold from the economic downturn that blew in at the end of the decade; and before the storm could blow out, the development of a new hurricane in the form of accounting irregularities and other questionable practices of 2001 and 2002 that tipped the scales.

Consider Tyco and the alleged pocketing of millions by the CEO, Dennis Kozlowski, that was not rightfully his; the members of the Rigas family, who were charged with the fraud in the Adelphia scandal; the WorldCom executives, who were charged with accounting fraud; and the fall of Enron and the related indictments against Ken Lay, Jeff Skilling, Andy Fastow, and others in that massive fraud. The stage was set. Something had to be done, and it was. Congress and regulators acted swiftly, and while the aftermath may linger for years to come, its immediate effects are already being felt.

Some of those immediate effects come about by virtue of the provisions of the law. Others, which many are finding more ominous, arise due to the ways that the requirements are being implemented. Essentially, the government is again attempting to prevent individuals from criminal acts by passing more stringent legislation. This approach brings to mind Einstein's definition of insanity: doing the same thing over and over again and expecting different results. Nonetheless, Sarbanes now requires:

- Audit committees that consist solely of independent directors and at least one that is designated as a financial expert.
- Auditing standards that are set by the newly formed Public Company Accounting Oversight Board (PCAOB). Auditing firms are required to register with and be monitored by the PCAOB.
- Auditors are required to issue two additional opinions. One of those opinions covers management's process of establishing and evaluating their controls. The second is the auditor's opinion on the effectiveness of those controls.
- CEOs and CFOs are required to:
  - Certify that it is their responsibility to establish and maintain adequate internal control over financial reporting.
  - Identify the framework used to evaluate the effectiveness of internal control over financial reporting.
  - Conduct an assessment of the effectiveness of the company's internal control over financial reporting as of the year-end.
  - State that its auditor has issued an attestation report on management's assessment.

It is clear that COSO failed to alter the fixation on financial reporting controls and the importance placed on such controls in deterring financial reporting fraud. Perhaps it's true that people tend to drift to the familiar, especially in times of crisis. The response to Sarbanes is no different. The fixation on financial controls overrode any of the other considerations when Sarbanes was being implemented, so the financial reporting controls took center stage, and only those elements of COSO were considered. With the AS2 requirements, the auditors held all the trump cards. Accordingly, driven by the need to satisfy the auditor's requirement, management fell into the trap of blind obedience.

10.3 Q2: WHERE CAN WE GO FROM HERE?

We now turn to the second question: Where do we go from here—is there any hope that the Sarbanes control and review requirements can be incorporated into an organization's DNA? Yes, it can become part of the very fabric of the way companies are managed. In April 2005 and again in May 2006, the SEC held roundtable discussions in Washington, D.C. Both were a "who's who" list of panelists,[6] as well as all SEC commissioners and board members of the PCAOB. Over 60 experts participated in a number of panel discussions, and although they were a diverse group, the themes were consistent throughout. The message at each session was: "It is not the legislation that needs to be fixed, but rather the implementation of 404 through the auditors, PCAOB, and SEC that needs to be addressed."[7] The most popular topic was the need to control the substantial and unanticipated costs of Section 404 compliance.

(a) SEC and PCAOB Issue New Interpretations

Subsequent to the first roundtable held in 2005, the SEC and the PCAOB issued interpretations to address the issues raised. In its statement, the SEC said:

> An overarching principle of this guidance is the responsibility of management to determine the form and level of controls appropriate for each company and to scope their assessment and the testing accordingly. Registered public accounting firms should recognize that there is a zone of reasonable conduct by companies that should be recognized as acceptable in the implementation of Section 404.[8]

Shortly after this guidance was issued, SEC Commissioner and acting chair Cynthia A. Glassman noted some of the strengths and failures of SOX Section 404. She commented that:

> There is no question in my mind that the implementation [of SOX Section 404] has been misdirected. What was meant to be a top-down, risk-focused management exercise became a bottom-up, "check the box," auditor-driven exercise.[9]

From these interpretations it is clear the SEC and the PCAOB heard the message and acknowledged that an auditor-led process is not the intent of this legislation and are taking the steps to move these requirements in the right direction.

Has the message been heard? Considering that immediately after this guidance was issued, accounting firms stopped pressing sample size and key controls issues and have begun to listen to other control mechanisms that are equally effective, the answer appears to be yes. Before these interpretations, guidance to the accounting firms' clients and staff was that their approaches needed to be essentially the same as what the firm had prescribed.

(b) The Case for Moving Beyond Compliance Is Compelling

So, what should we do now? Over 50 emissaries went to Washington for two straight years to argue the case, and each year the SEC and PCAOB acknowledged that the implementation of Sarbanes was costing too much and that auditors might have been too conservative in their interpretations. The SEC acknowledged that management should take the lead. After all, as one panelist pointed out, "We have been designing, monitoring, and improving these processes longer than many of the personnel assigned to audit my firm have been alive."

Former SEC Chairman William Donaldson saw this as a three-step process: comply, sustain, and improve. Comply because there is a legal obligation to do so. That thought can become the lever needed to move managers from the status quo. He then called for companies to sustain their initial momentum by enlisting other functions into the initiative. It has become apparent to many people that compliance cannot be sustained as a finance-only work product. It becomes a one-off project conducted once a year driven by finance with a clean year-end Sarbanes opinion as its only goal. The only measure of success is no material weaknesses. There is no exploring opportunities to improve internal controls, improve performance, or improve reporting. Like other similar

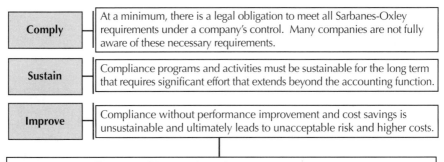

| Comply | At a minimum, there is a legal obligation to meet all Sarbanes-Oxley requirements under a company's control. Many companies are not fully aware of these necessary requirements. |

| Sustain | Compliance programs and activities must be sustainable for the long term that requires significant effort that extends beyond the accounting function. |

| Improve | Compliance without performance improvement and cost savings is unsustainable and ultimately leads to unacceptable risk and higher costs. |

SEC Chairman William Donaldson s Perspective

"Simply complying with the rules is not enough. They should, as I have said before, make this approach part of their companies' **DNA**. For companies that take this approach, most of the major concerns about compliance disappear. Moreover, if companies view the new laws as opportunities—opportunities to improve internal controls, improve the performance of the board, and improve their public reporting—they will ultimately be better run, more transparent, and therefore more attractive to investors."

SEC Chairman William Donaldson
National Press Club
July 30, 2003

EXHIBIT 10.1   Sarbanes–Oxley Point of View

initiatives, it languishes on the laptops in the "Oh, my God, do I really have to do that again?" folder. And what's worse, managers are left with auditor-designed processes laden with all the documentation, sign-offs, approvals, and controls that strangle any attempt to implement lean systems.

However, this can be viewed as an opportunity to reclaim responsibility from the auditor. Yes, reclaim it. Currently, there are no standards for management's assessment of internal control. The only place one can find any direction—but only indirectly—is in the PCAOB's AS2. In that standard, the PCAOB provided direction on what items need to be in place for the auditor to issue a clean opinion on management's assessment and on the internal control procedures in place. The PCAOB thereby indirectly established the management assessment practices needed. A finance executive at another company stated in a moment of shear frustration with this process: "Damn it, this is our company, and these are our processes. We have designed them to be effective, efficient, and provide the necessary control. I'm not going to change them just to satisfy an auditor when I know it's nonsense."

This approach really does not make sense and it has not gone unnoticed. The representatives at each SEC/PCAOB roundtable suggested what is needed in the long term. They suggested that an appropriate panel be formed consisting of representatives from management empowered by the SEC to develop a standard or provide guidance to management on how to conduct a proper assessment of an internal control system. It is the only thing that makes sense. The benefits of such an approach include:

- It moves the responsibility and the authority to where it belongs. If managers create the guidance, other managers more readily accept it, because the assessments are directly and explicitly suited to their overall business needs. When regulators tell the auditors what they need to do and the managers they audit need to have before they can issue a clean opinion, auditors have too much say in how the controls are designed and how the assessment process should be conducted.

  With concepts of control limited to internal accounting control, auditors are hardly in a position to determine what controls are necessary. It is simply more logical to have a standard developed by managers who have the ability to make more of those decisions and have the auditors make determinations of whether management has met the management standard.

- The guidance provides managers with a comprehensive framework to the assessment by focusing on more than just internal accounting controls. Operational and other strategic managerial controls that get little to no consideration from auditors could be incorporated and provide a cost-effective means of designing and assessing the controls.

- Ownership reduces cost. If managers set the standards, design the controls, and determine how the assessments are conducted, less auditor time is needed. They simply review the process and evaluate the controls, not redo or design management's assessment process.

10.4 Q3: ARE THERE COMMON DENOMINATORS BETWEEN SARBANES AND LEAN THAT CAN BE USED AS A SPRINGBOARD FOR THE FUTURE?

Some companies are beginning to see the benefits of integrating Sarbanes and using it to their advantage in reengineering their financial processes. What they found during their initial Sarbanes reviews was how disparate some of their systems have become in especially decentralized environments. Everyone does it differently. Each location offers different prices, terms, and discounts to the same customers; pays employees differently; uses different approaches to acquiring, receiving, and paying suppliers; uses manual processes extensively; and uses multiple data-processing platforms. With these findings, they began standardizing their processes (often by moving transaction processing to shared service centers), they began automating manual processes, and they began eliminating controls that added no value. They used model locations to develop and test a process, and once it was perfected they moved those to other locations. Finally, they incorporated many of those model processes into acquisition integration plans. In short, they found a surprise benefit from Sarbanes. It forced them to review their processes, and that review has identified opportunities for improvements.

(a) Where Do We Begin to Integrate Lean with Sarbanes?

For those who are not familiar with lean, a short description is a good place to start.[10] Essentially, a lean enterprise is one that focuses on value to the customer, creates value streams to support the customer needs, designs its processes to eliminate waste by creating a continuous flow from order to delivery, and zealously seeks perfection through identifying and eliminating waste that impedes the flow. Toyota pioneered lean production approaches and has typically required half the human effort, half the manufacturing space, and a fraction of the product development time than its mass-production counterparts. In short, Toyota's successes—and the successes of other lean manufacturers—come from managing their core processes brilliantly.

In searching for the desired "flawless process," lean manufacturers look to create processes that are capable, available, simple, and understandable— capable in that they are able to perform at the level needed to ensure the results meet the defined objectives; available in that they can be called upon when needed to perform what is needed; simple in that they do not include unnecessarily complicated steps that cause delays (i.e., they can be repeated easily and speedily); and understandable in that they can be explained in laymen's terms and readily grasped by those who need to execute the steps.

In creating and improving their processes, lean manufacturers step through a rigorous approach that includes understanding the existing process flow by creating value stream maps, creating process stability by removing waste and reorganizing the work, simplifying the process through connecting one series of activities to another, and institutionalizing the processes through documenting the standard best-way approach to the work that uses performance measures to signal when to stop and fix problems as they occur. All this occurs within a culture that values the input of the individual, focuses on values that are larger than the company itself, and places company profits and individual compensation as secondary and as the consequence of a executing a near perfect process, flawlessly.

Sarbanes attesters and regulators articulated similar criteria. They counsel management to:

- Document the significant processes and provide examples of major classes of transactions (e.g., revenues, procurement of goods or services, etc.) that should be documented.
- Understand the flow of transactions from when they are initiated to when they are recorded, processed, and reported.
- Identify and document the points within the process that could fail.
- Identify and document controls that address these potential failures.

Comparing the two, Sarbanes and lean actually have a lot in common. They both are process oriented; are concerned with the adequacy of control; are risk management focused; believe the processes need to be documented, evaluated, and improved; stress the importance of culture; and value integrity and respect for people. In short, they both seek a flawless process.

The differences are the lenses through which each is viewed. In Sarbanes (up to now), the accountant's view has prevailed. It's understandable because, from the early definitions through Sarbanes, the public accountants have taken an active role in defining internal accounting control because they had the most at stake. In lean, senior management leads. The definitions, direction, and philosophies are not at all consistent from one firm to another, because the concepts are just beginning to be understood and take root. Unlike COSO, there is no group of organizations that has come together to define lean. All that is available is case study driven, and most of those deal with designing or manufacturing a product. Notwithstanding the dearth of guidance, some have attempted to integrate the major elements of lean with COSO's integrated framework. While this approach is still in its formative stages, here are the steps followed.

(b) Step 1: Integrate the COSO Elements into Lean Categories and Create Process Owners

The first step is to take the elements contained in the COSO framework and regroup them into organizational categories. As shown in Exhibit 10.2, the categories used are procurement, conversion, distribution, and support. They were chosen because they generally follow the flow of product, and some lean organizations, by the way, are using those categories to report unit earnings. Since COSO is process oriented as well, it is easy to fit the COSO elements into each category. This also becomes helpful in identifying the process owners. For example, purchasing managers can easily fit as the procurement process owner, the manufacturing or operation's managers as the conversion process owners, and sales or marketing managers as the distribution owners. The objective is to use the existing organizational structure and fit the elements of COSO under that structure. It visually identifies who is responsible for each COSO element. In this way, as lean Kaizen events are conducted (shown as numbered Kaizen bursts in Exhibit 10.2), these COSO elements are subject to review, evaluation, and improvement during that event. Likewise, the associated COSO risks are also explicitly addressed.

(c) Step 2: Conduct Kaizen Events and Integrate the COSO Elements

Step 2 is done during a Kaizen event. Most events begin by doing a process map to identify the work steps, the flow of the work, and the time taken (cycle time). As shown in Exhibit 10.3, all the work elements appear with a process map and time elements. The map's unique color coding of activities that relate to Sarbanes risks makes those activities visual to the entire team and signals that this activity is the responsibility of the financial expert on the team. The rule is "no change can be made to that particular activity without the approval of the financial expert." Similar to the expert in the "stop-and-fix" lean environments, each team has a financial representative whose role is to be the "custodian" of those activities addressing a Sarbanes risk. To help them show that integration even more clearly, the financial expert prepares and maintains a report like the one depicted in Exhibit 10.4 that contains each risk in the COSO Integrated Framework with cross-references to the work steps contained in Exhibit 10.3. This makes the objective of the step—to address a specific internal

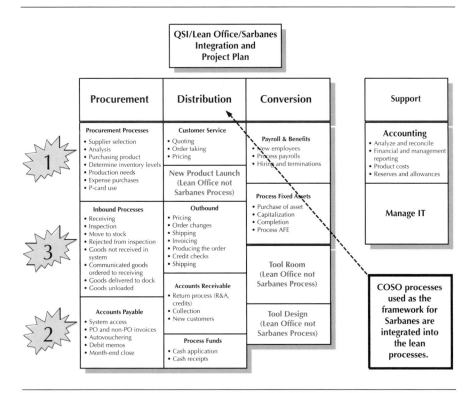

EXHIBIT 10.2   Integrating COSO Elements into Lean Categories

accounting control risk—explicit and visual. Another feature (not shown) is a cross-reference to the testing or monitoring activities performed within the process. In this way, all the Sarbanes requirements (documentation, risk identification, and testing) are a part of each lean event, thereby subjecting it to review and improvement, and that specific improvement is under the guidance of a financial expert.

(d) Step 3: Establish Entity-Level Processes that Make Material Weaknesses Unlikely

The third step in the integration with lean is articulating how a lean environment—with its philosophy, structure, accountability, and monitoring—

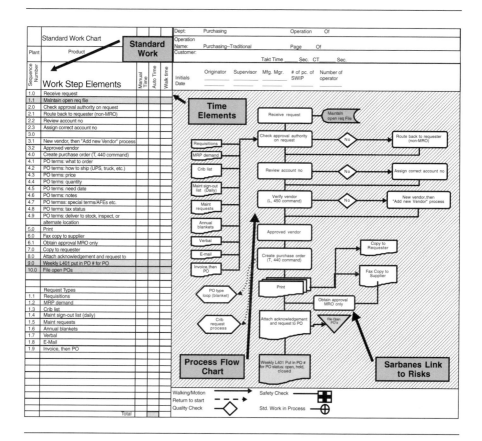

EXHIBIT 10.3 Sarbanes-Coded Process Map

reduces the risk of a material weakness in financial reporting occurring. The arguments that resonate well are:

- *Philosophy.* Perhaps the most important elements of what makes lean work are the core beliefs. COSO spends some time discussing the tone at the top and deploying such practices as audit committees, internal audit groups, codes of ethics, and whistleblower practices. Unfortunately, these are not the differentiators. Enron had all of these and failed. They wrote them, talked about them, but never put them into practice. In other words, they never walked the talk, and everyone in the company knew it. The differentiators between writing them as Enron and others had and "living"

EXHIBIT 10.4 Integrating Sarbanes Risks with Lean

	COSO Risks	COSO	COSO Ref	IAD Ref	Control Activities	Cross-References	Standard Work Reference
1	Out-of-date or incomplete price information —pay appropriate price	O	p. 80	p. 23	Monthly PO audit >$1,000 (PM) >$10,000 (Acctg) Spending controls AP reviews price lists & PO price match User access control Network Procurement Phases 1 and 2	Std Work Mtls Mgr (>$1,000) and Acctg (>$10,000) Std Work All Managers Std Work Acctg Std Work IT; Acctg Std Work Mtls Manager	Step 1.1 Step 1.1 Step 1.2 Step 1.2 Step 1.1 Step 1.3 step 1.3
2	Purchase orders may be lost —record authorized POs completely and accurately	OF	p. 82	p. 24	AP & Receiving compare against PO file	Std Work Acctg and Receiving Std work	step 1.4 step 1.1
3	Inadequate policies and procedures to prevent unauthorized use	OF	p. 82	p. 24	Yearly review of user access Access limited to authorized personnel P Card issuance is approved by dept. manager/controller P Card use is controlled by corporate policy	Std Work Team (IT and Acctg) Std Work IT Std Work Acctg Std Work Acctg	Step 1.1 Step 1.3 Step 1.2 Step 1.5 Step 1.5
4	Inadequate vendor screening, including periodic requalification of existing vendors —identify and purchase from vendors capable of meeting the entity s needs	O	p. 78	p. 21	Network Procurement Phases 1 and 2 Supplier performance report reviewed quarterly	Std Work Mtls Mgr for all items in this category	Step 1.3 Step 1.4

#	Risk				Control	Std Work Owner	Step
					New inventory suppliers complete self-evaluation form		Step 1.5
					Majority of production suppliers are third-party certified		Step 1.6
5	Unavailable or inaccurate info on inventory levels or production needs—order appropriate quantity at appropriate time	O	p. 81	p. 23	DSI	Std Work and Performance Measure Mtl Mgr	Step 1.7
					Kanbans	Std Work Mtls Mgr to oversee and develop Kanban Stds.	Step 1.8
					OTD for supplier	Others implement performance measure that is tracked by purchasing	Step 1.9
					MRP report	Std Work Mtls Mgr	Step 10.0
6	Purchase orders are not entered into the system on a timely basis	O	p. 81	p. 24	PO requisitions in queue—visual perf measures standard work	Standard Work Purchasing	Step 1.1
7	Unavailable or inaccurate info on items ordered but not received	O	p. 81	p. 24	Past-due report reviewed weekly for production items	Std Work Mtls Manager	Step 1.11
					Daily task includes maintaining open POs	Std Work Purchasing	Steps 9 and 10

Other Risks Not Included

Unavailable or inaccurate information about fraudulent acts or other improper activities or vendors	p. 79
Poor communication of operations' or other activities' needs	p. 79
Inappropriate production specifications	p. 79

253

them seems to be more about what lean authors spend considerable time discussing and what Jim Collins's *Good to Great*[11] seems to possess: They have and deploy core philosophies that are timeless and principles based, not just short-term, rules-based mandates as Enron. They build companies that have a sense of purpose beyond the quarter and annual financial results. In fact, they believe that when you put the customer first, take care of your people, and have great processes, the financial results will take care of themselves. They are not slavishly wedded to "making the quarter or the year" as Enron leaders were. In short, they *live* the principles of fairness, integrity, and ethics, not just write them.

- *Small units.* Create small organizational units. Small units motivate people, not only because they are more exciting places to work, but when they are small, financial errors become obvious. Consider the size of a typical value stream that some experts suggest be limited to 25 to 125 people. When financial results are reported and frequently monitored for units of that size, even small reporting errors are more likely to be noticed and acted on. It is no different than highly decentralized environments. Where operating divisions are all less than 5 percent of sales, the likelihood of undetected material errors, whether they are intentional or unintentional, becomes less as the units become smaller.

- *Accountability.* Provide people only what they need to control their immediate work processes. Separate the categories of assets, liabilities, and related operating results to that which they need to and can control. For example, what employees need are the resources necessary to service the customer. That includes designing product, taking orders, procuring materials, producing the product, and finally shipping and billing the product. From a financial statement standpoint, that means they need billing and receivables, purchasing and payables, fixed assets, and payrolls. From a systems standpoint, they need simple approaches that are governed by standard work and the appropriate information technology (IT) support systems. All the other accounting and administrative stuff is *muda* that creates complexity, which unnecessarily increases risk. Move all the other stuff into shared service centers that specialize in particular areas. For example, move external reporting, treasury, and tax matters to a corporate center where you can have specialists focus on those disciplines.

- *Monitor.* Review the financial and nonfinancial results weekly, monthly, quarterly, and annually. The hallmark of a lean environment is that the work is monitored continuously and immediate action is taken when a problem is noted. This is no different. Develop key performance indicators (KPIs) that are aligned down through each organization level. This requires a thoughtful process of determining organizational objectives, translating those into both financial and nonfinancial KPIs, and developing a reporting system to monitor results. It does not have to be a formal reporting system on enterprise resource planning (ERP) systems with colorful charts and graphs. Instead, keep it simple. Put the data on whiteboards or on graph paper pinned to a corkboard. Just make it visual, and use it to meet and review with others. The purpose is to use the data to take appropriate action to correct the process, not punish the person. To paraphrase W. Edwards Deming: All failures are with the process, not the people. Punishing people for process failures leads to the Enron mess—people manipulating the information to meet the goal. The lean answer is to determine the underlying cause and improve the process.

(e) Step 4: Develop a Monitoring Process that Forgoes the Need to Test Transactions

This is perhaps the most controversial area of all. There is some overlap with the monitoring discussed in step 3, but step 4 works to remove the requirement for management testing and replace it with a rigorous entity-level monitoring process. The first three steps should not be contentious since they merely overlay much of what is required into a lean environment. This step, however, is one that looks at the very essence of a requirement—that management must test the processes to reach its conclusion about the effectiveness of its internal accounting control procedures—and disputes the need to do so.

To reiterate, the concept of management testing was introduced indirectly in AS2; in paragraph 42 it states that: "When determining whether management's documentation provides reasonable support for its assessment, the auditor should evaluate whether such documentation includes the . . . results of management's testing and evaluation."[12] From that directive, the accounting firms established the minimum testing requirements for each process (e.g., purchasing, payrolls, sales, and receivables) and used the number of times a control operated as a criterion. So if the control operated daily, a certain number of transactions would need to be examined.

Similar requirements existed when the control operated weekly, monthly, quarterly, or annually. Likewise, they set additional criteria for exceptions found in the testing. For example, if testing revealed an error, the procedure needed to be remediated, regardless of significance, in sufficient time before year-end so that a minimum number of repetitions could be observed. Otherwise, it was still considered a weakness. The auditors considered all these matters (sample sizes, remediation, and retesting) in making their determinations about whether management's process was adequate. For many who went through this exercise, the "Chinese fire drill" metaphor is an understatement. While it will probably take years to unravel these requirements, managers need to look back to the well-established management practices of monitoring and ask themselves, "Why aren't they sufficient to form an opinion on whether our processes are working?"

Other questions naturally arise when an organization begins to look at this issue. Why do we have managers in the first place? Aren't they needed to orchestrate the planning, organizing, and *controlling* as Peter Drucker described, or the planning, doing, *checking*, and acting that Deming outlined? Can organizations abandon the current responsibilities that managers fulfill? Are these managerial tasks and responsibilities that thousands of managers have been trained to perform actually useless? Or were the failures at Enron, WorldCom, Tyco, Adelphia, and the like due to a few bad managers?

So, rather than throw out the baby with the bath water, this lean practitioner favors returning to those age-old management tasks and responsibilities, reinforcing them, enhancing them for the approaches that lean manufacturers have deployed, and using them as the basis for determining the adequacy of the processes.

(f) What Are the Approaches at the Process Level?

Simply put, they are no different than the monitoring process described in step 4. In developing KPIs, focus on what can go wrong with the process and what performance measures would signal the system is not working as planned. As on the manufacturing floor, where the day-by-hour KPI signals a disruption in production flow and first time through a failure in standard work, similar measures can be used for administrative processes. In simple list form, a few examples include:

- For the procurement to supplier payment process, the number of suppliers, purchase orders, receiving reports, invoices, and people; cycle times and throughput times for processing each; supplier ratings; the number, amount, and aging of debit memos, unpaid balances, and reconciling items; and the number of and amount of exceptions in matching receiving reports to purchase orders and/or to invoices. A useful operating measure is average days' payables outstanding.

- For the revenue to collection process, the number of customers, invoices, shippers, and people; cycle times and throughput measures for processing orders and invoices; customer service statistics for on-time delivery; the number, amount, and aging of credit memos and unpaid balances in receivables. A useful operating measure is days' sales outstanding.
- For the production process, the amount of inventory aged to show excess, obsolete for each category (raw, work in process, and finished goods). A useful operating measure is inventory turnover.
- For the accounting process, the time to close and the numbers and amounts of manual adjusting journal entries and reconciling items.

This list is by no means exhaustive, but it illustrates the types of measures developed at the process level. In effective lean environments, the associates display the KPIs in their respective areas, review them with their managers each day, and make them the subject of the weekly and monthly continuous improvement meetings. Most are time phased with notations of when an improvement initiative was implemented.

(g) What Are the Processes at the Entity Level?

Looking at it from the top of the organization, there are many items that are necessary under Sarbanes that are equally necessary in lean. Audit committees, codes of ethics, fraud prevention strategies, internal audit departments, and disclosure committees all exist in a lean environment as well. Additional items directed at the entity level that eliminate the need for management detail testing the process include:

- Staffing each location with competent, experienced financial and operational people.
- Creating and distributing accounting policies that provide the necessary direction to the units in accounting for and reporting of assets, related reserves, and liabilities for which the unit is accountable.
- Using annual operational plans with interim updates. Items forecasted include revenues, earnings, assets and liabilities, and KPIs for the corporate initiatives along with other operating measures.

- Using monthly reviews with rolling forecasts to review the unit's actual forecast and provide explanations for variances in actual-to-actual, actual-to-rolling forecast, and actual-to-original plan. Monthly and/or conference calls are used for outlying locations.
- Using a quarterly certification and control questionnaire to review and communicate the progress on lean initiatives and to reaffirm that specific control practices are being followed at the units.
- Peer group reviews (e.g., a staff from another operating unit) in which operating results, progress on lean initiatives, and control practices are reviewed and commented upon by that group.

10.5 EXAMPLES OF INTEGRATING LEAN WITH SARBANES

In each of the examples that follow, there were no material weaknesses or even significant weaknesses in internal accounting control noted. However, a number of operational improvements were identified that have simplified the processes at each location. Publishing these findings internally resulted in a number of changes to other locations' practices as well.

(a) Procurement Reengineering Initiative that Needed a Boost

The first example was the procurement area included in the exhibits shown above. The improvements identified and implemented included a more extensive use of procurement cards (P-cards) and of the evaluated receipts settlement (ERS) process in settling vendor payables and revising the procedures for supplier invoice retention.

Several years ago, this Fortune 100 company went through a substantial financial reengineering initiative in which both P-cards and ERS were introduced. After monitoring divisions' implementations for nearly a year, the reengineering team was disbanded and went on to other areas. Implementations and monitoring were left to the units. As a result, when the process was reviewed in connection with Sarbanes/lean integration in mind, little was done to modify, extend, or improve these previous initiatives. One of the team's first efforts was a Pareto analysis of how many and in what amounts invoices were still being received and processed by the unit. The team next grouped and redefined which additional items could be subject to the P-card and what additional suppliers could be included in the ERS process. Overall, 50 percent of the invoices were no longer necessary, significantly reducing the accounts payable time previously required to complete the three-way match (comparing invoices to receiving reports and purchase orders).

The final area was invoice filing, where the team found that the accounts payable clerks were sorting and alphabetically filing supplier invoices, which took nearly two hours per day. This was part of the process, even though the batch number of the payment was contained in the electronic data file. When asking "why," it became apparent there was no need to alphabetically file, so they immediately moved this process to a batch file.

(b) Payroll Processing that Simply Took Too Long

The second example relates to payroll payments and processing time in same Fortune 100 company with the same reengineering circumstance. In this example, two opportunities became immediately apparent to the team. Both were identified when the value stream map and the cycle-time metrics were prepared for each of the three plants being studied. The team discovered that the hourly payrolls were still being paid weekly, even though the remainder of domestic U.S. hourly payrolls was paid biweekly. The second discovery was that the processing at one plant took eight times longer than the best plant, while the second took four times longer than the best. The team found that the computer program application was different for each of the three plants, and although a request had been submitted some time ago, it still had not been acted on due to limited resources and presumably "higher" priorities. Once the amount of time taken to process these payrolls was made visible to senior location personnel, the changes (moving to biweekly payrolls and the changes to the software) were made almost immediately.

(c) Three Initiatives that Desperately Needed Each Other

The third and final example is from yet another business unit of the same Fortune 100 company—this one with a slightly different twist. The unit needed to comply with ISO 9000 and had implemented a rather sophisticated tracking tool to review, document, monitor, and provide version control over their processes so they could report that they were ISO 9000 compliant and to retrieve the process documentation for any given year. This retrieval capability is essential, especially for prior-year quality claims.

Along came Sarbanes, and this unit used yet another database prescribed by the corporate headquarters to review, document, and evaluate their processes for compliance—same processes, but with a slightly different twist. For example, they had to use bullet-point outlines to document the processes. The ISO 9000 database used flowcharts extensively. It had some other differences, such as outlining key controls, incorporating COSO risks, and testing, each of which could have been easily incorporated into the ISO 9000 database.

It became readily apparent to the team and, quite frankly, to all the units that were ISO certified (nearly 90 percent) that there was considerable redundancy in evaluating the same process several times depending on who was imposing the requirement. Like many others, this company has lean or other reengineering or continuous improvement initiatives, ISO, and, depending on the industry, many other regulatory or customer requirements to review, document, and disclose their processes. Why not use the one-to-many rather than the many-to-one approach? Take one process, one process owner, and one team within the process and incorporate all the requirements into one review. Establish the necessary frequency of review, the timing of changes needed, and be done with it. It certainly makes more sense than reviewing the process many times—one for each requirement—so that is what they began doing.

These three examples illustrate that managers do not ordinarily schedule time to review processes for continuous improvement. Many mass producers would never do it at all if it weren't required. ISO certification began that process. Sarbanes also requires it. Lean manufacturers do it naturally. But, oddly enough, many companies moving to lean struggle with these reviews. While they want it done and require it, it seldom is. Many outlying units game the system and do only what is inspected, not what is expected. And perhaps that is where Sarbanes can provide some leverage. If a company must do it for that purpose, why not do it the right way and make it comprehensive? Include all the requirements (lean, ISO, Sarbanes, etc.) in one review and set the objective of the search for the "perfect process" as the goal.

10.6 WHAT'S NEEDED TO INTEGRATE LEAN WITH SARBANES

Overall, the practices described in this chapter (philosophy, structure, accountability, and monitoring) are not any different than those espoused over the years by Henry Ford, Alfred Sloan, Peter Drucker, W. Edwards Deming, and others. The practice of management is not new. Entrepreneurs, visionaries, and experts have been inventing and refining these practices over the past century. The problem has been the wandering few, who interpreted everything at face value, structuring transactions and interpreting reporting criteria according to the letter of the law, not the spirit. They caused us to lose sight of the truly important matters in operating our companies.

So, what is needed is basically a return to what lean manufacturers know works. What is needed is active participation—not cheerleading from the sidelines. Managers cannot simply play the role of Enron's Ken Lay and disclaim all knowledge of what the others are doing. They really need to be more like Wiremold's Art Byrne and get involved. Beyond that, managers need to:

- *Understand* the internal control program and the financial reporting process.
- *Map* the systems that support internal control and the financial reporting process.
- *Identify* risks related to the systems.
- *Design and implement* controls designed to mitigate the identified risks.
- *Document* controls.
- Ensure that controls are *updated and changed*, as necessary, to correspond with the processes currently in effect.
- *Develop KPIs and monitor* controls for effective operation over time.

The choices are simple. Either you accept the challenge to incorporate Sarbanes into your lean initiative or you do not. If you choose to integrate, each process can be reviewed once and contain the requirements of each. If you choose not to integrate, processes will need to be examined as many times as there are initiatives. The many-to-one approach is simply not an efficient way of approaching process reviews. Each initiative then requires a separate review, with the scope of each designed to meet separate objectives. This is hardly a way of incorporating any initiative into an organization's DNA. Alternatively, in the one-to-many approach, each process review would be designed to contain all the requirements of each initiative (lean, Sarbanes, total quality management) and designed to meet all the objectives. This is clearly a more effective way of addressing any process requirements and easily sustained by becoming part of the organization's DNA. It is your choice.

NOTES

1 In the United States, the Committee of Sponsoring Organizations (COSO) of the Treadway Commission published *Internal Control-Integrated Framework*. Known as the COSO report, it provides a suitable and available framework for purposes of management's assessment in connection with determining compliance and reporting under the Sarbanes-Oxley Act of 2002. The COSO framework identifies three primary objectives of internal control: efficiency and effectiveness of operations, financial reporting, and compliance with laws and regulations. The COSO perspective on internal control over financial reporting does not ordinarily include the other two objectives of internal control, which are the effectiveness and efficiency of operations and compliance with laws and regulations.

2. PCAOB Release No. 2004-001 March 9, 2004, "An Audit of Internal Control over Financial Reporting Performed in Conjunction with an Audit of Financial Statements," Auditing Standard No. 2, pp, 1–2.

3. Much of this section is taken from Chapter 3 of Steven J. Root's *Beyond COSO: Internal Control to Enhance Corporate Governance* (Hoboken, N.J.: John Wiley & Sons, 1998).

4. See note 3, p. 54.

5. www.navanet.org/res/outlook/novdec02Out/ConnerArticle_novdec02.pdf. Frederick R. Bellamy and W. Thomas Conner, "Sarbanes-Oxley Act of 2002: The Perfect Storm," NAVA OUTLOOK, November/December 2002, Vol. 11, No. 6 p. 1–2.

6. SEC reference www.connectlive.com/events/secicrp/. Panelists included top executives or board members from the NYSE, NASDAQ, CalPERS, GAO, the Big-4 accounting firms, and some of the biggest names in corporate America, including General Electric, Microsoft, Dow Chemical, Lockheed Martin, Eli Lilly, and Aetna.

7. Ron Kral, "Star Panel Re-evaluates Sarbanes-Oxley One Year in at SEC Headquarters," *Wisconsin Technology Network*, April 13, 2005.

8. SEC reference www.sec.gov/news/press/2005-74.htm. Commission Statement on Implementation of Internal Control Reporting Requirements RELEASE 2005-74.

9. SEC reference www.sec.gov/news/speech/spch061505cag.htm. Speech by SEC Commissioner Cynthia A. Glassman, "SEC in Transition: What We've Done and What's Ahead," Washington, D.C., June 15, 2005.

10. For more complete definitions of lean, refer to the Lean Enterprise Institute's *Lean Lexicon: A Graphical Glossary for Lean Thinkers*, version 1.0, January 2003. Also refer to Jim Womack's publications, including a speech given in Monterrey, Mexico, May 8, 2003, entitled "In Search of the Perfect Process," www.lean.org/Community/Resources/Presentations/NewMonterreyMexico.pdf; and to Jeff Liker and David Meier's *The Toyota Way Fieldbook* (New York: McGraw Hill, 2006).

11. Jim Collins, *Good to Great: Why Some Companies Make the Leap . . . and Others Don't* (New York: HarperCollins, 2001).

12. See note 2.

11

THE NEED FOR A SYSTEMS APPROACH TO ENHANCE AND SUSTAIN LEAN

DAVID S. COCHRAN, PHD

11.1 INTRODUCTION TO COLLECTIVE SYSTEM DESIGN

Systems evolve to achieve objectives that people consider to be important to enhance the performance of their social organizations. For many organizations, changes that people consider important can harm the organization in the long term. Many businesspeople are now painfully aware that existing practices for controlling costs and procedures for measuring and evaluating enterprise profitability are distorted and counterproductive to the long-term health of an enterprise. Collective system design™ (CSD) is an approach to understanding the ramifications of these dysfunctional choices, practices, and procedures. It is a process that seeks to clarify purpose and meaning in business systems today. It provides both a philosophy and a toolset for collective agreement about where organizations should focus during a lean transformation (i.e., for defining purpose), and it provides a common-sense toolset for designing any organization's enterprise manufacturing systems to assure long-term sustainability.

Regardless of product, customers of manufactured goods have similar needs throughout the world. They want rapid, on-time delivery; high quality; low cost; a variety of different products; and innovative fresh design. For this reason, Toyota's system design for delivering high-quality products rapidly and on time to customers has been applicable to many different manufacturing industries in many different countries. Any manufacturing system requires decisions about how to allocate resources (e.g., equipment, people, time). An effective system design defines how to achieve any manufacturing system's purpose with the least resources.

CSD is a methodology that defines how an organization achieves its purpose by characterizing the *functional requirements* of the organization's manufacturing system and the *physical solutions* that are required to achieve that purpose. Primary performance measures reinforce the achievement of purpose (functional requirements), and secondary performance measures reinforce the organization of work (physical solutions) to achieve purpose. The performance measures and managerial accounting structure come *after* a team creates the thinking layer of a CSD, which defines how the physical solutions achieve the functional requirements for any system. When the functional requirements and physical solutions change, enterprise leadership can readily change the performance measures and supporting managerial accounting structures to become consistent with the newly changed enterprise functional requirements and physical solutions (see Exhibit 11.1).

Most implementations of the Toyota Production System (TPS) and *lean*, the term commonly used to describe the result of implementing TPS, are not sustained even as long as one year. The purpose of the CSD process is to provide an enhancement to lean transformations so that implementations become sustainable. The CSD process creates a growth-oriented and learning environment within an enterprise by first emphasizing collective agreement about enterprise

- Measures (M) are chosen after the functional requirement (FR) and physical solution (PS) relationships are designed/defined.

- The cost challenge is to choose physical solutions that achieve the functional requirements for the least cost.

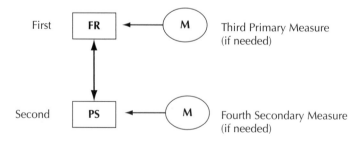

EXHIBIT 11.1   Collective System Design Language

purpose. The purpose of the enterprise is then stated in terms of functional requirements. CSD is the practice of defining purpose and the physical solutions to achieve and to sustain enterprise purpose.

One cautionary note: As with all accounting tools, lean system tools can be applied without sufficient rigor engendering the risk of implementation without adequate consideration of the objectives or functional requirements that the system tools are designed to achieve. The objective of this chapter is to provide an approach to ensure that accounting for lean is applied from a systems perspective.

11.2 ACCOUNTING FOR LEAN COMMUNICATIONS

This chapter discusses the principles and practice for designing, communicating, and sustaining manufacturing systems that meet customer needs. The design of sustainable manufacturing systems must include coordinated thinking, decisions, and actions by the people within that system. The CSD focus invites people to look at and discuss the enterprise differently—in terms of interdependent human and structural relationships that are ultimately designed to meet and fluidly adapt to changing customer needs.

CSD provides a powerful tool for conducting discussions about lean accounting. The methodology requires the logical separation of an organization's objectives (functional requirements) from the means to achieve those objectives (physical solutions) with a language that makes sense to both accountants and nonaccountants. A key purpose of this separation is to focus attention on the difference between an organization's goals and the physical solutions it must cultivate to achieve those goals. Being clear about this difference helps organizations avoid the *common mistake* of believing that if people focus intently enough on goals, they will achieve their desired outcomes regardless of how the organization conducts its operations.

Objectives and means thinking, analogous to what H. Thomas Johnson refers to as management by means (MBM),[1] distinguishes *what* a system must do (i.e., its functional requirements) from *how* it does it (i.e., its physical solutions). CSD uses a language for system design that distinguishes functional requirements from *physical solutions* through collective agreement and understanding. In many lean programs the tools—the physical solutions—become the objective or the "functional requirements" of the new system. Consequently, implementation of the lean *tool* replaces designing a *system* that reliably meets customer needs and that can effectively adapt to changing customer needs. In contrast, CSD uses a language for system design that treats physical solutions as a hypothesis for the functional requirements the enterprise will need to meet customer needs. Then the practice of dialogue enables the group to hold the physical solutions as hypotheses rather than as necessities.

A guiding principal of CSD is that long-term business success and profitability requires effectively meeting customer needs. When the people within an organizational system are not on the same page and do not have shared knowledge and understanding about internal and external customer needs (functional requirements) and how the corresponding business structures (physical solutions) meet the needs, those systems eventually fail without the guidance of a language to communicate the system design that is grounded by lean principles. CSD provides a road map for long-term business viability that focuses on and helps communicate the design of the human relationships and business processes to meet customer needs. The road map prevents what W. Edwards Deming characterized as "chasing variability."[2] The CSD process provides a language for system design that distinguishes the functional requirements of customer needs from the physical solutions necessary to achieve the customer needs that can be understood by accountants and nonaccountants. CSD quantifies the effectiveness of a system design by separating the *objectives* (functional requirements) from the *means* (physical solutions) of a system. If a system design is able to meet the functional requirements of that system for the least cost, it is said to arrive at a state of "lean" according to the CSD process. Therefore, lean is not simply a bag of tools or learned through a series of courses. Lean returns to its original description as the result of the application of the principles embedded in the Toyota Production System,[3] which CSD posits as the reference system design model. Thus, lean is a noun, not a verb. Lean is not what organizations need to do. Lean is what organizations should become through effectively designing, implementing, and sustaining their own system design.

11.3 THE JOURNEY TO ACCOUNTING FOR LEAN

In Henry Ford's Highland Park factory circa 1910, ninety-nine percent of the vehicles were presold and paid for. Ford took payment in advance of the manufacture of the vehicle. In the plant, there was no management accounting control system. Management accounting was not needed to run the facility. Only the "shortage chaser" was needed. The goal of the shortage chaser was to ensure that there were enough of the right parts on hand at the right time to ensure that final assembly made the customer-consumed quantity and variety of each vehicle. The original 1913 book by Arnold and Faurote provides an interesting description of the shortage chaser, styled as "a brisk young man, whose brow is etched from fine lines of concentration, boards the department drifting within sound of breakers, seizes the helm of component production, and pilots the department into smooth water again—sometimes but barely escaping the surf-line, it is true, but always managing to escape disaster."[4]

The functional requirements (manufacturing goals) of Ford's plant were to produce the customer-consumed quantity and variety on time. Toyota would later call the achievement of these functional requirements JIT or just-in-time.[5] Henry Ford's method of "JIT" was to ensure a minimum–maximum stock level ahead of assembly using the shortage chaser (Ford's physical solution). Toyota studied and then refined Ford's method by inventing a new physical solution called the kanban card.

Henry Ford identified the Toyota Manufacturing functional requirements that would be implicitly stated by Toyota nearly 50 years later. Toyota's contribution was to innovate and to improve the physical solution. Toyota accepted Ford's functional requirements, even though they were never explicitly stated by Ford. The benefit of the CSD process language is that it names and clarifies functional requirements and physical solutions for enterprise employees. The identification of functional requirements and physical solutions also provides a framework and guideline for improvement.

Since Henry Ford did not explicitly state the functional requirements of his operations, he left his company at risk of confusion of goals. Any system that does not clearly articulate its functional requirements is particularly susceptible to problems. For example, in the 1950s, the "Whiz Kids" at Ford Motor Company changed the functional requirements of manufacturing. They defined the company's operational goals in terms of management accounting goals. They could make waste *appear to be* an asset, as was the case with unnecessary inventory and storage, long production runs of the same part type not in demand by a customer, and deferred maintenance.

Several changes had to take place to implement the changes brought about by the Whiz Kids:

1. Members of the organization had to accept functional requirements that result from an imposed use of an abstract equation to define cost.

2. People had to accept the belief that accounting targets can in fact be used to control operations.

3. People also had to accept the idea that minimizing the unit cost of parts of the enterprise minimizes the whole cost.

4. Finally, everyone in the organization had to believe that minimizing the unit cost at one operation does not adversely affect other operations.

The management cost equation that is referred to in Equation 1 defines minimum total manufacturing cost as the sum of the minimum unit cost ($/unit) at each operation "i," where the minimum total cost is given by:

$$\text{Minimum Total Cost} = \Sigma\{\min[\text{Unit Cost}(op_i)]\} \text{ for } i = 1 \text{ to } n \text{ operations}$$

$$\text{Unit Cost}(op_i) = \frac{\text{Labor Hours}(op_i) \times \text{Wage Rate} + \text{Material\$}(op_i) + \text{Overhead\$}(op_i)}{N}$$

and,   (Eq. 1)

$$\text{Overhead\$}(op_i) = \frac{\text{Labor Hours}(op_i)}{\text{Labor Hours(total)} \times \text{Total Overhead\$}}$$

For managers asked to run operations according to the terms of this equation, the goal is to minimize the unit cost ($/unit) of each operation as if each operation is an isolated stand-alone entity whose inputs and outputs *do not affect and are not affected by* other operations.

When the Whiz Kids at Ford Motor Company began using this equation to define the goals of plant operations, they implicitly changed the organization's primary goal from meeting customer needs to minimizing each operation's cost as defined by this limited and shortsighted equation. Thus, by seeing the company's operations through the lens of this equation, they viewed sales volume as a given and an *input parameter* (N). In reality, however, N is a reflection of how well customer needs are met in terms of the design, quality, reliability, variety and availability of options, delivery speed, cost, service, and support of a product offered in the marketplace. The CSD methodology uses the language of system design to identify the functional requirements and physical solutions that are necessary to effectively meet these and other customer needs; whereas the preceding management accounting equation (Eq. 1) leads an organization to agree on quite different functional requirements and physical solutions that are not healthy in the long run.

The unhealthy functional requirements (FR) and physical solutions (PS) derived from using this traditional unit cost equation (Eq. 1) are:

FR1: Increase speed (N) of operation i   *PS1: High-speed machines*

FR2: Decrease direct labor content   *PS2: Automate the operation*

FR3: Decrease direct labor wage rate   *PS3: Low-wage environment*

One consequence of using the unit cost management accounting equation to make manufacturing system design decisions is to purchase for each department high-speed, automated machines and preferably operate them in low-wage countries. In contrast, CSD defines the functional requirements necessary to create stable flow and output to the customer operation in accordance with actual demand. Functional requirements could also address robustness to variation, long-run sustainability, self-diagnosis and correction of problems, quality, safety, and environmental needs of the manufacturing workplace. Such functional requirements lead the organization's members to focus on a quite different set of physical solutions than those listed. As the "C" in CSD indicates, *collective* agreement among members leads to the desired functional requirements and physical solutions of the manufacturing system.

In *Relevance Lost*, H. Thomas Johnson and Robert S. Kaplan identified the allocation of overhead as a major concern with this type of unit cost equation; they proposed activity-based costing (ABC) as the solution to this problem.[6] Johnson's 1992 book, *Relevance Regained*, refuted the idea of using ABC to control operations costs, as Johnson came to realize that the work itself creates the cost and that an improved overhead allocation schema does not, in itself, improve the work within a system.[7] In 2001, Johnson took his insights one step further in *Profit Beyond Measure* by arguing that numbers and accounting information cannot be used to control operations. The work by the people within a system affects the outcomes of the system, and a system is much greater than the sum of its parts.[8]

CSD places a different role on the use of numerical measures, as shown in the FR-PS relationships defined in Exhibit 11.1. Numerical measures come after defining the functional requirement–physical solution relationships. A performance measure (M) is used to determine how well a functional requirement is achieved by the physical solution selected to achieve it. The measure connected with a functional requirement is not a numerical target. The functional requirement defines what the manufacturing system must do to meet customer needs. It does not identify what the organization must do with an artificially defined numerical target like "reduce inventory by 30 percent." For example, a functional requirement could state, "Produce the Customer-Consumed Quantity." A measure for this particular functional requirement could be "Percentage of Parts to Takt Time." If the answer is not 100 percent, the upstream process has trouble replenishing material at the pace consumed by the downstream process. This measure can be stated as a "yes" or "no" answer. If the answer is "no," an alarm typically sounds in the plant and music plays to alert the appropriate team leader that production is not occurring at the right pace. The identification of the problem condition that production is not taking place at takt time sets in motion a predefined standardized problem-solving process that ensures that the root cause is identified and long-term corrective action is implemented.

Excessive cost in the context of CSD is seen as the result of not achieving the functional requirements of the system. Managers seek to resolve problems and conflicts to ensure that the functional requirements are met. To resolve a problem condition indicated by a measure like "Percentage of Parts to Takt Time" requires understanding the process (i.e., the work and the people who do it). Managers' roles change from command-and-control concerns to understanding why problems occur and why the outcome associated with the achievement of each functional requirement is and is not being created. Therefore, *cost is understood to be the result of not achieving the functional requirements of the manufacturing system design.*

From the system-design perspective, it is more appropriate to use the phrase "Accounting for Lean" or "Accounting for the System Design," rather than "Lean Accounting." System design defines the purpose (functional requirements) for any manufacturing system and the physical means (physical solutions) to achieve that purpose. Management accountability should occur *after* the system design functional requirements and physical solutions are defined. When a system design changes, leaders and managers must change the management measurements to be aligned and congruent with the new FR-PS relationships. The phrase "Accounting for Lean" or "Accounting for the System Design" has at least a fighting chance of conveying this precedence of measures coming after the selection of the FR-PS relationships. By contrast, "Lean Accounting" appears to convey the use of a tool, one that may or may not be aligned with the required purpose (functional requirements) and the practice (physical solutions) of a system designed to achieve enterprise purpose.

11.4 OBSTACLES TO SUSTAINABLE LEAN

This section examines five obstacles that prevent sustainable lean initiatives with a discussion of the ways that the CSD process resolves each of these obstacles:

1. Unconsciously using a management costing approach that emphasizes vertical improvement rather than horizontal improvement.
2. Unconsciously establishing performance targets instead of defining the system design to achieve enterprise purpose.
3. Not knowing how to define purpose and the physical solutions to achieve it because of an ambiguous organizational understanding of lean.
4. Unconsciously using an approach to "cost reduction" at the expense of long-term real cost reduction: cutting "costs" (the cart) before implementing a stable system design (the horse).
5. Managers within enterprises not being an integral part of the system design.

A CSD that defines the functional requirements, the physical solutions, and the corresponding measures enables both cost reduction and the achievement of enterprise purpose.

(a) Sustainable Lean Obstacle 1

Unconsciously using a management costing approach that emphasizes vertical improvement rather than horizontal improvement.

A unique feature of TPS is the approach it takes to reduce cost. Management accounting assumes that the way to reduce cost is to minimize cost in each and every individual operation (called *vertical improvement*). TPS, by contrast, focuses on improving the entire work system, or "value stream," used to meet customer needs (called *horizontal improvement*). Shigeo Shingo emphasized the horizontal improvement of the entire system used to meet customer needs instead of the vertical improvement of individual operations.[9] The management accounting focus on vertical improvement of operations affects the thinking of managers. The false premise that vertical cost reduction results in total system (i.e., horizontal) cost reduction is the main reason why smart managers, who are thoughtful and work hard at what they do, are misled into making wrong decisions. Vertical improvement creates "islands of automation" within factories that improve the operation and not the flow. To demonstrate this, Exhibit 11.2 provides a process map of product flow at a production facility that is in operation today.

The decision to purchase an automated storage and retrieval systems (AS/RS) is an example of automating ("improving") the storage operation, which Shingo called the "mechanization (automation) of waste."[10] Likewise, the decision to buy automated guided vehicles (AGVs) is an example of automating the waste of transportation within the factory. The decisions to automate waste occur unconsciously and as a matter of business practice when managers make investment decisions using the unit cost equation (Equation 1). This equation focuses on optimizing individual operations instead of systems. The danger in this approach is to keep and automate operations that are unnecessary in the first place. Notice in the lower half of Exhibit 11.2 that the automated operations became unnecessary once the system design approach was taken.

CSD looks at systems from four aspects: the tone, the thinking, the business structure, and the work (Exhibit 11.3). The thinking layer of CSD is used to diagnose and to understand the false premise of vertical improvement to reduce cost. CSD uses a Diagnosis to Design™ process. Diagnosis is used to understand the existing process. Diagnosis goes into the flame to understand the root cause thinking and tone. CSD moves out of the center of the flame starting with the tone.[11] The thinking layer of CSD is also used to define the design selection of horizontal (system) improvements to reduce total cost.

The underlying tone that led to the false notion of vertical improvement (the thinking) is a belief that one part of a system can win at the detriment of other parts in a system. Thinking follows from tone. This tone is false because it manifests the assumption that *I can win, even though you lose.* The tone and the thinking within an enterprise can be implicit and unstated. The actions and activities that result from the people within an organization not consciously acknowledging the existing tone and thinking is one reason why lean operations are so difficult to sustain. We see a system's activities, action, and value stream, what we don't see is the tone and thinking that is present within an organization. TPS is based on the tone that "problems are an opportunity." Often, "lean practices and tools" are applied to an organization having the tone that problems lead to blaming (and perhaps firing) the guilty. A lean implementation cannot be sustained when people know they will be blamed for identifying problems and waste.

Thinking follows tone, and structure follows thinking. The structure of full-absorption costing leads managers to make wrong decisions and assertions

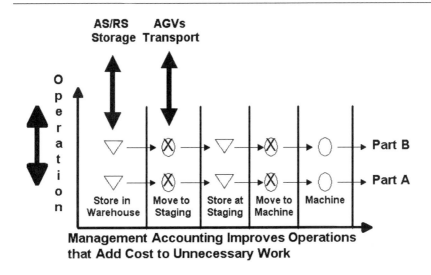

Management Accounting Improves Operations that Add Cost to Unnecessary Work

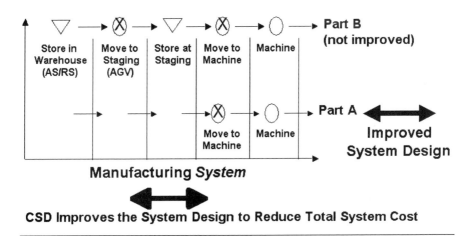

CSD Improves the System Design to Reduce Total System Cost

EXHIBIT 11.2   Process Map of Product Flow

about the profitability of the enterprise. Full-absorption costing means that indirect cost is not deducted from revenue, and therefore does not reduce net profit until a product is sold. Thus, an enterprise is rewarded for producing product that is not needed by the customers and is stored in inventory. When a manufacturing system produces quality products to the pace of customer demand (i.e., to takt time), the structure of the system design supports the thinking that horizontal improvement reduces cost. In addition, when a system produces

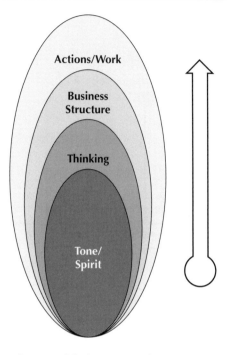

Flame Model of System Design

EXHIBIT 11.3   Integrating Human–Technical System Designs with CSD

at the pace of customer demand, it does not produce excess inventory, by definition.

There is no better way of controlling a production system than by producing at the pace of customer demand (i.e., at takt time). Takt time is the physical solution to achieve the functional requirements of *Producing the Customer Consumed Quantity* every time period. If the system is making product too fast, there is something wrong. Likewise, if product is made too slowly, there is something wrong. The ability to control a system requires rapid feedback as to whether the production pace is exactly as required.

A production system should be viewed as an orchestra or a band in which each member plays the music at the same tempo. The individual members are not rewarded for playing too fast or too slowly. They must play the right note at exactly the right time. This is the required structure. Vertical improvement (individual members trying to play faster than other members) would no longer be music. The conductor ensures that the orchestra plays at the right pace. The drummer in a rock band sets the right pace. A good rock-and-roll band starts with an outstanding drummer.

Balancing and regulating a system requires knowing the proper pace. When the pace becomes improper, people must know about it immediately. This is the statement of FR5 in Exhibit 11.10, which shows six functional requirements of system stability to meet customer needs in a customer-focused CSD system. When a problem condition occurs (i.e., not producing at the right pace), people need to know about the condition immediately and resolve it in a predefined, standardized way. The CSD methodology requires the implementation of a system that achieves this requirement. Balancing and regulating the system are not accomplished through or by accounting information. System regulation is built into the design of the system. Systems are regulated and balanced by the members of the system (just like the members of the band or an orchestra). A system that is properly designed integrates controllability of that system.[12] An effectively designed manufacturing system requires that, when the system is not in production, the members work and practice to learn how to work at exactly the right pace and identify and resolve problem conditions when they do occur.

System regulation and balance should not be left to accountants. Accounting alone cannot regulate a system. An accountant cannot and should not be a controller of a system. Designing a system that can be regulated and balanced is an industrial engineering function, not an accounting function. For this reason, CSD calls for and sponsors the integration of accounting, industrial engineering, and management as disciplines to achieve the agreed-to functional requirements of their enterprise.

(b) Sustainable Lean Obstacle 2

Unconsciously establishing performance targets instead of defining the system design to achieve enterprise purpose.

Many organizations require managers to enforce numerical targets on systems that are not capable of delivering the desired, targeted result. The organizational design either consciously or unconsciously requires managers to focus on a numerical target rather than focus on the system design to achieve that target. For example, assume the author's wife placed a numerical target on the author to run a marathon in two and a half hours. No matter how much his wife cajoled and prodded the author to achieve the target, the author simply could not achieve this desired result. The author's system is incapable of producing the desired result. There are two problems with this management-by-edict approach: First, the author's system design is such that he will continue to be incapable of delivering the desired result. Furthermore, the author does not agree that the two-and-a-half-hour marathon is a necessary target to achieve.

The approach to cost reduction with CSD follows from Deming's ideas about system stability.[13] He said that an unstable system cannot achieve performance goals or targets. By definition, the author's system for running a marathon is unstable. If a system is unstable it is unpredictable and not reliable. Therefore, the author's wife places a numerical target on the author's system, which is unpredictable; the act of placing that kind of goal on the author is a type of waste and could lead to disharmony because the wife and husband do not agree (and have not tried to agree).

Johnson notes that this practice is what most MBO (management by objectives) programs do. The managers place targets on inherently unstable systems, and continue to do so expecting a different result other than failure.[14] This is no different than forcing the author to try to run a two-and-a-half-hour marathon. It could do more harm than good when a system is unstable and will produce unpredictable results. A CSD first establishes collective agreement on purpose, called the functional requirements. The author's purpose is to be healthy; the author's wife may want him to be healthy, too. But she thinks that running a marathon very fast would ensure that the author is healthy. So the author and his wife may, in fact, agree on the following functional requirement:

FR1: Ensure that the author is healthy.

However, it is evident that they do not agree on the performance measure and the author is irritated by the suggestion (since after all, she can't run a two-and-a-half-hour marathon, either). In this example, the wife assumes that the physical solution to achieving the author's health FR1 is running.

PS1: Running

The author and his wife have not even discussed whether running is a physical activity that the author wants to do. Perhaps the author's wife does not know, for example, that he has an old football injury and cannot run very well. What the author really needs is a comprehensive health program that includes proper diet and adequate exercise. So the true PS1 is not running, the true PS1 can be stated as:

PS1: Total Health Program

Sometimes lean is similarly implemented by this MBO approach. It is analogous to trying to pour fresh water into salt water, with the hope of getting only fresh water.[15]

(c) Sustainable Lean Obstacle 3

Not knowing how to define purpose and the physical solutions to achieve it because of an ambiguous organizational understanding of lean.

An organization's success requires a common vision, such as Toyota's "true north." When 30 people are asked what lean means, there are typically 30 different answers about its meaning. In some cases, the answers are consistent with what lean is supposed to represent; but in most cases the definitions are contrary to its real purpose or practice. For these reasons, CSD uses a language to describe the thinking about a system's design.

Exhibit 11.4 provides language for the functional requirements and the physical solutions in detail.[16] The functional requirements define what a system must do to achieve purpose. The primary purpose of an organization must be to satisfy internal and external customer needs. The physical solutions define how purpose is achieved. Functional requirements are normally defined with

EXHIBIT 11.4   Collective System Design Language

Functional Requirements	Physical Solutions
• Define *what* the system must accomplish	• Define *how* the system must accomplish tasks
• Are *functions*	• Are *physical things*
• Cannot be compromised for "cost reduction"	• May be changed to improve performance
• First word is:	• First word is:
—Achieve	—Process
—Reduce	—Procedures
—Increase	—Machines
—Control	—Module

the first word being a verb, whereas, since the physical solutions identify physical entities, the first word is a noun. Once a functional requirement is identified and is part of the system design map, it must be achieved. However, many program managers delete functional requirements to "save cost," and there is inherent long-run cost in the system design that does not achieve the defined functional requirements.

Performance measures (M) are chosen *after* defining the functional requirements and physical solution design relationships shown in Exhibit 11.1. The measures reinforce achieving the functional requirements or performing the physical solutions in a rigorous standardized way. Not every functional requirement and physical solution must have an associated measure. Measures are selected only to reinforce the system design. For example, Toyota uses a measure that reinforces the PS:

PS4: Standard Work-in-Process (WIP) Inventory

The measure that is used by Toyota to reinforce the PS is a binary question: "Is the Standard WIP full?" If the answer is no, the measure indicates that production is not keeping pace with the system takt time. This measure is used after each shift. A person is responsible for diagnosing why the standard inventory is not full and for putting actions in place immediately to correct this problem condition. PS4 is designed to achieve FR4, *Achieve FR1 through FR3 in spite of internal (Plant B) and external (Plant A) variation*, which is described in the next section.

The system design language creates the structure of an interdependent network of functional requirements, physical solutions, and performance measures (M) that defines detailed (lower-level) functional requirements based on the chosen higher-level functional requirement and physical solution relationship (Exhibit 11.5). Before moving to the next lower level of the CSD map, the effectiveness of the design FR-PS relationship must be validated. This validation requires the evaluation of the type of design.[17] Exhibit 11.6 shows three design types. An uncoupled design is the most effective design relationship. One physical solution satisfies one functional requirement. This design produces predictable results (see the upper third of Exhibit 11.6). A path-dependent design is also robust, but less predictable than an uncoupled design (middle third of Exhibit 11.6). In this example, PS1 affects the achievement of both FR1 and FR2. The design is path dependent since PS1 must be implemented prior to FR2.

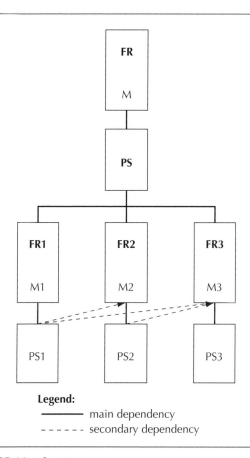

EXHIBIT 11.5   CSD Map Structure

A coupled design is unpredictable, not robust, and consumes a lot of resources to implement. The system design mapping cannot go to the next lower level if a coupled design exists (lower third of Exhibit 11.6). A coupled design is unacceptable and should not be implemented. Two other designs are unacceptable: an incomplete design (not enough physical solutions to achieve the functional requirements) and a redundant design: too many physical solutions (more than one) to achieve a functional requirement.

Exhibit 11.7 uses these three design types to describe why "offshoring" customer technical support in an effort to reduce labor cost actually increased cost for a computer company. In response to the measure-driven FR2, *Reduce Direct Labor Cost*, the company used PS2, *Offshoring*. To achieve the customer

Type 1: Predictable (Uncoupled) Design

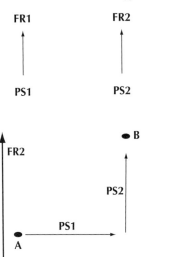

- Implementing PS1 affects only FR1
- Implementing PS2 affects only FR2

Uncoupled Design

PS1 implements FR1 fully.
PS2 implements FR2 fully.

This design is the most robust to a change in FR1 or FR2, as the PSs do not effect each other. This design is the most flexible and defines the least waste condition.

Points A and B represent the desired level of achievement of FR1 and FR2. Point B has a combined higher level of FR1 and FR2 achievement than A.

Type 2: Path-Dependent Design

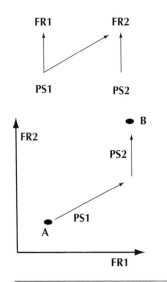

Implementing PS1 affects both FR1 and FR2. Implementing PS2 affects only FR2.

Path Dependent Design: The sequence of PS implementation is important.

Correct Implementation: Implement PS1 first, then PS2.
PS1 implements FR1 to the desired level.
FR2 changes with PS1.
PS2 implements FR2 to the desired level.

Incorrect Implementation: If PS2 implemented first, then PS1 changes FR2 and PS2 must be reimplemented. The wasteful sequence is PS2, then PS1, then PS2.

EXHIBIT 11.6   Type 1, 2, and 3 System Design Relationships

Type 3: Trial-and-Error (Coupled) Design

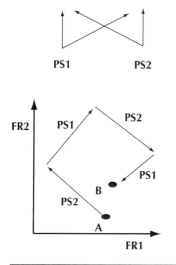

Implementing PS1 affects both FR1 and FR2. Implementing PS2 affects both FR2 and FR1.

Coupled Design

PS2 attempts to implement FR2 to the desired level (but runs out of resources). PS1 attempts to implement FR1 and overshoots FR1 and completely changes FR2.

Next, PS2 attempts to implement FR2 and dramatically changes FR1. Each PS iteration adds time and unnecessary cost. The target B may never be reached with absolute certainty since the FRs are not achieved independently by the PSs.

EXHIBIT 11.6   Continued

service FR1, *Resolve Problems to Satisfy the Customers*, the linked PS1 asked the less-skilled, lower-wage workers to use a *Standard Script* to diagnose problem conditions. Notice that PS1 negatively affected the achievement of FR2 (indicated by the minus sign). This negative result was the consequence of the selected PS1, since the standard script of questions *increased the time* required to diagnose a problem relative to the time required by a skilled technician.

The coupled design is unacceptable. Company management then discovered that using highly skilled technicians to diagnose problems over the phone actually saved time, which obviated the cost benefit of hiring lower-wage workers. The second design illustrates this point; it also illustrates the new PS1: *Skilled workers to diagnose and resolve problem*, which has a positive impact on cost reduction. However, the first design is an *incomplete* design, since there is no PS2 identified to achieve FR2, which is to reduce direct labor costs. After thinking about the problem and expanding the scope from focusing on just the telephone support operation to the process of support, the team discovered that information about computer failures was not being fed back to the design engineers. The significance of this CSD process discovery is that when service

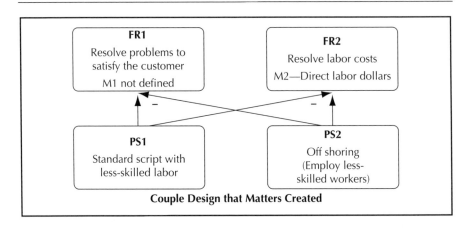

Couple Design that Matters Created

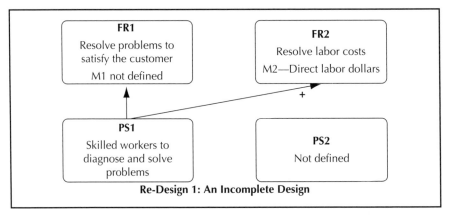

Re-Design 1: An Incomplete Design

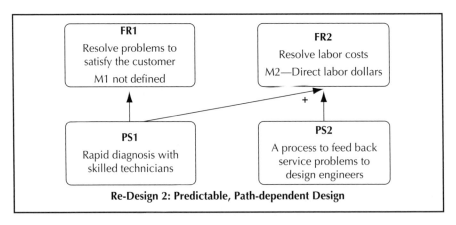

Re-Design 2: Predictable, Path-dependent Design

EXHIBIT 11.7   System Design for Offshoring Customer Technical Support

problems are fed back to design engineering, the number of service problems is reduced, which in turn reduces customer service direct labor cost (FR2). The team wrote PS2: *Process to feedback service problems to design engineers.* The third design is a path-dependent design. The selection of PS1: *Skilled Workers* affects the achievement of both FR1 and FR2. PS1 must be implemented first and effectively, followed by PS2, because the final design is a path-dependent design (panel 3 in Exhibit 11.7). Exhibit 11.8 summarizes the typical types of designs encountered during the CSD process. Notice the conversion that occurred in the previous example from coupled, to incomplete, to a path-dependent design.

Exhibit 11.9 expands the system design map to include system objectives and product design relationships for a large design and manufacturing company (Cochran et al. 2000 describes the construction of the Manufacturing System Design Decomposition [MSDD] in detail).[18] The expanded design map describes the design relationships that exist within TPS using the system design

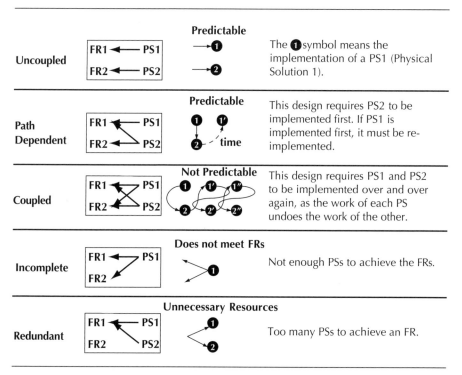

EXHIBIT 11.8 Typical Designs Encountered in the CSD Process

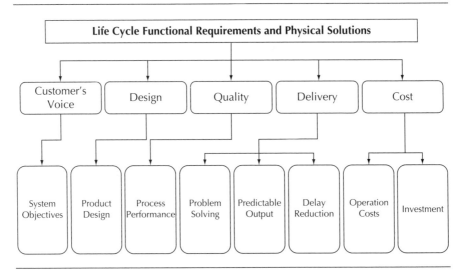

EXHIBIT 11.9   Collective System Design Map

language format. The system design language and the system design mapping provide the thinking layer of CSD as illustrated by Exhibit 11.3.

(d) Sustainable Lean Obstacle 4

Unconsciously using an approach to "cost reduction" at the expense of long-term real cost reduction: cutting "costs" before implementing a stable system design.

A stable system achieves the system design functional requirements consistently. The functional requirements of the system design are the result of translating the needs of the internal and external customers into functional requirement statements combined with the CSD principles of robust system design and rapid problem resolution. A stable, low-cost system achieves the functional requirements with the least resources. CSD treats cost reduction in two major steps. The first step uses collectively learning to design and implement a stable system. The second step is the practice of Kaizen to reduce waste. Cost is the derivative of waste. Once a system has been designed and has proven to be stable, additional cost is reduced by improving the work practices and methods that are required to operate the system design.

This two-step process enhances and articulates Toyota's approach, which is to first implement the system design and to make the system become stable and consistent; the second step is the implementation of work and workplace method improvements to further reduce cost. Work-method Kaizen occurs once the system design has been implemented within Toyota. CSD provides a method to formally define the functional requirements, physical solutions, and measures needed to define a system design to meet customer needs.

A CSD nurtures and improves the physical solutions so that they do achieve the functional requirements. For this reason, MBO programs use an approach that is opposite to the CSD approach. An MBO program seeks to achieve numerical targets in systems that are typically unstable, and that have not been collectively designed to achieve customer needs. The first step in the CSD approach involves designing the system to achieve the six functional requirements of system stability shown in Exhibit 11.10. Once the system design achieves system stability, cost is again reduced by improving the system and eliminating variation by "working on the work" to fully meet the functional requirements of the system design.

A supply-chain system example with two links illustrates the derivation of stable system design functional requirements. The first link is the Plant A to Plant B link. The second link is the Plant B to the final customer link—A to B to final customer. For this example, we will focus on Plant B; the input link from A to B that supplies B and the output link from Plant B to the final customer. Plant B supplies a variety of different products to its final customer. Plant A provides a variety of different products to Plant B. The internal customers of this system are the people who operate their piece of the system in

EXHIBIT 11.10   The Six Functional Requirements of System Stability to Meet Customer Needs

FR1—Produce the customer-consumed quantity every demand-time interval.
FR2—Produce the customer-consumed mix/variety evey demand-time interval.
FR3—Ship perfect-quality products to the customer every demand-time interval.
FR4—Achieve FR1 through FR3 in spite of internal (Plant B) and external (Plant A) variation.
FR5—Immediately identify a problem condition in achieving any of the system functional requirements and resolve in a standardized way.
FR6—Provide a safe, clean, ergonomically sound working environment.

the plants. These customers need to work in a safe and healthy environment. The associated functional requirement (FR6 in Exhibit 11.10) is stated as:

FR6: Provide a safe, clean, ergonomically sound working environment.

Plant B must meet the quality needs of the final customer. The final customer needs to receive only products that meet the design specification; the final customer wants to receive no defects. The functional requirement that Plant B must achieve to satisfy the final customer's need is stated as:

FR3: Ship perfect-quality parts to the customer every demand-time interval.

This FR sets the minimum expectation that is placed on Plant B with respect to providing quality to the final customer.

Regarding delivery, the final customer also expects to receive the quantity, part mix, and part variety at an expected time. Production at Plant B does not always go as planned due to unexpected downtime, unanticipated changes in customer demand, unanticipated absenteeism, and other unpredictable sources of variation (including defects), which a production plan or schedule cannot predict. Therefore, the production plan or schedule is not always what Plant B demands from Plant A. The managers at Plant A know that they can compensate for all of these sources of variation by replenishing the products that Plant B consumes. Similarly, the final customer's demand is always changing for various reasons. Plant B also cannot rely on the production schedule that the final customer provides.

Plant A and B's management uses the production plan or schedule only for rough-cut capacity estimation. Production operations have to be controlled by replacing exactly the mix and quantity that their respective customer consumes. Plant B states two functional requirements, in addition to FR3:

FR1: Produce the customer-consumed quantity every demand-time interval.
FR2: Produce the customer-consumed mix/variety every demand-time interval.
FR3: Ship perfect-quality parts to the customer every demand-time interval

Applying the CSD principle of robust design, the managers at Plant B state FR4.

FR4: Achieve FR1 through FR3 in spite of internal (Plant B) and external (Plant A) variation.

For Plant B to have a robust system design, it must be able to achieve its purpose (i.e., to meet the final customer's functional requirements 1 through 3) even though Plant B suffers from internal sources of variation (i.e., defects, downtime, absenteeism) and must deal with incoming defects, an external source of variation, from its supplier, Plant A. FR4 defines the robustness functional requirement for Plant B's supply of parts to the final customer.

Stability is the result of the ability of Plant B to meet its commitment—defined by the functional requirements 1 through 6 of the system design—to its final customer. In this case, Plant B may have to *add* inventory to achieve FR4. This is an example of the two-step approach to cost reduction—stability first, then improvement of all facets of production (work methods, equipment design and maintenance, engineering change management).

As all sources of variation are reduced within the context of the system design to achieve the FRs of system stability, the standard WIP inventory level can be reduced without compromising system stability. Long-term and sustained cost reduction is a two-step process that requires: (1) implementing the system design to achieve stability, then (2) Kaizen to further improve the reliability of the work and the manufacturing processes. The use of financial measures and metrics to "drive" improvement does not ensure long-term and lasting cost reduction since the functional requirements of the system under consideration are not clearly defined and communicated.

The final functional requirement of a stable system design, FR5, establishes a type of human intervention–based control system to ensure that problems are really identified and corrected instead of being ignored or swept under the rug.

FR5: Immediately identify a problem condition in achieving any of the system functional requirements and resolve in a standardized (predefined) way.

This functional requirement means that the system must be designed to immediately identify any problems in producing the customer-consumed quantity and variety. The system must also identify immediately any quality or health and safety issues. This functional requirement also means that there must be a preplanned way of resolving the problem condition. Therefore, standardized work is performed to resolve identified problem conditions in achieving the functional requirements of the system design.

Customers always demand low cost. The solution to obstacle 4 is not contrary to fulfilling this expectation. The key idea is to select physical solutions that achieve the functional requirements for the least cost. The tendency of most enterprises is to first ignore designing a system that achieves the functional requirements in the first place. Second, those companies that do wish to achieve the functional requirements, typically the ones trying to implement lean, fall into the trap of spending lots of money on automating the physical solutions. For example, instead of implementing a manual kanban system first, they attempt to automate before completely debugging and testing their manual system to achieve the functional requirements of stability.

CSD in practice requires the construction of a physical model of the manufacturing or service system that is needed to achieve the functional requirements. This physical model implements the physical solutions in terms of the physical structure and the standardized work that is necessary to fulfill the functional requirements. Everyone who uses the manufacturing system takes part in the design of this physical model. Everyone at this company worked together to redesign their manufacturing system to achieve the functional requirements of system stability. The team included union workers, area managers, supervisors, information technology (IT) support, production planning specialists, purchasing personnel, shipping personnel, and quality department personnel. Every function within the factory was touched by this system design, including the performance measurement and evaluation functions, which had to be changed from rewarding "the more the better" to producing to takt time, which rewards producing exactly the quantity consumed by the customer.

CSD requires collective agreement. Collective agreement means that there are no hidden agendas, and no gaming of the system. The team knew that the existing performance measures could potentially destroy the new system's implementation if they did not take action to change them. For this reason, the plant manager, directors, and vice presidents of the company had to change the way the plant and the plant manager's performance were evaluated. Otherwise, the new system could not survive. The existing system was the result of business structures and practices that evolved to satisfy implicitly defined functional requirements (traceable to the structure of the unit cost equation) and the existing performance measures, which rewarded running the machines all the time and made products that the customers did not need right then.

Costs cannot be reduced until there is system stability to achieve system functional requirements. The lure of producing products in low-wage countries does not ensure that total costs are reduced. Even though a cost equation may indicate that producing in a lower-wage country has lower cost, the cost equation does not consider the entire functional requirements of the manufacturing or product delivery system. The cost equation does not consider whether quality, for example, is equivalent to that of the higher-wage country. In addition, the cost equation does not consider whether delivery will be on time and reliable relative to that of the higher-wage country. Also, the cost equation does not consider the costs of engineering changes, workforce turnover, protection of intellectual property rights, fluctuations in transportation costs, and more. All of these points are factors in a CSD and redesign. The CSD map, which defines FR-PS relationships, establishes the thinking that the people within an enterprise have about these factors. A stable system, then, must achieve the functional requirements. After all, the functional requirements that are on the CSD map have been collectively agreed to and have been placed on that map as an expression of purpose for the enterprise.

When a system is not stable and does not meet the functional requirements, unnecessary cost is incurred. A CSD map can be used to evaluate the cost of not achieving the functional requirements. In one company, for example, the map showed that 25 percent of the total direct labor hours were waste because the existing system could not achieve six functional requirements of the system design.[19] These additional labor hours are the cost of not achieving the functional requirements of a system design. In many cases, the quantified cost of not achieving the system design functional requirements is much greater than the benefit of any Six Sigma or vertically/operation-focused lean implementations.

The management of the company recognized that the existing system had to be redesigned to achieve the functional requirements. The CSD process quantified the cost benefit of implementing a new system design based on the opportunity costs associated with the existing system not achieving the collectively desired functional requirements. The CSD map gave the managers the rationale and logic that enabled them to invest resources (capital, people, material) to achieve the deficient functional requirements. The CSD map enhanced the lean TPS program for the company since the managers had a common definition and understanding of the thinking of what lean meant for their company.

CSD offers an alternative to the thinking that is implicit in traditional management accounting. Using the CSD approach, cost is reduced by selecting the least costly physical solutions that do achieve the functional requirements that meet true customer needs. When the functional requirements are not achieved, a manufacturing system incurs unnecessary cost. Long-term cost reduction requires the stable achievement of system-design functional requirements. The CSD map defines the system design itself in terms of functional requirements, physical solutions, and associated performance measures. The map may also be used to evaluate the effectiveness of the system design and to guide decisions about investment and resource allocation so that the system design functional requirements are reliably achieved.

Once the CSD functional requirements are met and achieved with stability, additional cost reduction is achieved through system Kaizen (improvements). When Kaizen is done before the system achieves the functional requirements of system stability (i.e., a stable system design), the improvement work typically focuses on vertical operations, rather than horizontal system improvement. CSD embellishes how value stream mapping and other tools may be used in the design of an enterprise[20] (see Exhibit 11.11).

(e) Sustainable Lean Obstacle 5

Managers within enterprises not being an integral part of the system design.

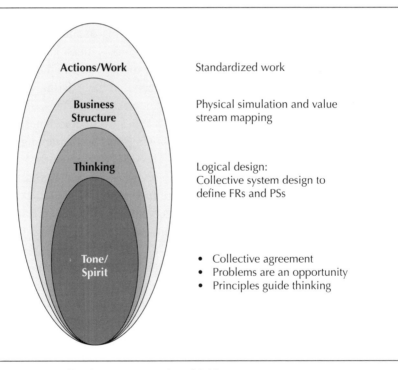

EXHIBIT 11.11   Collective System Design Thinking

The practice of CSD integrates collective leadership, the learning organization, and dialogue as part of the leadership through design process. Organizational system design starts with the tone as illustrated by Exhibit 11.12. However, to understand its tone, an existing organizacion may have to start with understanding the actions that come to the surface of the system. These surface actions are the result of existing business structures and processes. The CSD map in turn is used to express the thinking that creates the existing system's structure. The tone guides the thinking of an existing system. This process of *going into the flame* is the diagnosis of the existing system's design.

The existing system's thinking (FR-PS relationships) is inferred based on the processes and structures that the business uses. The existing system's structure is diagnosed by observing the existing actions (of the people). For example, if

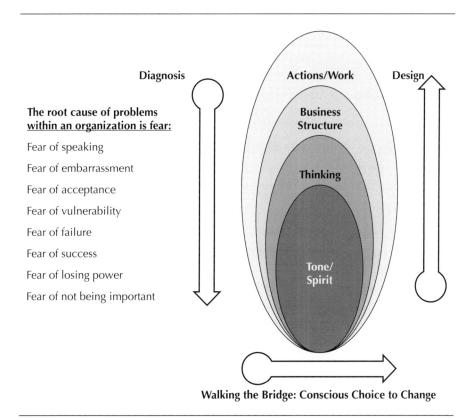

EXHIBIT 11.12   Exposing the Fear of Transformation

a surface action is to "produce more parts the better," the diagnostic process seeks to determine the structural cause of this action. In this example, assume that the structural cause is the unit cost equation. This equation imposes a structure on the system that encourages the action of producing the more the better, regardless of demand.

$$\text{Unit Cost(op}_i) = \frac{\text{Labor Hours(op}_i) \times \text{Wage Rate} + \text{Material\$(op}_i) + \text{Overhead\$(op}_i)}{N}$$

and

$$\text{Overhead\$(op}_i) = \frac{\text{Labor Hours(op}_i)}{\text{Labor Hours(total)} \times \text{Total Overhead\$}}$$

The diagnostic process continues by determining the functional requirements of the existing system's thinking. The functional requirements are:

FR1: Reduce labor cost of the operation   (M: labor cost $\rightarrow$ 0)

FR2: Reduce material cost of the operation   (M: material cost $\rightarrow$ 0)

FR3: Increase the quantity produced (N)   (M: N $\rightarrow$ ∞)

FR4: Decrease direct labor content/time (t)   (M: t $\rightarrow$ 0)

The corresponding physical solutions are:

PS1: Low-wage countries/environments

PS2: Material type

PS3: High-speed machine/operation

PS4: Automation

These physical solutions in response to the structure of the unit cost equation explain why so many businesses implement high-speed, automated operations in low-wage environments.

The underlying tone of this system design expresses qualities that influence and affect the thinking. Describing tone is sometimes difficult with words. However, the tone here is that the system of production is independent of the customer. The thinking reflects this tone, since the system makes products that customers do not demand or consume! So the paradox is that the overall system design produces products that customers do not want and, even worse, indicates to managers that the cost is lower and the profit is higher than if the system produces exactly what the customers demand at the time demanded. Of course, Toyota started with a different tone than this.

An important role of leadership is to understand how fear affects an existing system's design. Fear also affects the decision shown in Exhibit 11.12, to *walk the bridge to make a conscious choice to change*. The conscious choice that is made is to do the system design that is necessary to change the organization's product delivery or service system design. CSD emphasizes the decision to change more than the implementation of lean tools. When an organization implements the lean tools in absence of a real and a collective decision to change, the lean-tool implementation typically does not last.

There are too many factors that can negatively impact the ability to sustain lean tools within an enterprise. CSD demonstrates how business structures and measures affect actions. Lean tools impose a structure and require certain actions by the people within an organization to work. Collective agreement ensures that the tone and the thinking within an organization are in step with the lean tool and structure implementation. Since this congruence is required for the new system design to survive, the leadership within an organization must be an integral part of the diagnosis and design process. The leadership must "walk the talk."

The fear of change must be integrated into the fabric of new system design. Integration means that fear must be acknowledged and dealt with, not brushed aside or put under the rug. The aspiration of the business should be to meet the needs of the internal customers in addition to meeting the needs of the external customers and to be able to adapt to changing customer needs. The tone that moved Toyota far away from the total drudgery of high-speed, one-person-one-machine operations, called mass production was "respect for the worker."[21] Leaders facilitate the discussions about tone. Leaders are also a critical part of the process to determine the functional requirements and physical solutions of the system design. Once the system design map has been developed and agreed to, the leaders and managers become responsible for achieving the functional requirements.

Investment and resource allocation decisions are an important part of day-to-day management of the system design in the journey to implement and sustain lean. The problem that occurs with many lean implementations is that as some of the lean tools and techniques are implemented, the results reported are very good, and then the lean team stops. When the point of view by leaders and managers is that lean is a program, lean is implicitly a separate activity. Instead, for lean to be sustainable, it must be viewed as the system that is used to operate and manage the business. Lean is also a journey that seeks to perfect the achievement of the functional requirements.

The following example illustrates what happens when lean is implemented as a program rather than as a system design. The CSD map was not used to guide this implementation. The implementation was motivated by the fact that the product cost was too high. The plant managers and employees were threatened by the possibility that the product would be outsourced to Mexico. The team was motivated by fear to change the system design to reduce cost. The team developed a work control board and work cells to produce the product to takt time.

Exhibit 11.13 shows the outstanding performance results, and Exhibit 11.14 compares how well the functional requirements are achieved before and after the system redesign. The use of the performance results alone would indicate to a team that they had done well and could stop the implementation. With the use of the CSD map to evaluate the system design's achievement of the functional requirements, however, a team would understand that after the implementation only 5 of the functional requirements are poorly achieved, whereas prior to the implementation 28 functional requirements are poorly achieved. The map indicates to the leadership and to the teams that the system design is very good, but it is not complete and they should not stop working on the system design and improvement just because the financial results and performance measures have been improved.

The concept of system design, instead of a lean implementation, should be for leaders and managers to not view lean as a program that is separate from "the system."[22] Instead, the key to sustaining lean is to view lean as a journey of perfecting and improving the CSD.

EXHIBIT 11.13   Normalized Performance Metrics Comparison

	Before	After
Floor area	1	.59
WIP	1	.43
Direct workers	1	.43
Indirect workers	1	1.0
Rework cost	N/A	1.0
Labor hour/good harness	1	.23
Assembly content (days) per wiring harness	1	.29
Number of variations	1	1.0
# Different parts shipped	1	1.0

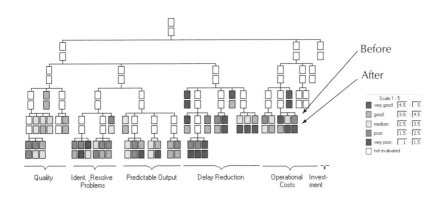

Total	Very Poor	Poor	Medium	Good	Very Good	N/A
WH #1	0	28	6	2	1	2
WH #2	0	5	10	19	6	2

EXHIBIT 11.14   System Design Evaluation

11.5 THE ESSENTIALS OF SYSTEMS DESIGN WHEN ACCOUNTING FOR LEAN

The language of system design (functional requirements and physical solutions and measures) helps people define and articulate the health of an enterprise. Lean is the name for the result of implementing the Toyota Production System. Toyota did not need "lean accounting" to become lean (i.e., to reach a given state). Toyota's measurement and managerial accounting practices had to be consistent with the thinking and the tone that are part of the Toyota Production System design. To the degree that Toyota or any enterprise confuses managerial accounting and measurement with their purpose (functional requirements) and practice (physical solutions), system redesign is required. Collective system redesign includes four layers: the tone, the thinking and measures, the business processes/structures, and the actions/work. CSD acknowledges that to sustain any change to account for lean, the new system design requires alignment and integration of the four aspects of a system. Therefore, performance measures and managerial accounting must reinforce the ability of any product delivery or service system to achieve the system design functional requirements.

Decisions about cost should not be an accounting function; this should be an industrial engineering function, because the system design creates cost and has the ability to control cost. Industrial engineers should be responsible for the system design and should be an integral part of a CSD process. Accountants and accounting should perform the measurement function and have a new role to ensure that resources are allocated and investments are made to ensure the achievement of the system design functional requirements. System design can determine whether a system can be balanced and regulated or not. When measures are placed on a system in the absence of a system design, a system evolves to achieve those measures, whether or not those measures will prompt actions with harmful long-term consequences.

The CSD process provides a proven process for long-term reduction of total cost through system design for stability and the elimination of pre-existing business structures like the unit cost equation that prevent sustainable changes from being made.

NOTES

1. H. Thomas Johnson and Anders Bröms, *Profit Beyond Measure: Extraordinary Results through Attention to Work and People* (New York: Free Press, 2000).
2. W. Edwards Deming, *Out of the Crisis* (Cambridge, Mass.: MIT Press, 2000).
3. James P. Womack, Daniel T. Jones, and Daniel Roos, *The Machine that Changed the World: The Story of Lean Production* (New York: Harper Collins, 1991).
4. Horace Lucien Arnold and Fay Leone Faurote, *Ford Methods and the Ford Shops* (Boston: Adamant Media Corporation, 2006; facsimile reprint of 1919 Engineering Magazine Company version).
5. Taiichi Ohno, *Toyota Production System: Beyond Large Scale Production* (New York: Productivity Press, 1988).
6. H. Thomas Johnson and Robert S. Kaplan, *Relevance Lost: The Rise and Fall of Management Accounting* (Boston: Harvard Business School Press, 1987).
7. H. Thomas Johnson, *Relevance Regained: From Top-Down Control to Bottom-Up Empowerment* (New York: Free Press, 1992).
8. See note 1.
9. Shigeo Shingo, *A Study of the Toyota Production System from an Industrial Engineering Viewpoint* (New York: Productivity Press, 1989). This is an extremely important book that distinguishes operation improvement versus process (what I call system) improvement. The system must be implemented first before operation improvements (and operation-focused Kaizens) are made.

10. Ibid.
11. David S. Cochran and William Isaacs, "System Design and Leadership Program: NASA Workshops," 2002 and 2003. Issacs offered the flame model from his work with dialogue; the author added the Thinking Layer to the Flame model and made the Tone, the inner (hottest part) of the flame. Bill originally described the importance of "Tone" in organizations while we were cycling past Walden Pond (of all places!).
12. J. Temple Black, *The Design of the Factory with a Future* (New York: McGraw-Hill Series in Industrial Engineering and Management Science, 1991). Also, see H.Thomas Johnson in this book, Chapter 1, section 1.4.
13. J. Won, D. Cochran, H. T. Johnson, S. Bouzekouk, and B. Masha, "Rationalizing the Design of the Toyota Production System: A Comparison of Two Approaches," Proceedings of the 34th CIRP International Seminar on Manufacturing Systems, June 5–7, 2001, Stockholm, Sweden (see also www.sysdesign.org/pdf/paper 15.pdf). This paper expands on Deming's ideas and contrasts Steve Spear's excellent work.
14. See note 1.
15. David S. Cochran and Makoto Kawada, "Joint Strike Fighter (JSF) Product Build and Delivery System Design Map," (Society of Automotive Engineers Conference—Joint Presentation with JSF Production Engineering, Makoto Kawada [accounting for Toyota Production System emphasis], September 2003).
16. Nam P. Suh, *Principles of Design* (Cambridge: Oxford University Press, 1990). The CSD language for design acknowledges the art in human design intended by a seemingly mechanistic approach.
17. Ibid.
18. David S. Cochran, J. F. Arinez, J. W. Duda and J. Linck, "A Decomposition Approach for Manufacturing System Design," *Journal of Manufacturing Systems* No. 6, 2001/2002.
19. Steven Hendricks, "System Design Implementation in Aircraft Manufacturing Industry," MIT master of science thesis, Prof. D. S. Cochran, advisor (Cambridge: MIT Libraries, September 2002).
20. Mike Rother and John Shook, *Learning to See* (Brookline, Mass.: Lean Enterprise Institute, June 2003).
21. Yasuhiro Monden, *Toyota Production System: An Integrated Approach to Just in Time*, 3rd ed. (Engineering and Management Press, December 1998). Monden describes the significance of respect for the worker within the Toyota Production System. He provides hierarchical trees of Toyota Production System relationships. Womack et. al., in *The Machine that Changed the World*, use the term *mass production* to describe the antithesis of lean (see note 3).
22. Peter M. Senge, *The Fifth Discipline: The Art and Practice of the Learning Organization*, (New York: Doubleday, 2006).

GLOSSARY

Autonomation   Automation with the human touch, which allows a person to automatically stop a machine, process, or system when an abnormality is detected. This term is also frequently referred as *detect and stop*. Also see *Jidoka*.

Batch production   Manufacturing large quantities of products without regard to demand or customer requirements to reduce costs of overhead, labor, and equipment by spreading the costs over a large amount of product.

Cell   The arrangement of people, equipment/machines, materials, and methods so that processing takes place in sequential order with continuous one-piece flow. Often this arrangement is put into a "U"-shaped configuration, called a U-shaped cell.

Chaku-chaku   Literally translated as *load-load*. It means that a part is cleared from a fixture automatically so that an operator can load the next part without having to manually remove the previous part from the fixture.

Continuous flow   A concept that, in its ideal state, means that items are processed and moved directly from one processing step to the next, one piece at a time. Each processing step operator works on only the one piece that the next step needs just before that step needs it, and the transfer batch size is one. Also called *one-piece flow*, *single-piece flow*, *1 × 1*, or simply *flow*.

Cost management for lean environments   The use of cost information to evaluate how efficaciously a business consumes resources to create products or services that have value to customers by developing and executing superior systems (instead of traditional cost-management accounting techniques), in which cost information is direct (see the definition of *direct costs*), simple, and accurate. In this type of system, cost management is a tool used to support and reflect the operations, not drive the operations and the behavior of those who manage it.

Direct costs Costs that can be directly associated with a product in the context of its incidence of manufacture. (*Not* as has been traditionally defined—costing that treats only the variable manufacturing costs as a part of product cost and fixed manufacturing costs being considered as period costs and unrelated to product cost, also referred to as *variable costing*.)

Flow The movement of a product through the value stream without stoppages or defects.

Flow manufacturing Manufacturing operations that utilize continuous flow as the method of production.

Focus factory Sometimes referred to as a factory within a factory. Usually a collection of manufacturing cells, which manufacture components that supply a value stream for a product or product family, or a collection of component value streams, which supply (and are a part of) a value stream for a product or product family. A focus factory has its own autonomous support, resources, and management and functions as an independent entity and support resources (also called *focused factory*).

Hoshin The literal translation of Hoshin Kanri is "control of the organization's direction," from hoshin (compass) and kanri (management control). Hoshin Kanri is a formal process that helps organizations develop and implement their strategy throughout all levels of the organization while maintaining alignment with the overriding objectives. It coordinates detailed process activities by linking them to the high-level strategy set by executive management, but allows for enterprise-wide participation in the management of process details at each level of the organization with the support and coordination of multifunctional teams. This participation feature facilitates strategic alignment, proper prioritization, and employee buy-in. It is a very key element and practice to achieving an effective lean organization.

Jidoka The ability to detect an abnormality and stop before moving to the next process. It supports the ability for manufacturing to build the part correctly the first time. Also see *Autonomation*.

Just-in-time A production system that manufactures and delivers exactly what is needed, when it is needed, and in the amount needed.

Kaikaku Generally translated as rapid or radical improvement.

Kaizen (continuous improvement) Continuous improvement in lean is anything that eliminates waste or something that inhibits continuous flow. It is also a methodology for improving ergonomics, safety, operational downtime, scrap or rework, and productivity (based on takt time).

Kanban   The card system that controls inventory and movement in a pull system.

Lean production   Coined by John Krafcik, a research assistant at MIT with the International Motor Vehicle Program in the late 1980s, lean production is a business system for organizing and managing product development, operations, suppliers, and customer relations that requires less human effort, less space, less capital, and less time to make products with fewer defects to precise customer desires, compared with the previous system of mass production.

Management by means (MBM)   An approach that organizes work systematically, in contrast to management by results (see following) business outcomes that emerge spontaneously from mastering practices that harmonize with patterns inherent in the production system itself.

Management by results (MBR)   Driving work with financial goals through the use of quantitative targets to run the operations of a business.

Managerial cost accounting   The branch of accounting that uses both historical and estimated data in providing information that management uses in conducting daily operations, planning future operations, and developing overall business strategies by accumulating manufacturing costs.

Mass production   Manufacturing large amounts of product or producing large volumes. A traditional or lean manufacturer can be a mass producer. For example, Toyota and General Motors are mass producers because the both manufacture a large volume of products—automobiles.

Muda   Japanese term for waste or non-value-added. See *Waste*.

One-piece flow   The same as flow but only one piece at a time.

One-touch start   A machine or process being cycle started by the touch of only one start button, lever, or paddle that is in line with the movement of the operator in their standard operation procedure (as opposed to needing to backtrack to start a machine), which actuates the machine cycle. It also infers that proper precautions, devices, sensors, and guards are in place where needed to maintain a safe machine or process.

Pull system   A system in which product does not move to the next process until signaled by the next process.

Quick change (SMED)   The ability to rapidly change over machines, processes, or manufacturing lines in ten minutes or less. The acronym SMED stands for single-minute exchange of dies, which is a technique and procedure developed by Shigeo Shingo to reduce changeover times down to less than ten minutes.

Right-design   Designing machines, processes, cells, and value streams for one-piece flow based on lean principles and techniques. (Sometimes referred to as *right-sizing* when referencing equipment or machine tools.)

Rules-in-use   The essence of the Toyota Production System, these rules specify how work is expected to occur before performing it, embedding tests in work designs to immediately signal when work is not occurring as expected so that employees can quickly respond to signals with problem-solving processes.

5S   Five words that represent the principles for cleanliness and organization. Originally based on five Japanese words: *seiri*, sort; *seiton*, straighten; *seiso*, scrub; *seiketsu*, systematize; *shitsuke*, standardize.

Takt time   The rate of production based on customer demand, calculated by dividing the time available (usually per shift) by the quantity required per shift.

Toyota Production System (TPS)   The methods, procedures, principles, philosophy, and enterprise-wide system used by Toyota. TPS has its roots in Henry Ford's Highland Park plant, the TWI Service (see following), and its own needs and situation. Toyota has continuously evolved its system since pre–World War II and particularly post–World War II events. Its fundamental basis is eliminating or avoiding waste in order to implement continuous flow.

   The production system provides best quality, lowest cost, and shortest lead time through the elimination of waste. TPS is comprised of two platforms, just-in-time production and Jidoka. The system is maintained and improved through iterations of standardized work and Kaizen following the plan-do-check-act cycle.

Training within industry (TWI)   The TWI Service was established in 1940 during World War II to increase production output to support the Allied Forces' war effort. It focused on the operator-supervisor interface and had four main training programs, called the "J" programs (Job Instruction, Job Methods, and Job Relations). It was so successful that during the occupation of postwar Japan, it was extensively used to help rebuild and democratize Japanese industry.

Value   Any activity that contributes to transforming a product or information into the customer requirements.

Value stream   The activities required to design, order, and manufacture a product or information from raw material to the customer.

Waste   Any activity that consumes time and resources and does not contribute to conforming a product or information into the customer requirements. See *Muda*.

Zero defect   The ability to manufacture products with no defects, scrap, or
rework.

Index